Basic and Clinical Science Course

Thomas A. Weingeist, PhD, MD, Iowa City, Iowa
Senior Secretary for Clinical Education

Thomas J. Liesegang, MD, Jacksonville, Florida
Secretary for Instruction

M. Gilbert Grand, MD, St. Louis, Missouri
BCSC Course Chair

Section 4

Faculty Responsible for This Edition

Hans E. Grossniklaus, MD, *Chair,* Atlanta, Georgia

Harry H. Brown, MD, Little Rock, Arkansas

Ben J. Glasgow, MD, Los Angeles, California

Timothy G. Murray, MD, Miami, Florida

Debra J. Shetlar, MD, Houston, Texas

David J. Wilson, MD, Portland, Oregon

Rick D. Isernhagen, MD, Lexington, Kentucky
Practicing Ophthalmologists Advisory Committee for Education

Each author states that he or she has no significant financial interest or other relationship with the manufacturer of any commercial product discussed in the chapters that he or she contributed to this publication or with the manufacturer of any competing commercial product.

Recent Past Faculty

David H. Abramson, MD
Lee S. Anderson, MD
John Douglas Cameron, MD
R. Jean Campbell, MD
Robert Folberg, MD
Marilyn C. Kincaid, MD
Martha Luckenbach, MD
Curtis E. Margo, MD

Jan McDonnell, MD
Alan D. Proia, MD
Alan M. Roth, MD
Joseph W. Sassani, MD
Andrew P. Schachat, MD
Elise Torczynski, MD
John D. Wright, Jr, MD

In addition, the Academy gratefully acknowledges the contributions of numerous past faculty and advisory committee members who have played an important role in the development of previous editions of the Basic and Clinical Science Course.

American Academy of Ophthalmology Staff

Kathryn A. Hecht, EdD
Vice President, Clinical Education

Hal Straus
Director, Publications Department

Margaret Denny
Managing Editor

Fran Taylor
Medical Editor

Maxine Garrett
Administrative Coordinator

Ruth Modric
Production Manager

Beth T. Berkelhammer
Production Editor

American Academy of Ophthalmology
655 Beach Street
Box 7424
San Francisco, CA 94120-7424

Basic and Clinical Science Course
Section 4

Ophthalmic Pathology and Intraocular Tumors

1999-2000

LEO

LIFELONG
EDUCATION FOR THE
OPHTHALMOLOGIST

American Academy of Ophthalmology

The Basic and Clinical Science Course is one component of the Lifelong Education for the Ophthalmologist (LEO) framework, which assists members in planning their continuing medical education. LEO includes an array of clinical education products that members may select to form individualized, self-directed learning plans for updating their clinical knowledge. Active members or fellows who use LEO components may accumulate sufficient CME credits to earn the LEO Award. Contact the Academy's Clinical Education Division for further information on LEO.

This CME activity was planned and produced in accordance with the ACCME Essentials.

The Academy provides this material for educational purposes only. It is not intended to represent the only or best method or procedure in every case, nor to replace a physician's own judgment or give specific advice for case management. Including all indications, contraindications, side effects, and alternative agents for each drug or treatment is beyond the scope of this material. All information and recommendations should be verified, prior to use, with current information included in the manufacturers' package inserts or other independent sources, and considered in light of the patient's condition and history. Reference to certain drugs, instruments, and other products in this publication is made for illustrative purposes only and is not intended to constitute an endorsement of such. Some material may include information on applications that are not considered community standard, that reflect indications not included in approved FDA labeling, or that are approved for use only in restricted research settings. The FDA has stated that it is the responsibility of the physician to determine the FDA status of each drug or device he or she wishes to use, and to use them with appropriate patient consent in compliance with applicable law. The Academy specifically disclaims any and all liability for injury or other damages of any kind, from negligence or otherwise, for any and all claims that may arise from the use of any recommendations or other information contained herein.

CONTENTS

GENERAL INTRODUCTION

The Basic and Clinical Science Course (BCSC) is designed to provide residents and practitioners with a comprehensive yet concise curriculum of the field of ophthalmology. The BCSC has developed from its original brief outline format, which relied heavily on outside readings, to a more convenient and educationally useful self-contained text. The Academy regularly updates and revises the course, with the goals of integrating the basic science and clinical practice of ophthalmology and of keeping current with new developments in the various subspecialties.

The BCSC incorporates the effort and expertise of more than 70 ophthalmologists, organized into 12 section faculties, working with Academy editorial staff. In addition, the course continues to benefit from many lasting contributions made by the faculties of previous editions. Members of the Academy's Practicing Ophthalmologists Advisory Committee for Education serve on each faculty and, as a group, review every volume before and after major revisions.

Organization of the Course

The 12 sections of the Basic and Clinical Science Course are numbered as follows to reflect a logical order of study, proceeding from fundamental subjects to anatomic subdivisions:

1. Update on General Medicine
2. Fundamentals and Principles of Ophthalmology
3. Optics, Refraction, and Contact Lenses
4. Ophthalmic Pathology and Intraocular Tumors
5. Neuro-Ophthalmology
6. Pediatric Ophthalmology and Strabismus
7. Orbit, Eyelids, and Lacrimal System
8. External Disease and Cornea
9. Intraocular Inflammation and Uveitis
10. Glaucoma
11. Lens and Cataract
12. Retina and Vitreous

In addition, a comprehensive Master Index allows the reader to easily locate subjects throughout the entire series.

References

Readers who wish to explore specific topics in greater detail may consult the journal references cited within each chapter and the Basic Texts listed at the back of the book. These references are intended to be selective rather than exhaustive, chosen by the BCSC faculty as being important, current, and readily available to residents and practitioners.

Related Academy educational materials are also listed in the appropriate sections. They include books, audiovisual materials, self-assessment programs, clinical modules, and interactive programs.

Study Questions and CME Credit

Each volume includes multiple-choice study questions designed to be used as a closed-book exercise. The answers are accompanied by explanations to enhance the learning experience. Completing the study questions allows readers both to test their understanding of the material and to demonstrate section completion for the purpose of CME credit, if desired.

The Academy is accredited by the Accreditation Council for Continuing Medical Education to sponsor continuing medical education for physicians. CME credit hours in Category 1 of the Physician's Recognition Award of the AMA may be earned for completing the study of any section of the BCSC. The Academy designates the number of credit hours for each section based upon the scope and complexity of the material covered (see the Credit Reporting Form in each individual section for the maximum number of hours that may be claimed).

Based upon return of the Credit Reporting Form at the back of each book, the Academy will maintain a record, for up to 3 years, of credits earned by Academy members. Upon request, the Academy will send a transcript of credits earned.

Conclusion

The Basic and Clinical Science Course has expanded greatly over the years, with the addition of much new text and numerous illustrations. Recent editions have sought to place a greater emphasis on clinical applicability, while maintaining a solid foundation in basic science. As with any educational program, it reflects the experience of its authors. As its faculties change and as medicine progresses, new viewpoints are always emerging on controversial subjects and techniques. Not all alternate approaches can be included in this series; as with any educational endeavor, the learner should seek additional sources, including such carefully balanced opinions as the Academy's Preferred Practice Patterns.

The BCSC faculty and staff are continuously striving to improve the educational usefulness of the course; you, the reader, can contribute to this ongoing process. If you have any suggestions or questions about the series, please do not hesitate to contact the faculty or the managing editor.

The authors, editors, and reviewers hope that your study of the BCSC will be of lasting value and that each section will serve as a practical resource for quality patient care.

OBJECTIVES FOR BCSC SECTION 4

Upon completion of BCSC Section 4, *Ophthalmic Pathology and Intraocular Tumors,* the reader should be able to:

- Explain the functioning, capabilities, and limitations of an ophthalmic pathology laboratory

- Summarize the histopathology of common ocular conditions in order to improve diagnostic acumen

- Explain the basic histopathology of common ocular conditions as viewed by light microscopy

- Correlate clinical and pathologic findings

- Identify characteristics that differentiate intraocular tumors

- Describe the basic principles of immunohistochemistry, flow cytometry, and polymerase chain reaction (PCR)

- Communicate with the ocular pathologist

- Select from the many textbooks available on ocular pathology

- Identify ophthalmic lesions that indicate systemic disease

- Summarize new information about the most common primary tumors of the eye

- Identify those lesions that are life-threatening to patients

- Assess modern treatment modalities for ocular tumors that offer the patient the best possible survival and that minimize disfigurement and loss of function

- Describe new and current treatment modalities for intraocular tumors

- Provide useful genetic data to those at risk of developing retinoblastoma

- Describe useful ancillary tests that help the clinician to differentiate the various ocular tumors

INTRODUCTION TO SECTION 4

This volume of the Basic and Clinical Science Course (BCSC) is divided into two parts: Part 1, Ophthalmic Pathology; and Part 2, Intraocular Tumors: Clinical Aspects. Although these are two distinct disciplines, there is overlap, and it is critically important for the sight and life of the patient that the physician understand both the clinical and pathologic aspects of ocular neoplasia. The importance of correlating the clinical findings of other ophthalmic disciplines, such as cornea and retina, with the corresponding pathologic findings should not be neglected.

Part 1, Ophthalmic Pathology, uses a hierarchy that moves from general to specific to help derive a differential diagnosis for a specific tissue. This concept was introduced by Curtis E. Margo, MD, and Hans E. Grossniklaus, MD, in the book *Ocular Histopathology: A Guide to Differential Diagnosis,* and it may be used as an organizational framework for the study of ophthalmic pathology.

Part 2, Intraocular Tumors: Clinical Aspects, is a compilation of selected clinical aspects of importance to the general ophthalmologist. Since intraocular tumors may be both vision- and life-threatening, ophthalmologists must be aware of the basic principles of their diagnosis and treatment.

We are grateful to the former chair of BCSC 4, Elise Torczynski, MD, for her leadership and guidance prior to this current revision.

The History of Ophthalmic Pathology

The establishment of ocular pathology as an independent science depended, obviously, on the development of our knowledge of the normal anatomy of the eye. Although animal eyes had been dissected for thousands of years, both Aristotle and Hippocrates held rather vague ideas about ocular anatomy. Only much later did the Greek school of Alexandria establish a formal structure of ocular anatomy. The first reports are by Rufus of Ephesus. He lived at the end of the first and the beginning of the second century AD and worked at least for a time in Egypt. His observations were astute, and, while he still believed that the crystalline lens was the seat of all vision, he wrote excellent descriptions of the anatomy of the eye and the orbit.

His counterpart in Rome was Aulus Cornelius Celsus, who lived from 25 BC to AD 50 and was the first to give us a systematic treatise on ophthalmology. However, he did not contribute anything original on the anatomy of the eye but rather followed the Greek authors in a slavish way.

The high point of anatomical work during the classical time was reached by the Greek physician Claudius Galenus (Galen). Galenus was born in AD 131 in Pergamon (Asia Minor) and died in Rome in AD 201. He was by far the most prominent of the physicians of Rome, and his anatomical descriptions remained in use until Zinn created the modern study of anatomy when he published his book in Goettingen in 1755.

Johann Gottfried Zinn was born in 1727 in Germany and was only 24 years old when he was appointed professor of medicine in Goettingen. At the same time, he became the director of the botanical gardens, and his important contributions to botany led Linnaeus to name a large family of flowers the zinnias. He died before he was 32. For a short time, Zinn was a pupil of the famous Swiss naturalist and physiologist Albrecht von Haller, who first described the cribriform plate and the ophthalmic artery with its branches. Zinn's book has remained the foundation of modern anatomy for the eye. The exact and detailed descriptions have made this work famous. The superb text by Zinn was later complemented by the beautiful atlas published by Samuel Thomas Soemmerring (1755–1830), which appeared in Frankfurt in 1801.

The next advance in normal anatomy study was a book by Julius Arnold that appeared in Leipzig in 1832, when the author was only 29 years old. He already used the microscope but not yet thin tissue sections.

The anatomical studies in the 19th century culminated in the book by Ernst Brucke, who was born in Berlin and became a professor of physiology and anatomy in Vienna. In 1847 he wrote his anatomical description of the human eye. Brucke was the first to use thin sections to investigate the anatomical structures, and he found the longitudinal fibers of the ciliary muscle.

The first book on histology of the eye, written by Samuel Moritz Pappenheim (1811–1882), appeared in Breslau in 1842. The next step forward in this field was made by William Bowman in his book *Lectures on the Part Concerned in the Operations on the Eye,* which appeared in 1849.

The first indications of a pathologic anatomy concerning vision appeared in the book *Sepulchretum,* published by Theophile Bonet. Bonet, who was born in 1620 in Geneva, died from rabies in his hometown in 1689. The book appeared in 1700 in Lyons. Among the cases described are an optic atrophy due to a brain tumor, a case of syphilis of the frontal bone, a large retinoblastoma, and a chiasmal cyst with optic atrophy.

A more systematic and extensive discussion of ocular pathology was written by Giovanni Battista Morgagni, who was first an assistant to Valsalva (the pupil of Malpighi) in Bologna and then became professor of anatomy in Padua. He published his classic work *De Sedibus et Causis Morborum* in 1761, when he was nearly 80 years old. His 13th letter gives an extensive description of pathologic changes of the visual organ. It contains excellent discussions of the pathologic anatomy of the cataract, vitreous opacities, and traumatic exophthalmos.

The first anatomical examination of diseased eyes occurred in the 18th century. The peculiar structure of the eye required special examination techniques, and these techniques developed slowly. It is therefore not surprising that the first real textbook on general pathologic anatomy, published by Mattias Baillie in London in 1793, does not discuss the visual organ at all.

The first book devoted entirely to ophthalmic pathology was written by James Wardrop (1782–1869), one of the foremost ophthalmologists of his time in the United Kingdom. He was born in Scotland but soon moved to London, where he became a member of the Royal College of Surgeons. After he had successfully treated the eye of a horse that belonged to the Prince Regent, he became the monarch's surgeon, and in 1828 he became surgeon to King George IV. His essays on the morbid anatomy of the human eye appeared in 1808, and a second volume was added in 1818. In his book Wardrop summarized numerous quotations from the world literature, adding valuable and important personal observations.

Although Wardrop was recognized for his scientific contributions, his personal life soon brought him into conflict with the establishment. As a convinced liberal, he was an ardent supporter of the Reform Movement, and his abrasive personality made him many enemies, especially at court. He withdrew from public life at an early age, hardly ever attended medical meetings, and was practically forgotten.

Albrecht von Graefe tells of being at a banquet in London in 1850. Next to him happened to sit James Wardrop. After they had introduced themselves, von Graefe asked Wardrop whether the author of the book on retinoblastoma, which had appeared in 1809, was his father or grandfather; Wardrop smiled and explained that he himself was the grandfather. Julius Hirschberg, a well-known ophthalmologist and historian, regarded Wardrop's books on pathology as a rich source of new and important facts destined to be of continuing value.

The second textbook on ocular pathologic anatomy was published by Dr. Matthias Johannes Albrecht Schoen in Hamburg in 1828. Schoen was born and practiced in that city. The book is complete in its contents and extremely well organized.

The third textbook was published by Friedrich August von Ammon. He was born in Goettingen in 1799 and became professor of pathology and pharmacology in Dresden in 1828. He later became surgeon to the court of Saxony. Many feel that von Ammon's contribution inaugurated the modern era of the study of pathologic anatomy of the eye.

von Ammon's book was followed by a few important monographs, including one by John Dalrymple in English (1849–1852), one by Alan Williams Sichel in French (1852–1859), and one by George Theodor Ruete in German (1854–1860).

Heinrich Müller (1820–1864), a professor in Wurzburg, is considered the founder of pathologic histology of the eye. He described the microscopic anatomy of the eye and its pathologic alterations. Müller made a number of important anatomical discoveries: the glial cells in the retina, the annular part of the ciliary muscle, and the smooth eyelid muscles are all named after him. At the same time, R. Albert Kolliker, one of the foremost histologists of his time, and Rudolf Virchow, the creator of modern pathology, worked at the University of Wurzburg. It is not surprising that this university became the focal point of modern pathologic anatomy.

Müller attracted numerous pupils, but with his death and with Virchow's move to Berlin, Vienna became the center of ocular pathology. Here Karl Freiherr von Rokitansky pioneered in modern pathology. One of his pupils, the pathologist Carl Wedl, dedicated 10 years of his life to the study of ocular pathology. He published his famous atlas in 1861 in collaboration with the ophthalmologist Stellwag von Carion. Wedl greatly influenced the clinicians of that time, especially Carl Ferdinand Ritter von Arlt, the teacher of Ernst Fuchs (1851–1930), whose numerous contributions to ophthalmic pathology are well known.

A second center developed in Paris. Poncet de Cluny (died 1899) was one of the most prominent pupils of Louis Antoine Ranvier. The first French textbook on pathologic anatomy was published by Panas and André Rochon-Duvigneaud (1898).

The first histologic eye examinations in London were reported by J. W. Hulke (1859). This compilation was soon followed by the works of Edward Nettleship, the excellent textbook by J. Herbert Parsons, and the monograph by E. Treacher Collins and H. Stephen Mayou.

In Italy the science was taken up first by C. de Cincentiis (1872) and later by G. Circincione. Later German textbooks were by Adolf Alt of Toronto (1880), Wedl and Bock of Vienna (1886), and Otto Haab of Zurich (1890).

By the end of the 19th century, ophthalmic pathology had become a firmly established science that was more often than not advanced by ophthlamologists rather than pathologists. Only during the last few decades have general pathologists again become interested in the eye, thereby contributing greatly to our understanding of disease processes and enabling us to initiate a more purposeful therapy.

Frederick C. Blodi, MD

PART 1

OPHTHALMIC PATHOLOGY

CHAPTER I

Introduction to Part 1

The purpose of BCSC Section 4, *Ophthalmic Pathology and Intraocular Tumors,* is to provide a general overview of the fields of ophthalmic pathology and ocular oncology. This book contains numerous illustrations of entities commonly encountered in an ophthalmic pathology laboratory and in the practice of ocular oncology. In addition, important, but less common, entities are included for teaching purposes. For more comprehensive reviews of ophthalmic pathology and ocular oncology, the reader is referred to several excellent textbooks listed in Basic Texts at the end of this volume.

Part 1 of this text provides a framework for the study of ophthalmic pathology with the following hierarchical organizational paradigm, which is explained in detail below: topography, disease process, general diagnosis, differential diagnosis. Chapter II briefly covers basic principles and specific aspects of wound repair as it applies to ophthalmic tissues, which exhibit distinct responses to trauma, including endstage processes such as *phthisis bulbi.* Chapter III discusses specimen handling, including orientation and dissection, and emphasizes the critical communication between the ophthalmologist and pathologist. Although most ophthalmic pathology specimens are routinely processed and slides are stained with hematoxylin and eosin (H&E), special procedures are used in selected cases. Chapter IV details several of these procedures, including immunohistochemical staining, flow cytometry, polymerase chain reaction (PCR), and electron microscopy. Also discussed are indications in some instances for special techniques in obtaining the specimen, such as fine-needle aspiration biopsy, and special ways of preparing slides for examination, such as frozen sections. Chapters V through XV provide specific examples in the framework of the ophthalmic pathology organizational paradigm.

Organization

Chapters V through XV in Part 1, Ophthalmic Pathology, are each devoted to a particular ocular structure. Within the chapter the text is organized from general to specific according to the following hierarchical framework:

☐ Topography

☐ Disease process

☐ General diagnosis

☐ Differential diagnosis

Topography

The microscopic evaluation of a specimen, whether on a glass slide or depicted in a photograph, should begin with a description of any normal tissue. For instance, the topography of the cornea is characterized by nonkeratinized stratified squamous epithelium, Bowman's layer, stroma, Descemet's membrane, and endothelium. By recognizing a particular structure, such as Bowman's layer or Descemet's membrane in a biopsy specimen, an examiner might be able to identify the topography in question as cornea. It may not be possible to identify the specific tissue source from the topography present in a given glass slide or photograph. For example, a specimen showing the topographic features of keratinized stratified squamous epithelium overlying dermis with dermal appendages may be classified as skin; however, it is not necessarily from the eyelid, unless specific eyelid structures such as tarsal plate, etc, are identified. The reader is referred to BCSC Section 2, *Fundamentals and Principles of Ophthalmology,* for a review of ophthalmic anatomy.

Disease Process

After identifying the tissue source, the student should attempt to categorize the general disease process. These processes include

☐ Congenital anomaly

☐ Inflammation

☐ Degeneration and dystrophy

☐ Neoplasm

Congenital anomalies   Congenital anomalies usually involve abnormalities in size, location, organization, or amount of tissue. An example of congenitally enlarged tissue is congenital hypertrophy of the retinal pigment epithelium (CHRPE) (Figs I-1, I-2). Many congenital abnormalities may be classified as choristomas or hamartomas.

A *choristoma* consists of normal, mature tissue at an abnormal location. It occurs when one or two embryonic germ layers form mature tissue that is abnormal for a given topographic location. One example of a choristoma is a *dermoid:* skin

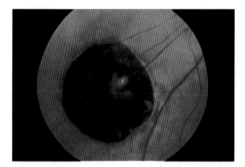

FIG I-1—Congenital hypertrophy of the RPE is darkly pigmented and surrounded by a lightly pigmented rim.

FIG I-2—The darkly pigmented retinal pigment epithelium (RPE) (arrow) is adjacent to lightly pigmented RPE containing lipofuscin and corresponding to the rim (arrowhead).

that is otherwise normal and mature present at the abnormal location of the limbus. A tumor made up of tissue derived from all three embryonic germ layers is called a *teratoma.*

In contrast, the term *hamartoma* describes an exaggerated hypertrophy and hyperplasia (abnormal amount) of mature tissue at a normal location. One example of a hamartoma is a *cavernous hemangioma,* an encapsulated mass of mature venous channels in the orbit. Examples of congenital abnormalities encountered in specific tissues (such as cornea, conjunctiva, etc) are illustrated in the appropriate chapters. Some important congenital conditions are listed in Table I-1 on pp 14–16.

Inflammation The next disease process in our schema, inflammation, is classified in several ways. It may be acute or chronic in onset and focal or diffuse in location. Chronic inflammation is subdivided further as either granulomatous or nongranulomatous. For example, a bacterial corneal ulcer is generally an acute, focal inflammatory process, while sympathetic ophthalmia is a chronic, diffuse granulomatous inflammation.

Polymorphonuclear leukocytes (PMN), eosinophils, and basophils all circulate in the blood and may be present in tissue in early phases of the inflammatory process (Figs I-3, I-4, I-5). The types of leukocytes present at the site of inflammation

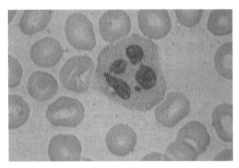

FIG I-3—Polymorphonuclear leukocyte with multilobulated nucleus.

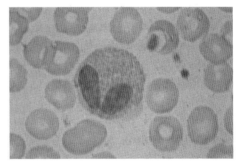

FIG I-4—Eosinophil with bilobed nucleus and intracytoplasmic eosinophilic granules.

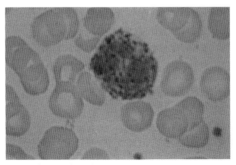

FIG I-5—Basophil with intracytoplasmic basophilic granules.

TABLE 1-1

IMPORTANT CONGENITAL CONDITIONS

CONDITION	DESCRIPTION	ASSOCIATED OCULAR CONDITION	ASSOCIATED CONDITIONS AND RISKS	TRANSMISSION
Oculodermal melanocytosis (nevus of Ota)	Increased number of dendritic melanocytes in uvea, sclera, episclera, conjunctiva, and skin	Uveal melanoma, increased incidence	Malignant melanoma, orbit	None
Buphthalmos (megaloglobus)	Enlargement of globe in association with glaucoma	Glaucoma, congenital	Neurofibromatosis Sturge-Weber syndrome	Autosomal dominant None
Aniridia	Rudimentary, shortened iris leaflet without sphincter	Corneal pannus, macular hypoplasia, nystagmus, cataracts	In sporadic cases: Wilms tumor with deletion of 11p13, microcephaly, mental retardation, genital abnormalities	Autosomal dominant and recessive forms
Cataract	Lens opacification: nuclear, cortical, or combination forms	Retinal pigment epithelial disturbance and cataract (rubella), lens subluxation (Marfan), PHPV, Peters anomaly, aniridia, Axenfeld-Rieger anomaly	Lowe syndrome; Alport syndrome; Sjögren syndrome; Hallermann-Streiff syndrome; Pierre Robin syndrome; Treacher Collins syndrome; Bloch-Sulzberger syndrome; congenital ectodermal dysplasia; Rothmund syndrome; Schafer syndrome; Conradi syndrome; trisomies 21, 13, and 18; 11p– syndrome; third-trimester asphyxia	Autosomal dominant and recessive forms
Persistent hyperplastic primary vitreous (PHPV)	Retrolenticular fibrovascular mass; sometimes containing adipose tissue, cartilage, or smooth muscle; with elongated ciliary processes	Microphthalmos, cataract, persistent hyaloid vessels, retinal detachment or fold, macular hypoplasia, developmental glaucoma		Usually sporadic

TABLE I-1

IMPORTANT CONGENITAL CONDITIONS (continued)

CONDITION	DESCRIPTION	ASSOCIATED OCULAR CONDITION	ASSOCIATED CONDITIONS AND RISKS	TRANSMISSION
Hypoplastic optic disc	Decreased disc diameter and axonal mass	Decreased caliber, central retinal vessels; aniridia; PHPV	11p– syndrome; septo-optic dysplasia; maternal diabetes mellitus	Usually sporadic
Optic nerve pit	Depression in optic disc, usually inferotemporally, communicating with subarachnoid space	Serous detachment of macula with macular hemorrhage, cysts, or holes		Usually sporadic
*von Hippel–Lindau disease (retinal angiomatosis)	Retinal angioma supplied by dilated tortuous arteriole and venule; may be multiple	Retinal exudates, hemorrhages, retinal detachment, glaucoma	Cerebellar capillary hemangiomas, malformation of visceral organs	Autosomal dominant, chromosome 3p25
*Sturge-Weber syndrome (encephalofacial angiomatosis)	Capillary hamartia (nevus flammeus) of skin, conjunctiva, episclera, and/or uveal tract, and of meninges	Glaucoma (especially with upper eyelid involvement by nevus flammeus)	Diffuse meningeal hemangioma with seizure disorder, hemiplegia or hemianopia, or mental retardation	Sporadic
*Neurofibromatosis (von Recklinghausen disease)	Occasionally congenital, widespread hamartomas of peripheral nerves and tissue of neural crest derivation	Neurofibromas of lid and orbit, uveal melanocytic nevi, retinal glial hamartomas, congenital glaucoma, optic nerve glioma, absence of greater wing of sphenoid with pulsating exophthalmos	Similar hamartomas of central nervous system, peripheral and cranial nerves, gastrointestinal tract; malignant transformation possible	Autosomal dominant NF-I: chromosome 17q11.2

* These are among the six entities that constitute the group of congenital conditions referred to as *phakomatoses.*

TABLE I-1

IMPORTANT CONGENITAL CONDITIONS (continued)

CONDITION	DESCRIPTION	ASSOCIATED OCULAR CONDITION	ASSOCIATED CONDITIONS AND RISKS	TRANSMISSION
*Tuberous sclerosis (Bourneville disease)	Mental deficiency, seizures, and adenoma sebaceum	Angiofibromas of eyelid skin; glial hamartomas of retina and optic disc	Adenoma sebaceum (angiofibromas), cerebral glial hamartomas	Autosomal dominant, chromosome 9q34
*Ataxia-telangiectasia (Louis-Bar syndrome)	Progressive cerebellar ataxia, ocular and cutaneous telangiectasis, pulmonary infections	Conjuctival telangiectasis, anomalous ocular movements, and nystagmus	Dysarthria, coarse hair and skin, immunologic deficiency, and mental and growth retardation	Autosomal recessive, chromosome 11q22
*Wyburn-Mason syndrome (racemose angioma)	Retinal and midbrain arteriovenous (AV) communication (aneurysms and angiomas) and facial nevi	AV communication (racemose angioma) of retina, with vision loss depending on location of AV communication	AV aneurysm at midbrain; intracranial calcification	Sporadic
Xeroderma pigmentosa	Lack of ability to repair DNA damaged by ultraviolet light	Xerosis of conjunctiva and cornea with degeneration; squamous cell carcinoma of conjunctiva	Atrophy, erythema, pigmentary disturbances of skin (including eyelids), with squamous and basal carcinomas, melanomas and fibrosarcoma ensuing	Autosomal recessive
Cephalocele, meningocele, meningo-encephalocele	Intraorbital herniation of cerebral and/or meningeal tissue, sometimes with communication between orbit and intracranial space	Mass at nasal bridge, medial canthus or upper eyelid nasally; subcutaneous; usually soft and collapsible. Sometimes proptosis of ipsilateral eye is present.	Injudicious surgical exploration can produce cerebral damage or meningitis	Sporadic

* These are among the six entities that constitute the group of congenital conditions referred to as *phakomatoses.*

Isselbacher KJ, Braunwald E, Wilson JD, eds. *Harrison's Principles of Internal Medicine.* 13th ed. New York: McGraw-Hill; 1994:2207–2210.

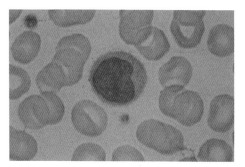

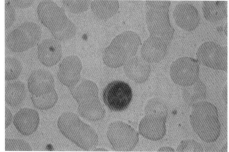

FIG I-6—Monocyte with indented nucleus.

FIG I-7—Lymphocyte with small, hyperchromatic nucleus and scant cytoplasm.

vary according to the inflammatory response. *PMN*, also known as *neutrophils*, typify acute inflammatory cells and can be recognized by a multisegmented nucleus and intracytoplasmic granules. They may be present in a variety of acute inflammatory processes; for example, they are associated with bacterial infection and found in the walls of blood vessels in some forms of vasculitis. *Eosinophils* have bilobed nuclei and prominent intracytoplasmic eosinophilic granules. They are commonly found in allergic reactions, although they may also be present in chronic inflammatory processes such as sympathetic ophthalmia. *Basophils* contain basophilic intracytoplasmic granules. *Mast cells* are the tissue-bound equivalent of the bloodborne basophils.

Inflammatory cells that are relatively characteristic of chronic inflammatory processes include monocytes (Fig I-6) and lymphocytes (Fig I-7). *Monocytes* may migrate from the intravascular space into tissue, in which case they are classified as *histiocytes,* or *macrophages.* Histiocytes have eccentric nuclei and abundant eosinophilic cytoplasm. In some instances, histiocytes may take on the appearance of epithelial cells, with abundant eosinophilic cytoplasm and sharp cell borders, hence becoming known as *epithelioid histiocytes.* Epithelioid histiocytes may form a ball-like aggregate, known as a *granuloma,* the sine qua non for granulomatous inflammation. These granulomas may contain only histologically intact cells ("hard" tubercles, Fig I-8), or they may exhibit necrotic centers ("caseating" granulomas, Fig I-9). Epithelioid histiocytes may merge to form a syncytium with multiple nuclei known as a *multinucleated giant cell.* Giant cells formed from histiocytes come in several varieties, including

☐ Langhans' cells characterized by a horseshoe arrangement of the nuclei (Fig I-10)

☐ Touton giant cells, which have an annulus of nuclei surrounded by a lipid-filled clear zone (Fig I-11)

☐ Foreign body giant cells with haphazardly arranged nuclei (Fig I-12)

Lymphocytes are small cells with round, hyperchromatic nuclei and scanty cytoplasm. Circulating lymphocytes infiltrate tissue in all types of chronic inflammatory processes. These cells terminally differentiate in the thymus *(T cells)* or bursa equiv-

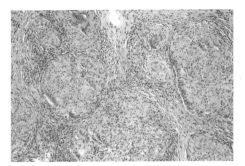

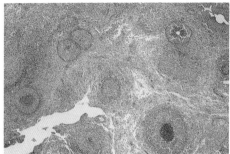

FIG I-8—Noncaseating granulomas, or "hard" tubercles, are formed by aggregates of epithelioid histiocytes.

FIG I-9—Granulomas with necrotic centers are classified as caseating granulomas.

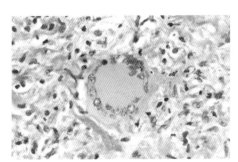

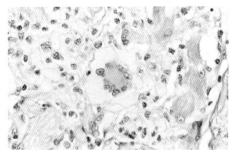

FIG I-10—Langhans' giant cell.

FIG I-11—Touton giant cell.

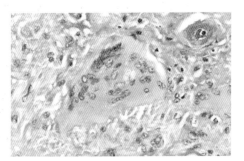

FIG I-12—Foreign body giant cell.

alent *(B cells)*, although it is not possible to distinguish between B and T lymphocytes with routine histologic stains. B cells may produce immunoglobulin and differentiate into *plasma cells,* with eccentric "cartwheel," or "clockface," nuclei and a perinuclear hof corresponding to the Golgi apparatus. These cells may

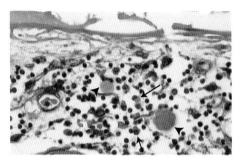

FIG I-13—This aggregate of plasma cells (arrows) is associated with Russell bodies (arrowheads).

become completely distended with immunoglobulin and form *Russell bodies,* which may be extracellular (Fig I-13). BCSC Section 9, *Intraocular Inflammation and Uveitis,* discusses the cells involved in the inflammatory process in depth in Part 1, Immunology.

Degeneration and dystrophy   The term *degeneration* refers to a wide variety of deleterious tissue changes that occur over time. Degenerative processes are not usually associated with a proliferation of cells; rather, there is often an accumulation of acellular material or a loss of tissue mass. Extracellular deposits may result from cellular overproduction of normal material or metabolically abnormal material. These processes, which have a spectrum of pathologic appearances, may occur in response to an injury or an inflammatory process. *Dystrophies* are defined as bilateral, symmetric, inherited conditions that appear to have little or no relationship to environmental or systemic factors.

Degeneration of tissue may be seen in conjunction with other general disease processes. Examples include calcification of the lens (degeneration) in association with a congenital cataract (congenital anomaly); corneal amyloid (degeneration) in association with trachoma (inflammation); and orbital amyloid (degeneration) in association with a lymphoma (neoplasm). The ophthalmic manifestations of diabetes mellitus can be classified as degenerative changes associated with a metabolic disease. Although "degeneration" may appear to be a somewhat artificial category, it is helpful within the hierarchical classification scheme used in this text.

Neoplasia   A *neoplasm* is a stereotypic, monotonous new growth of a particular tissue phenotype. Neoplasms can occur in either benign or malignant forms. Examples found in particular tissues include

- Adenoma (benign) versus adenocarcinoma (malignant) in glandular epithelium
- Topography + *oma* (benign) versus topography + *sarcoma* (malignant) in soft tissue
- Hyperplasia/infiltrate (benign) versus leukemia/lymphoma (malignant) in hematopoietic tissue

TABLE I-2

CLASSIFICATION OF NEOPLASIA

TISSUE ORIGIN	BENIGN	MALIGNANT	GROWTH PATTERN
Epithelium	Hyperplasia/adenoma	Carcinoma Adenocarcinoma	Cords Tubules
Soft tissue	Topography + *oma*	Topography + *sarcoma*	Coherent sheets
Hematopoietic tissue	Hyperplasia/infiltrate	Leukemia Lymphoma	Loosely arranged

Some neoplastic proliferations are called *borderline*, in that they are difficult to classify histologically as benign or malignant. Although most of the neoplasia illustrated and discussed in this text are classified as benign or malignant, the reader should be aware that tissue evaluation in a particular disease can give only a static portrait of a dynamic process. Thus, it may be impossible to determine whether the process will ultimately be benign or malignant, and in some instances "indeterminant" or "borderline" is a legitimate interpretation. Table I-2 summarizes the origin, general classification of benign versus malignant, and growth pattern of neoplasia originating in various tissues.

The growth patterns described in Table I-2 are shown in Figure I-14 on p 21. General histologic signs of malignancy include cellular pleomorphism, necrosis, hemorrhage, and mitotic activity.

General Diagnosis

After considering the topography and disease process, the examiner formulates the general diagnosis. Recognizing a tissue *index feature* is a critical step in arriving at the general diagnosis. Index features are morphologic identifiers that help to define the disease process more specifically. Examples include presence of pigment in a pigmented neoplasm, necrosis in a necrotizing granulomatous inflammation, and accumulation of smudgy extracellular material in a smudgy eosinophilic corneal degeneration. The index feature should differentiate the particular specimen from others demonstrating the same general disease process. For instance, retinoblastoma and melanoma are both intraocular malignant neoplasms; the former is a retinal malignancy, and the latter is a uveal tract malignancy. Other index features for distinguishing between these lesions could be "small, round blue cell tumor" for the retinoblastoma and "melanocytic proliferation" for the melanoma. Although the most basic index features can be recognized without great difficulty, it takes experience and practice to identify subtle index features.

General Classification of Malignant Tumors

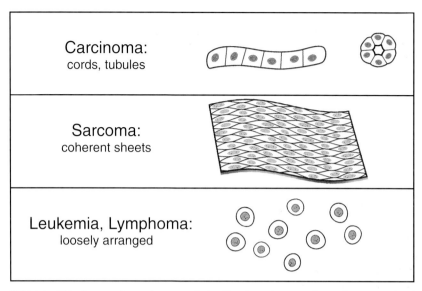

Carcinoma:
cords, tubules

Sarcoma:
coherent sheets

Leukemia, Lymphoma:
loosely arranged

FIG I-14—This diagram shows the general classification scheme and growth pattern of malignant tumors. (Illustration by Christine Gralapp.)

Differential Diagnosis

After the examiner has distinguished a key index feature and formulated a general diagnosis, developing a differential diagnosis is the next step. The differential diagnosis is a limited list of specific conditions resulting from pathologic processes that were identified in the general diagnosis. For instance, the differential diagnosis based on the features of noncaseating granulomatous inflammation of the conjunctiva includes sarcoidosis, foreign body, fungus, and mycobacterium. The differential diagnosis of melanocytic proliferation of the conjunctiva includes nevus, primary acquired melanosis, and melanoma.

The reader is encouraged to practice working through the hierarchical framework by verbalizing each step in sequence while examining a pathologic specimen. Chapters V through XV of this book provide tissue-specific examples of the differential diagnoses for each of the four disease process categories. The expanded organizational paradigm is shown in Table I-3.

TABLE I-3

ORGANIZATIONAL PARADIGM FOR OPHTHALMIC PATHOLOGY

Topography

Conjunctiva

Cornea

Anterior chamber/trabecular meshwork

Sclera

Lens

Vitreous

Retina

Uveal tract

Eyelids

Orbit

Optic nerve

Disease Process

Congenital anomaly

    Choristoma versus hamartoma

Inflammation

    Acute versus chronic

    Focal versus diffuse

    Granulomatous versus nongranulomatous

Degeneration (includes dystrophy)

Neoplasm

    Benign versus malignant

    Epithelial versus soft tissue versus hematopoietic

General Diagnosis

Index feature

Differential Diagnosis

Limited list

CHAPTER II

Wound Repair

General Aspects of Wound Repair

Wound healing, though a common physiological process, requires a complicated sequence of tissue events. The purpose of wound healing is to restore the anatomic and functional integrity of an organ or tissue as quickly and perfectly as possible. Repair may take a year, and the result of wound healing is a scar with variable consequences (Fig II-1). A series of reactions follows a wound, including an acute inflammatory phase, regeneration/repair, and contraction.

☐ The *acute inflammatory phase* may last from minutes to hours. Blood clots quickly in adjacent vessels in response to tissue activators. Neutrophils and fluid enter the extracellular space. Macrophages remove debris from the damaged tissues, new vessels form, and fibroblasts begin to produce collagen.

☐ *Regeneration* is the replacement of lost cells, and it occurs only in tissues composed of labile cells (e.g., epithelium), which undergo mitosis throughout life. *Repair* is the restructuring of tissues by granulation tissue that matures into a fibrous scar.

☐ Finally, *contraction* causes the reparative tissues to shrink so that the scar is smaller than the surrounding uninjured tissues.

Healing in Specific Ocular Tissues

The processes summarized below are also discussed in other volumes of the BCSC series. See Section 7, *Orbit, Eyelids, and Lacrimal System;* Section 8, *External Disease and Cornea;* Section 9, *Intraocular Inflammation and Uveitis;* Section 11, *Lens and Cataract;* and Section 12, *Retina and Vitreous.* See also the appropriate chapters in this volume for a specific topography.

Cornea

A corneal *abrasion,* a painful but rapidly healing defect, is limited to the surface corneal epithelium, although Bowman's layer and superficial stroma may also be involved. Within an hour of injury the parabasilar epithelial cells begin to slide and migrate across the denuded area until they touch other migrating cells; then *contact inhibition* stops further migration. Simultaneously, the surrounding basal cells undergo mitosis to supply additional cells to cover the defect. Although a large corneal abrasion is usually sealed within 24 hours, complete healing, which includes restoration of the full thickness of epithelium (4–6 layers) and re-formation of the anchoring fibrils, takes 4–6 weeks. The epithelial cells are labile; that is, some are

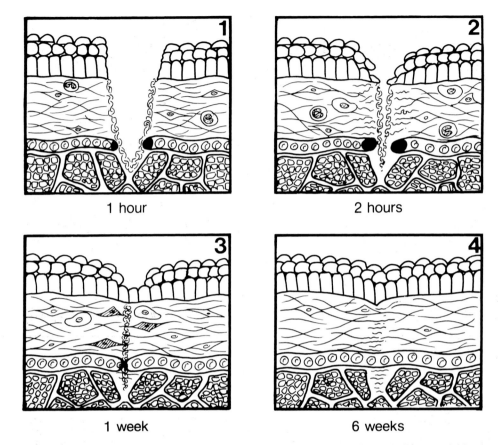

1 hour

2 hours

1 week

6 weeks

FIG II-1—Sequence of general wound healing with an epithelial surface. *1,* The wound is created. Blood clots in the vessels; neutrophils migrate to the wound; the wounded edges begin to disintegrate. *2,* The wound edges are reapposed with the various tissue planes in good alignment. The epithelium is lost over the wound but starts to migrate. The subcutaneous fibroblasts enlarge and become activated. Fibronectin is deposited at the wound edges. The blood vessels begin to produce buds. *3,* The epithelium seals the surface. Fibroblasts and blood vessels enter the wound and lay down new collagen. Much of the debris is removed by macrophages. *4,* As the scar matures, the fibroblasts subside. Newly formed blood vessels recanalize. New collagen strengthens the wound, which contracts. Note that the striated muscle cells (permanent cells) at bottom are replaced by scar.

continuously active mitotically and thus are able to completely replace the lost cells. If a slim layer of anterior cornea is lost with the abrasion, the shallow crater will be filled by epithelium, forming a facet.

Corneal stromal healing is avascular. Unlike other tissues, healing in the corneal stroma occurs by means of fibrosis rather than fibrovascular proliferation. This avascular aspect of corneal wound healing is critical to the success of penetrating keratoplasty as well as photorefractive keratectomy (PRK), laser in-situ keratomileusis (LASIK), and other corneal refractive surgical procedures.

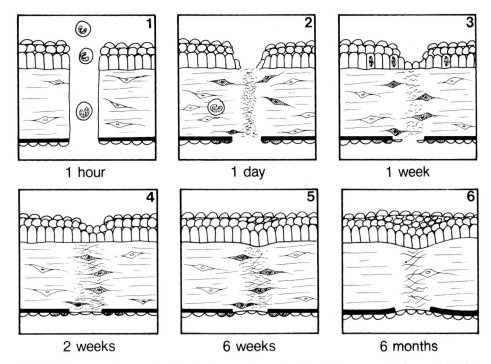

FIG II-2—Clear corneal wound. *1,* The tear film carries neutrophils with lysozymes to the wound within an hour. *2,* With closure of the incision, the wound edge shows early disintegration and edema. The glycosaminoglycans at the edge are degraded. The nearby fibroblasts are activated. *3,* At 1 week, migrating epithelium and endothelium partially seal the wound; fibroblasts begin to migrate and supply collagen. *4,* Fibroblast activity, collagen and matrix deposition continue. The endothelium, sealing the inner wound, lays down new Descemet's membrane. *5,* Epithelial regeneration is complete. Fibroblasts fill the wound with type I collagen and repair slows. *6,* The final wound contracts. The collagen fibers are not parallel with the surrounding lamellae. The number of fibroblasts decreases.

Following wounding of the central cornea, neutrophils arrive, carried by the tears (Fig II-2). The edges of the wound swell. Healing factors derived from vessels are not present. The matrix glycosaminoglycans, which in the cornea are keratan sulfate and chondroitin sulfate, disintegrate at the edge of the wound. The fibroblasts of the stroma become activated, eventually migrating across the wound, laying down collagen and fibronectin. The direction of the fibroblasts and collagen is not parallel to stromal lamellae. Hence, cells are directed anteriorly and posteriorly across a wound that is always visible microscopically as an irregularity in the stroma and clinically as an opacity. If the wound edges are separated, the gap is not completely filled by proliferating fibroblasts, and a partially filled crater results.

Both the epithelium and the endothelium are critical to good central wound healing. If the epithelium does not cover the wound within days, the subjacent stromal healing is limited and the wound is weak. Growth factors from the epithelium stimulate and sustain healing. The endothelial cells adjacent to the wound slide across the posterior cornea; a few cells are replaced through mitotic activity.

Endothelium lays down a new thin layer of Descemet's membrane. If the internal margin of the wound is not covered by Descemet's membrane, stromal fibroblasts may continue to proliferate into the anterior chamber as fibrous ingrowth, or the posterior wound may remain permanently open. The initial fibrillar collagen is replaced by stronger collagen in the late months of healing. Bowman's layer does not regenerate when incised or destroyed. In an ulcer the surface is covered by epithelium, but little of the lost stroma is replaced by fibrous tissue.

Sclera

The sclera differs from the cornea in that the collagen fibers are randomly distributed rather than laid down in orderly lamellae, and the glycosaminoglycan is dermatan sulfate. Sclera is relatively avascular and hypocellular. When stimulated by wounding, the episclera migrates down the scleral wound, supplying vessels, fibroblasts, and activated macrophages. The final wound contracts, creating a pinched-in appearance. If the adjacent uvea is damaged, uveal fibrovascular tissue may enter the scleral wound, resulting in a scar with a dense adhesion between uvea and sclera. Indolent episcleral fibrosis produces a dense coat around an extrascleral foreign body such as a scleral buckle.

Limbus

The limbus is a complex region of corneal, scleral, and episcleral tissues. Wounds of the limbus cause swelling in the cornea and shrinking of the sclera (Fig II-3). Healing involves episcleral ingrowth and clear corneal fibroblastic migration. Collector channels in the sclera do not contribute to the healing. Alterations in surgical technique between clear corneal and limbal incisions may produce different healing responses.

Uvea

Under ordinary circumstances wounds of the iris do not stimulate a healing response in either the stroma or the epithelium. Though richly endowed with blood vessels and fibroblasts, the iridic stroma does not produce granulation tissue to close a defect. The pigmented epithelium may be stimulated to migrate in some circumstances, such as excessive inflammation, but its migration is usually limited to the subjacent surface of the lens capsule, where subsequent adhesion of epithelial cells occurs. When fibrovascular tissue forms, it is usually on the anterior surface of the iris, as an exuberant and aberrant membrane (e.g., rubeosis iridis) that may cross iridectomy or pupillary openings. The fibrovascular tissue may arise from the iris, the chamber angle, or the cornea.

Stroma and melanocytes of the iris, ciliary body, and choroid do not regenerate after injury. Debris is removed, and a thin fibrous scar develops that appears white and atrophic clinically.

Lens

Small rents in the lens capsule are sealed by nearby lenticular epithelial cells. When posterior synechiae make the lenticular epithelium anoxic or hypoxic, a metaplastic response occurs, producing fibrous plaques intermixed with basement membrane.

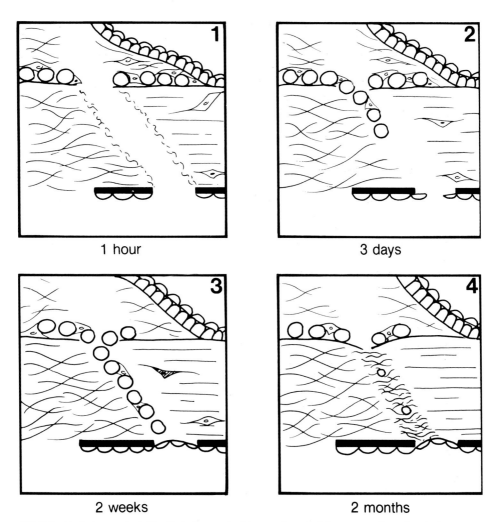

FIG II-3—Limbal wound. *1,* The limbal wound with a conjunctival flap passes through episclera externally and enters the globe through Descemet's membrane and endothelium. Sclera is on the left and cornea on the right. The wound edge shows early disintegration. Neutrophils and macrophages are omitted in this diagram. *2,* Episcleral vessels and fibroblasts migrate down the wound. Some activity is present in the corneal fibroblasts. *3,* Episcleral fibrovascular migration in the wound is stopped at the endothelium crossing the internal margin of the incision. *4,* The number of vessels decreases in the late stage of healing. Irregular collagen fibers and matrix fill the contracting wound.

Retina

The retina is made of permanent cells that do not regenerate when fatally injured. Instead, a glial plug pulls the retina together after closure. Surgical techniques to close openings in the peripheral retina are successful when the neurosensory retina and retinal pigment epithelium (RPE) are destroyed (e.g., cryotherapy, photocoagulation) and the surrounding tissues form an adhesive, atrophic scar.

Retinal scars are produced by glia rather than fibroblasts. After inflammatory cells have cleared away the debris, the tissues most damaged by the therapeutic modality remain as a thin, atrophic area in the center of the scar. Increasing numbers of residual viable cells ring the zone of greatest destruction. Adhesion between the residual neurosensory retina and Bruch's membrane develops according to the size of the original wound and the type of injury. The internal limiting membrane and Bruch's membrane provide the architectural planes for glial scarring. Adhesions from the internal limiting membrane to Bruch's membrane may incorporate a rare residual glial cell, and variable numbers of retinal cells and RPE may be present between the membranes. If the wound has damaged Bruch's membrane, choroidal fibroblasts and vessels may participate in the formation of the final scar. The end result is a metaplastic collagenous plaque in the sub–neurosensory retina and sub-RPE areas. The RPE usually proliferates rather exuberantly in such scars, giving rise to the dense black clumps seen clinically in scars of the fundus.

Vitreous

The vitreous has few cells and no blood vessels. Nonetheless, in conditions that cause vitreal inflammation, mediators stimulate the formation of membranes composed of new vessels and the proliferation of glial and fibrous tissue. With contraction of these membranes, the retina becomes distorted and detached.

Eyelid, Orbit, and Lacrimal Tissues

The rich blood supply of the skin of the eyelids supports rapid and complete healing. About the third day after injury to the skin, myofibroblasts derived from vascular pericytes migrate around the wound and actively contract, resulting in a volumetric decrease in the size of the wound. Early invasion of ocular wounds by myofibroblasts does not occur, and the resultant early contraction does not happen. The eyelid and orbit are compartmentalized by intertwining fascial membranes enclosing muscular, tendinous, fatty, lacrimal, and ocular tissues that are distorted by scarring. Exuberant contracting distorts muscle action, producing dysfunctional scars. The striated muscles of the orbicularis oculi and extraocular muscles are made of permanent cells that do not regenerate, but the viable cells may hypertrophy. Fat tissue atrophies when injured, hence the shrunken appearance of eyelids and globe following a crushing injury to the orbit.

Histologic Sequelae of Ocular Trauma

The anterior chamber angle structures, especially the trabecular beams, are vulnerable to distortion of the anterior globe. *Cyclodialysis* results from disinsertion of the longitudinal muscle of the ciliary muscle from the scleral spur (Fig II-4). This condition can lead to hypotony, because the aqueous of the anterior chamber has free access to the suprachoroidal space, and production of aqueous is decreased.

Traumatic recession of the anterior chamber angle is a rupture of the face of the ciliary body (Fig II-5). A plane of relative weakness starts at the ciliary body face and

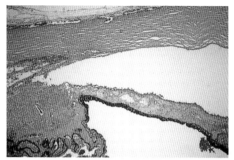

FIG II-4—Cyclodialysis shows disinsertion of ciliary body muscle from scleral spur.

FIG II-5—Angle recession shows a torn ciliary body muscle.

extends posteriorly between the longitudinal muscles of the ciliary body and the more centrally located oblique and circular muscle fibers. Concurrent damage to the trabecular meshwork may lead to glaucoma. The oblique and circular muscle fibers will usually atrophy, changing the overall shape of the cross-sectional appearance of the ciliary body from triangular to fusiform. The ciliary process will appear posteriorly and externally displaced as defined by a line drawn through the scleral spur parallel to the visual axis. In normal eyes this line intersects the first ciliary process.

The entire uveal tract is attached to the sclera at only three points: the scleral spur, the internal ostia of the vortex veins, and the peripapillary tissue. This anatomic arrangement is the basis of the evisceration technique and explains the vulnerability of the eye to expulsive choroidal hemorrhage. The borders of the dome-shaped choroidal hemorrhage are defined by the position of the vortex veins and the scleral spur (Fig II-6).

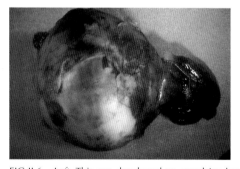

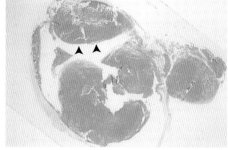

FIG II-6—*Left,* This eye developed an expulsive hemorrhage after a corneal perforation. *Right,* The intraocular choroidal hemorrhage is dome shaped (arrowheads), delineated by the insertion of the choroid at the scleral spur.

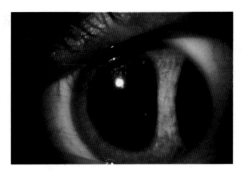

FIG 7—Iridodialysis shows a tear in the base of the iris.

An *iridodialysis* is a rupture of the iris at the thinnest portion of the diaphragm, the iris base, where it inserts into the supportive tissue of the ciliary body (Fig II-7). Only a small amount of supporting tissue surrounds the iris sphincter. If the sphincter muscle is ruptured, contraction of the remaining muscle will create a notch at the pupillary border. The iris diaphragm may be lost completely through a relatively small limbal rupture associated with 360° iridodialysis.

Vossius' ring appears when compression and rupture of iris pigment epithelial cells against the anterior surface of the lens occurs, depositing a ring of melanin pigment concentric to the pupil.

Cataract may form immediately if the lens capsule is ruptured. The lens capsule is thinnest at the posterior pole, a point farthest away from the lens epithelial cells. The epithelium of the lens may be stimulated by trauma to form an anterior lenticular fibrous plaque. The lens zonular fibers are points of relative weakness; if they are ruptured, displacement of the lens can be partial (subluxation) or complete (luxation). Focal areas of zonular rupture may allow formed vitreous to enter the anterior chamber.

Rupture of Descemet's membrane may occur after minor trauma (e.g., in keratoconus, Fig II-8) or major trauma (e.g., after forceps injury, Fig II-9). *Rupture of Bruch's membrane* can occur after compressive injuries (choroidal rupture); the rupture is often concentric to the optic disc. Ruptures of Bruch's membrane itself are not as functionally significant as the accompanying rupture of the overlying retina, which is usually undetectable clinically. A rupture of Bruch's membrane may also permit choroidal neovascularization by allowing the choroidal vasculature access to the subneurosensory retina space.

Retinal dialysis is most likely to develop in the inferotemporal or superonasal quadrants. The retina is anchored anteriorly to the nonpigmented epithelium of the pars plana. This union is reinforced by the attachment of the vitreous, which straddles the ora serrata. Deformation of the eye can result in a circumferential tear of the retina at the point of attachment of the ora or immediately posterior to the point of attachment of the vitreous base. Vitreoretinal traction may cause tears in a retina weakened by necrosis.

Commotio retinae (Berlin disease) usually complicates blunt trauma to the eye. Most prominent in the macula, commotio retinae can affect any portion of the retina. Originally, the retinal opacification seen clinically was thought to result from

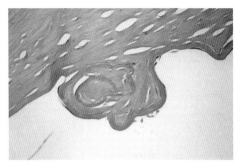 

FIG II-8—A break in Descemet's membrane in ker-atoconus shows anterior curling of Descemet's membrane toward the corneal stroma.

FIG II-9—A break in Descemet's membrane as a result of forceps injury shows anterior curling of the original membrane and production of a secondary thickened membrane.

retinal edema (extracellular accumulation of fluid), but experimental evidence shows that a disruption in the architecture of the photoreceptor elements causes the loss of retinal transparency.

Phthisis bulbi is defined as atrophy, shrinkage, and disorganization of the eye and intraocular contents. Not all eyes rendered sightless by trauma become phthisical. If the nutritional status of the eye and near-normal intraocular pressure (IOP) are maintained during the repair process, the globe will remain clinically stable. However, blind eyes are at high risk of repeated trauma with cumulative destructive effects. Slow progressive functional decompensation may also prevail. Many blind eyes pass through several stages of atrophy and disorganization into the endstage of phthisis bulbi:

☐ *Atrophia bulbi without shrinkage* (Fig II-10). Initially, the size and shape of the eye are maintained. The atrophic eye often has elevated IOP. The following structures are most sensitive to loss of nutrition: the lens, which becomes cataractous; the retina, which atrophies and becomes separated from the RPE by serous fluid accumulation; the aqueous outflow tract, where anterior and posterior synechiae develop.

☐ *Atrophia bulbi with shrinkage.* The eye becomes soft because of ciliary body dysfunction and progressive diminution of IOP. The globe becomes smaller and assumes a squared-off configuration as a result of the influence of the four rectus muscles. The anterior chamber collapses. Associated corneal endothelial cell damage results initially in corneal edema followed by opacification from degenerative pannus, stromal scarring, and vascularization. Most of the remaining internal structures of the eye will be atrophic but recognizable histologically.

☐ *Atrophia bulbi with disorganization (phthisis bulbi)* (Fig II-11). The size of the globe shrinks from a normal average diameter of 24–26 mm to an average diameter of 16–19 mm. Most of the ocular contents become disorganized. In areas of preserved uvea the RPE proliferates and drusen may be seen. Extensive calcification of Bowman's layer, lens, retina, and drusen usually occurs. Osseous metaplasia of the RPE may be a prominent feature. The sclera becomes massively thickened, particularly posteriorly.

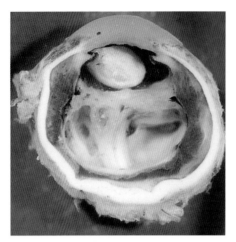

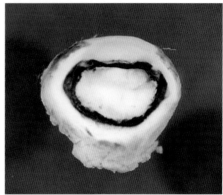

FIG II-10—Atrophia bulbi without shrinkage. Note the dense cyclitic membrane and the corresponding detachment of the ciliary body.

FIG II-11—Phthisis bulbi. The size of the globe is markedly reduced, the sclera is thickened, and the contents of the eye are totally disorganized.

CHAPTER III

Specimen Handling

Communication

Communication with the pathologist before, during, and after surgical procedures is an essential aspect of quality patient care. The final histologic diagnosis reflects successful collaborative work between clinician and pathologist. The ophthalmologist should provide a relevant and reasonably detailed clinical history when the specimen is submitted to the laboratory. This history facilitates clinicopathologic correlation and enables the pathologist to provide the most accurate interpretation of the specimen. Therefore, the clinical history portion of the pathology request form should not be neglected, even in "routine" cases.

In most cases where there is an ongoing relationship between a pathologist and ophthalmologist, communication can be accomplished through the pathology request form and the pathology report. However, if a malignancy is suspected or if the biopsy will be used to establish a critical diagnosis, direct and personal communication between the ophthalmic surgeon and the pathologist can be essential. For example, the pathologist may wish to have fresh tissue for immunohistochemical stains and molecular diagnostic studies, glutaraldehyde-fixed tissue for electron microscopy, and formalin-fixed tissue for routine paraffin embedding. If the tissue is simply submitted in formalin, the opportunity for a definitive diagnosis may be lost. Communication between clinician and pathologist is especially important in ophthalmic pathology, where specimens are often very small and require very careful handling.

Any time a previous biopsy has been performed at the site of the present pathology, the sections of the previous biopsy should be requested and reviewed with the pathologist who will interpret the second biopsy. The surgical plan may be altered substantially if the initial biopsy was thought to represent a basal cell carcinoma when in fact the disease process is sebaceous carcinoma. In addition, the pathologist will be able to interpret intraoperative frozen sections more accurately when the case has been reviewed in advance.

If substantial disagreement arises between the clinical diagnosis and the histopathologic diagnosis, the ophthalmologist should contact the pathologist directly and promptly to resolve the discrepancy. Mislabeling of pathology specimens or reports through a simple typing error, for example, can have serious consequences. Merely correcting the patient age on the pathology request form may change the interpretation of melanotic lesions of the conjunctiva. Benign melanotic lesions in children have a similar histologic appearance to malignant melanotic lesions in adults. Whether the patient is age 4 or age 44 makes a tremendous difference in interpretation.

Finally, the ophthalmologist who makes an effort to consult with the pathologist prior to surgery sends a clear signal both of special interest in the case and of respect for the contribution of the pathologist. The more collegial the relationship, the more precise the diagnosis.

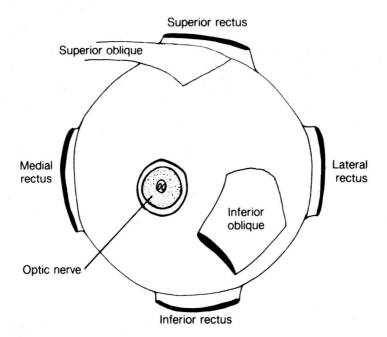

FIG III-1—Posterior view of right globe. (Modified from illustration by Thomas A. Weingeist, PhD, MD.)

Orientation

Globes may be oriented according to the location of the extraocular muscles and of the long posterior ciliary artery and nerve, which are located in the horizontal meridian. The medial, inferior, lateral, and superior rectus muscles insert progressively farther from the limbus. Locating the insertion of the inferior oblique muscle is very helpful in distinguishing between a right and left eye (Fig III-1). The inferior oblique inserts temporally over the macula, with its fibers running inferiorly. Once the laterality of the eye is determined, the globe may be transilluminated and dissected.

Transillumination

Eyes are transilluminated with bright light prior to gross dissection. This helps to identify intraocular lesions such as a tumor that blocks the transilluminated light and casts a shadow (Fig III-2). The shadow can be outlined with a marking pencil on the sclera (Fig III-3). This outline can then be used to guide the gross dissection of the globe so that the center of the section will include the maximum extent of the area of interest (Figs III-4 to III-6).

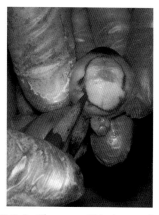

FIG III-2—Transillumination shows blockage to light secondary to an intraocular tumor.

FIG III-3—The area of blockage to light is marked with a marking pencil.

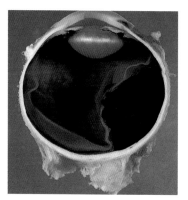

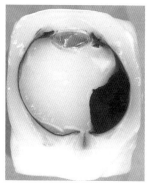

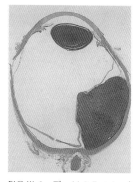

FIG III-4—The opened eye shows the intraocular tumor that was demonstrated by transillumination.

FIG III-5—The paraffin-embedded eye shows the intraocular tumor.

FIG III-6—The H & E-stained section shows that the maximum extent of the tumor demonstrated by transillumination is in the center of the section, which includes the pupil and optic nerve.

Gross Dissection

A globe is opened so as to display as much of the pathologic change as possible on a single slide. The majority of eyes are cut so that the pupil and optic nerve are present in the same section, the *PO section*. The meridian, or clock hour, of the section is determined by the unique features of the case, such as the presence of an intraocular tumor or a history of previous surgery or trauma. In routine cases, with no prior surgery or intraocular neoplasm, most eyes are opened in the horizontal meridian, which includes the macula in the same section as the pupil and optic nerve. Globes with a surgical or nonsurgical wound should be opened so that the wound will be perpendicular to and included in the PO section, which often means opening the globe vertically. Globes with intraocular tumors are opened in a fashion (horizontal, vertical, or oblique) that places the center of the tumor as outlined by transillumination in the PO section (Fig III-7).

The globe can also be opened coronally with separation of the anterior and posterior compartments. The tumor can be visualized directly with this technique, and a section including the maximum extent of the tumor may then be obtained.

Processing/Staining

Fixatives

The most commonly used fixative is 10% neutral buffered formalin. Formalin is a 40% solution of formaldehyde in water that stabilizes protein, lipid, and carbohydrates and prevents postmortem enzymatic destruction of the tissue (autolysis). In specific instances other fixatives may be preferred, such as glutaraldehyde for electron microscopy and ethyl alcohol for cytologic preparations.

Formalin diffuses rather quickly through tissue. Because most of the functional tissue of the eye is within 2–3 mm of the surface, it is not necessary or desirable to open the eye. Opening the eye prior to fixation may damage or distort sites of pathology, making histologic interpretation difficult or impossible. The adult eye measures approximately 24 mm in diameter, and formalin diffuses at a rate of approximately 1 mm/hr; therefore, globes should be fixed at least 12 hours prior to processing. It is generally desirable to suspend an eye in formalin in a volume of approximately 10:1 for at least 24 hours prior to processing to ensure adequate fixation.

Tissue Processing

The infiltration and embedding process removes most of the water from the tissue and replaces the water with paraffin. Organic solvents used in this process will dissolve lipid and may dissolve some synthetic materials. The specimen is processed through increasing concentrations of alcohol until it is in xylene or another clearing agent prior to infiltration with paraffin. The paraffin mechanically stabilizes the tissue, making possible the cutting of sections.

The processing of even a "routine" specimen usually takes overnight. Thus, it is unreasonable for a surgeon to expect an interpretation of a specimen sent for permanent sections to be available on the same day as the biopsy. Special techniques for the rapid processing of special surgical pathology material are generally reserved for certain biopsy specimens that require emergent therapy. Because the quality of histologic preparation after rapid processing is usually inferior to standard processed tissue, it should not be requested routinely. Surgeons should communicate directly with their pathologists about the availability and shortcomings of these techniques.

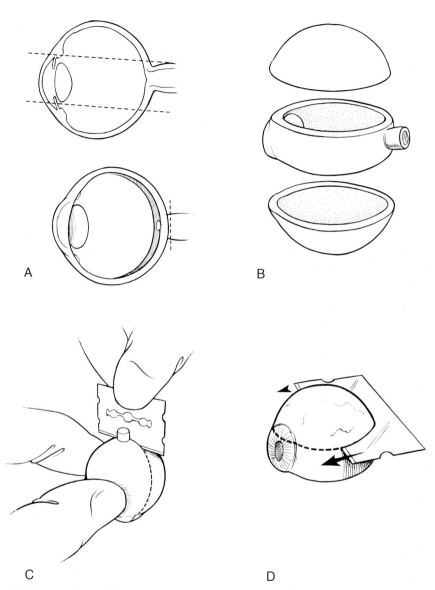

FIG III-7—*A*, The goal of sectioning is to obtain a pupil–optic nerve (PO) section that contains the maximum area of interest. *B*, Two caps, or *calottes*, are removed to obtain a PO section. *C*, The first cut is generally performed from posterior to anterior. *D*, The second cut will yield the PO section. (Illustration by Christine Gralapp.)

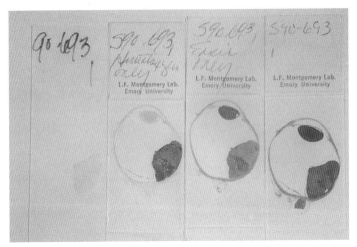

FIG III-8—The section of paraffin-embedded tissue at the far left is colorless except for mild indigenous pigmentation in the tissue. Moving to the right are shown slides stained with hematoxylin only, eosin only, and both hematoxylin and eosin.

Tissue Staining

Tissue sections are usually cut at 4–6 μm. A tissue adhesive is sometimes used to secure the thin paraffin section to a glass slide. The cut section is colorless except for areas of indigenous pigmentation, and various tissue dyes—principally hematoxylin and eosin (H&E) and periodic acid–Schiff (PAS)—are used to color the tissue for identification (Fig III-8). Other histochemical stains used in ophthalmic pathology are alcian blue or colloidal iron for acid mucopolysaccharides, Congo red for amyloid, Gram's stain for bacteria, Masson trichrome for collagen, Gomori's methenamine silver stain for fungi, and oil red O for lipid. A small amount of resin is placed over the stained section and covered with a thin glass coverslip to protect and preserve it. Table III-1 lists examples of common stains and their usage in ophthalmic pathology.

TABLE III-1

COMMON STAINS USED IN OPHTHALMIC PATHOLOGY

STAIN	MATERIAL STAINED	EXAMPLE
Hematoxylin/eosin (H&E)	Nucleus—blue Cytoplasm—red	General tissue stain
Periodic acid–Schiff (PAS)	Neutral mucopolysaccharide—magenta	Fungi
Alcian blue	Acid mucopolysaccharide—blue	Macular dystrophy
Alizarin red	Calcium—red	Band keratopathy
Colloidal iron	Acid mucopolysaccharide—blue	Macular dystrophy
Congo red	Amyloid—orange, red-green dichroism	Lattice dystrophy
Crystal violet	Amyloid—purple, violet	Lattice dystrophy
Gram's stain (tissue B&B or B&H stain)	Bacteria Positive—blue Negative—red	Bacterial infection
Masson trichrome	Collagen—blue Muscle—red	Granular dystrophy Red deposits
Perls' Prussian blue	Iron—blue	Hemosiderosis bulbi
Thioflavin t	Amyloid—fluorescent yellow	Lattice dystrophy
Verhoeff von Gieson	Elastic fibers—black	Temporal artery elastic layer
von Kossa	Calcium phosphate salts—black	Band keratopathy

CHAPTER IV

Special Procedures

Immunohistochemistry

Pathologists making a diagnosis take advantage of the property that a given cell will express specific antigens. The immunohistochemical stains commonly used in ophthalmic pathology work because an antibody binds to a specific antigen in or on a cell, and because that antibody is linked to a chromogen. The color product of the chromogens generally used in ophthalmic pathology is brown or red in tissue section, depending on the chromogen selected for use.

The precise cell or cells that display the specific antigen can be identified using these methods. Many antibodies are available:

☐ Cytokeratins for lesions composed of epithelial cells (adenoma, carcinoma)

☐ Desmin, myoglobin, or actin for lesions with smooth muscle or skeletal muscle features (leiomyoma, rhabdomyoma) (Figs IV-1, IV-2)

☐ S-100 protein or neuron-specific enolase for lesions of neuroectodermal origin (schwannoma, neurofibroma, melanoma)

☐ HMB 45 for melanocytic lesions (nevus, melanoma)

☐ Leukocyte common antigen for lesions of hematopoietic origin (leukemia, lymphoma)

These antibodies vary in their specificity, and sensitivities also vary among different antibodies. Considerable experience is required to use and interpret immunohistochemical stains. Antigen expression may also be used in tissue interpretation by flow cytometry, a sophisticated method with limited use in routine ophthalmic pathology.

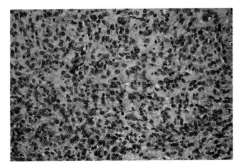

FIG IV-1—This H&E-stained section shows a poorly differentiated neoplasm.

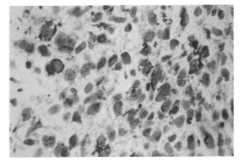

FIG IV-2—A desmin stain is positive in the poorly differentiated cells shown in Figure IV-1. The diagnosis is rhabdomyosarcoma.

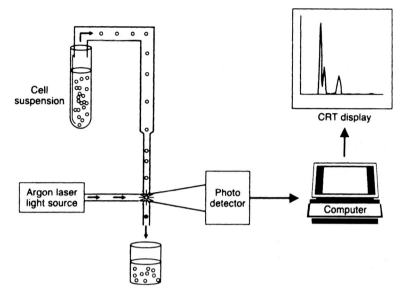

FIG IV-3—Schematic representation of the principles of flow cytometry. (Reproduced from Crotty TB, Campbell RJ. Flow cytometry. In: Grossniklaus HE, Margo CE, eds. *Advances in Ophthalmic Pathology. Ophthalmol Clin North Am.* 1995;8:38. Courtesy of Mayo Clinic and Mayo Foundation, Rochester, Minnesota.)

Flow Cytometry, Molecular Pathology, and Electron Microscopy

Flow Cytometry

This method is used to analyze the physical and chemical properties of particles or cells moving in single file in a fluid stream. An example of flow cytometry is immunophenotyping of leukocytes. Fluorochrome-labeled specific antibodies bind to the surface of lymphoid cells, and a suspension of labeled cells is sequentially illuminated by a light source (usually argon laser) for approximately 10^{-6} seconds. As the excited fluorochrome returns to its resting energy level, a specific wavelength of light is emitted that is received by a photodetector (Fig IV-3). This signal is then converted to electronic impulses, which are in turn analyzed by computer software. The results may be imaged by a dot-plot histogram.

Multiple antibodies can be analyzed, and the relative percentages of cells may be displayed. For example, CD4 (helper T cells), CD8 (suppressor T cells), both CD4+ and CD8+, or neither CD4+ or CD8+ may be displayed for a given lymphocytic infiltrate. The advantage of this method is that it actually shows the percentages of particular cells in a specimen. Disadvantages are the failure to show the location and distribution of these cells in tissue and the possibility of sampling errors. Flow cytometric data should therefore be used as an adjunct to morphologic interpretation. Flow cytometric analysis is particularly useful for the evaluation of lymphoid proliferations.

Molecular Pathology

Molecular pathology techniques are more sensitive than immunopathologic techniques since they may determine the actual presence or absence of a gene. These techniques are increasingly used in experimental and to some extent diagnostic ophthalmic pathology. A common molecular biologic technique is the *polymerase chain reaction (PCR)*, which amplifies a single strand of nucleic acid thousands of times, enabling the pathologist to recognize it (Fig IV-4). Molecular pathology is used to identify tumor-promoting or -inhibiting genes, such as the retinoblastoma gene; and viral DNA or RNA strands, such as those seen in herpesviruses.

In contrast to immunohistochemistry, molecular pathology recognizes the presence or absence of a strand of nucleic acid but generally does not precisely demonstrate which cell does or does not contain the nucleic acid. In contrast to flow cytometry, the PCR technique does not calculate percentages of the cells with a particular characteristic in a given specimen. An advantage of PCR is that it amplifies and may detect a single strand of nucleic acid, making it an extremely sensitive technique. The utility of molecular pathology as a diagnostic modality in ophthalmic pathology is currently evolving.

Diagnostic Electron Microscopy

Diagnostic electron microscopy is used primarily to indicate the cell of origin of a tumor of questionable differentiation rather than to distinguish between benign and malignant processes. For this purpose immunopathologic studies are less expensive and more rapidly performed than diagnostic electron microscopy. In some cases, however, diagnostic electron microscopy complements immunopathologic studies. Once again, the surgeon should consult with the pathologist before entering the operating room to determine if diagnostic electron microscopy might play a role in the study of a particular tissue specimen.

Special Techniques

Fine-Needle Aspiration Biopsy (FNAB)

This technique has been used in place of excisional biopsy by nonophthalmic surgeons and pathologists. It is especially useful if the physician performing the biopsy can grasp the lesion (usually between the thumb and forefinger) and make several passes with the needle to obtain representative areas. In the practice of general surgical pathology, FNAB is very useful in the assessment of enlarged lymph nodes, thyroid nodules, salivary gland masses, and breast masses.

Some ophthalmologists have attempted intraocular FNAB and have found that it is most useful in distinguishing between primary uveal tumors and metastases. It may be possible to visualize a uveal tumor through a dilated pupil and perform the FNAB during indirect ophthalmoscopy. Iris tumors may be accessible for FNAB during slit-lamp biomicroscopy. However, FNAB alone cannot reliably predict the prognosis of a uveal melanoma because the sample with intraocular FNAB is limited. Intraocular FNAB may also enable tumor cells to escape the eye; this possibility is an area of some controversy. In general, properly performed FNAB does not pose a risk for seeding of tumor, but retinoblastoma is a notable exception. FNAB of a

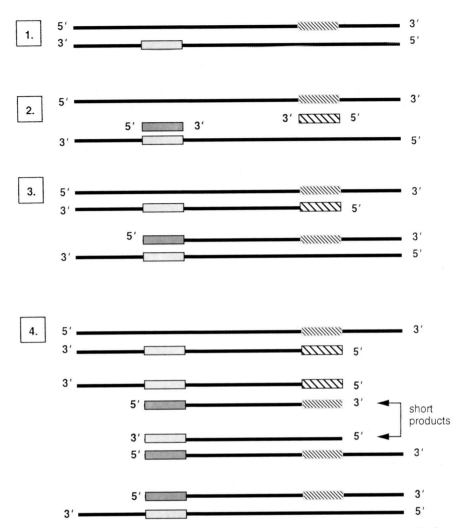

FIG IV-4—Polymerase chain reaction (PCR). *1*, Double-stranded DNA is heat-denatured in the first step of PCR. *2*, Oligonucleotide primers, which are complementary to sequences flanking the target DNA sequence on opposite strands, anneal to the denatured DNA. *3*, DNA synthesis proceeds in the 5′ to 3′ direction from the 3′ terminus of each primer by the action of a thermostable DNA polymerase. *4*, Newly synthesized DNA strands undergo denaturation, annealing of excess primers, and extension by DNA polymerase. Note the formation of short products that are of known base-pair length and that multiply exponentially with each PCR cycle. (Reproduced with permission from Garcia-Ferrer FJ, Blatt AN, Laycock KA, et at. In: Grossniklaus HE, Margo CE, eds. *Advances in Ophthalmic Pathology. Ophthalmol Clin North Am.* Philadelphia: Saunders; 1995;8:30.)

possible retinoblastoma lesion is indicated in very few cases and should be performed with extreme caution using specific protocols.

Some orbital surgeons have employed FNAB in the diagnosis of orbital lesions, especially presumed metastases to the orbit and optic nerve tumors. However, because it is difficult to make several passes at different angles through an intraorbital tumor, pathologists are concerned that surgeons obtaining FNAB of orbital masses are not sampling representative areas of the tumor. Specific indications for when and when not to perform intraocular or intraorbital FNAB are beyond the scope of this discussion, but some of these indications are discussed in Part 2, Intraocular Tumors: Clinical Aspects. Ophthalmic FNAB should only be performed when an ophthalmic pathologist and/or cytologist experienced in the preparation and interpretation of these specimens is available. The surgeon should be prepared to treat the patient appropriately when the FNAB results become known.

Frozen Section

This technique is indicated when the result of the study changes the management of the patient in the operating room. For example, frozen section may be used to determine if the resection margins are free of tumor or if the surgeon has biopsied representative material. Frozen sections are *not* indicated merely to satisfy the curiosity of the surgeon or patient's family; the utilization of frozen sections is carefully monitored by most hospital quality assurance committees. Surgeons must keep in mind that frozen sections are a time-intensive process.

The surgeon should communicate with the pathologist ahead of time if a frozen section is anticipated. It is considered inappropriate to order frozen sections and then proceed with a case before receiving the results from the pathologist. Finally, the surgeon must realize that the act of freezing tissue introduces artifacts that must be considered by the pathologist interpreting the tissue. Therefore, the entire specimen should not be frozen.

CHAPTER V

Conjunctiva

Topography

The conjunctiva is a mucous membrane lining the posterior surface of the eyelids and the anterior surface of the globe as far as the limbus. It can be subdivided into *palpebral, forniceal,* and *epibulbar* sections. The conjunctiva consists of stratified, nonkeratinized squamous epithelium that is interspersed with mucus-containing goblet cells, which are most numerous in the fornices and plica semilunaris (Fig V-1). The epithelial layer covers a substantia propria that is thickest in the fornices and thinnest covering the tarsus. Constituents of this stromal layer include loosely arranged collagen fibers; vessels; nerves; and resident lymphocytes, plasma cells, and mast cells. In the medial canthal area the conjunctiva forms a vertical fold, the *plica semilunaris,* and medial to this is the *caruncle.* The caruncle is covered by nonkeratinized stratified squamous epithelium, and within the stroma are sebaceous glands, hair follicles, and accessory lacrimal glands. BCSC Section 8, *External Disease and Cornea,* also discusses the conjunctiva in depth.

Congenital Anomalies

Choristomas

Choristomas are congenital proliferations of histologically mature tissue elements not normally present at the site of occurrence. Examples include

- Limbal dermoid
- Dermolipoma
- Ectopic lacrimal gland
- Episcleral osseous choristoma

Dermoids are firm dome-shaped, white-yellow papules at or straddling the limbus in the inferotemporal quadrant. Size varies from a few millimeters to more than 1 cm. They may occur in isolation or, particularly when bilateral, as a manifestation of a congenital complex such as Goldenhar syndrome or linear nevus sebaceous syndrome. A dermoid recapitulates the tissues of the skin; that is, epidermis and dermis including dermal adnexal structures. The surface epithelium may or may not be keratinizing. Figure VI-3 on p 65 shows an example of a corneal dermoid.

Dermolipomas occur more frequently in the superotemporal quadrant toward the fornix and may extend posteriorly into the orbit. A dermolipoma is softer and more yellow than a limbal dermoid, as a result of the adipose tissue component present in the deeper layers of the choristoma (Fig V-2). Histopathologically, it also differs from a dermoid in that the dermal adnexal structures are often absent. Dermolipomas may also be associated with Goldenhar syndrome or linear nevus sebaceous syndrome.

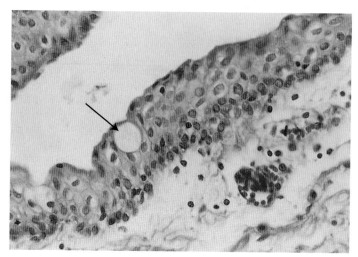

FIG V-1—Normal conjunctiva showing nonkeratinized epithelium with goblet cells (arrow).

FIG V-2—Dermolipoma differs from dermoid in that adnexal structures are often absent and significant amounts of mature adipose tissue are present in the deeper aspect of the choristoma.

Complex choristomas, in addition to having the features of a dermoid or dermolipoma, include other tissues such as cartilage, bone, and lacrimal gland. Clinically, they usually are indistinguishable from dermoids or dermolipomas.

Spencer WH, ed. *Ophthalmic Pathology: An Atlas and Textbook.* 4th ed. Philadelphia: Saunders; 1996: vol 1, chap 2.

Hamartomas

Hamartomas, in contrast to choristomas, are overgrowths of mature tissue normally present at that site. In the conjunctiva the most common variety of hamartoma is *hemangioma,* although a hemangioma can also be considered to be a true neoplasm. Although it may involve only the conjunctiva, typically the hemangioma is also present in the eyelid, face, and orbit. Congenital hemangiomas are detected at or shortly after birth as elevated, soft, red-purple nodules that may continue to grow in the first year of life before stabilizing. The majority of cases then begin a slow process of involution, resulting in complete regression. Intervention is necessary only when vision or ocular integrity is compromised. The histopathologic appearance varies depending on the stage at which the tissue is excised. Early, actively growing hemangiomas show a cellular proliferation of plump endothelial cells forming solid nests and cords within the connective tissue stroma. Mitotic figures are often present. In fully developed hemangiomas the endothelial cells flatten, forming easily recognizable capillary lumina. In the involutional phase the lobules of capillary proliferation are replaced by fibrous tissue.

Inflammations

Because the conjunctiva is an exposed surface, a variety of organisms, toxic agents, and allergens can initiate an inflammatory response known as *conjunctivitis.* Clinically, the response can be subdivided into acute or chronic conjunctivitis, according to the time frame of signs and symptoms. *Acute conjunctivitis* has a rapid onset of redness and irritation. Mucus production is particularly prominent in the acute phase, and, in concert with the sloughing of necrotic epithelium and outpouring of acute inflammatory cells and fibrin, a surface membrane may form. A true membrane is formed when the underlying epithelium is ulcerated, and granulation tissue forms beneath the fibrinopurulent exudate; attempts to remove a true membrane will result in petechial hemorrhages. However, if the underlying epithelium remains intact, removal does not cause bleeding and the surface material is known as a *pseudomembrane.*

The signs and symptoms of *chronic conjunctivitis* develop more insidiously. The inflammatory response is composed predominantly of lymphocytes and plasma cells, often causing localized nodules with infoldings of surface epithelium *(pseudo-glands of Henle).* Although more commonly a sequela of trauma, epithelial inclusion cysts and calcification of inspissated secretions may also occur in the post-inflammatory period (Fig V-3).

Papillary Versus Follicular Conjunctivitis

Conjunctivitis may be further subdivided into papillary and follicular types, according to the macroscopic appearance of the conjunctiva. Neither is pathognomonic for a particular disease entity. *Papillary conjunctivitis* shows a cobblestone arrangement of flattened nodules with a central vascular core (Fig V-4). It is most commonly associated with an allergic immune response, as in vernal and atopic keratoconjunctivitis, or a response to a foreign body such as a contact lens or ocular prosthesis. Papillae coat the tarsal surface of the upper eyelid and may reach large size *(giant papillary conjunctivitis).* Limbal papillae may occur in vernal keratoconjunctivitis

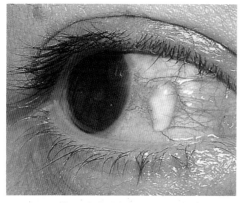
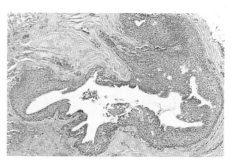

FIG V-3—*Left,* Epithelial inclusion cysts may follow conjunctival trauma. *Right,* The cyst is lined by non-keratinizing, stratified squamous epithelium, consistent with conjunctiva.

(Horner-Trantas dots). The histopathologic appearance is identical, regardless of the cause: closely packed, mesalike nodules lined by conjunctival epithelium, with numerous eosinophils, lymphocytes, and plasma cells in the stroma surrounding a central vascular channel. Mast cells may also be conspicuous.

Follicular conjunctivitis is seen in a variety of conditions including those caused by pathogens such as viruses, bacteria, chlamydiae, and toxins (Fig V-5). In contrast to papillae, follicles are small, dome-shaped nodules without a prominent central vessel. Histopathologically, they are composed of aggregates of lymphocytes and plasma cells in the superficial stroma between the tarsus and the fornix or within the palpebral and bulbar conjunctiva. Lymphocytes may form germinal centers within the follicles, complete with tingible body macrophages (histiocytes containing ingested intracytoplasmic nuclear debris).

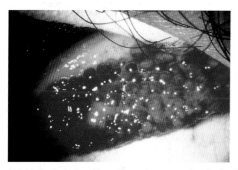
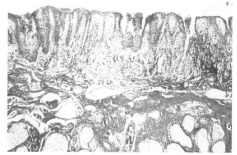

FIG V-4—*Left,* Papillae efface the normal palpebral conjunctival surface and form a confluent cobblestone pattern. *Right,* Low-power photomicrograph highlights the closely packed, flat-topped papillae with central fibrovascular cores (trichrome stain).

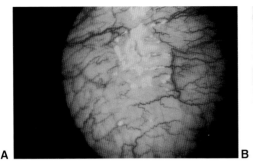

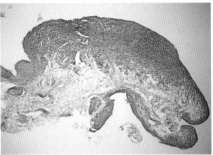

FIG V-5—*A*, Lymphoid follicles in the bulbar conjunctiva obscure the underlying congested conjunctival vasculature and cause an irregular light reflex. *B* and *C*, Nodular lymphoid aggregates may develop germinal centers.

Infectious Conjunctivitis

A wide variety of pathogens may infect the conjunctiva, including bacteria, chlamydiae, fungi, and viruses. The most common offending agents are viral, and the usual culprits are adenovirus and the herpesviruses (simplex and zoster). Viral infections, in addition to inciting a follicular conjunctivitis, often affect the cornea, resulting in ulcers in herpetic disease and subepithelial infiltrates in adenoviral disease.

Bacterial infections cause about 5% of cases of conjunctivitis. Microorganisms associated with an acute, often suppurative, conjunctivitis include *Neisseria gonorrhoeae, Streptococcus* species (particularly *S pneumoniae*), and *Haemophilus influenzae. Staphylococcus aureus* and *Moraxella lacunata* are associated with a more chronic process.

When the conjunctiva alone is infected, fungi are rarely the inciting pathogen. *Rhinosporidium seeberi,* which may cause an isolated conjunctivitis, is seen most often in endemic areas such as India and Southeast Asia.

Chlamydiae are obligate intracellular pathogens, among which *C trachomatis* is a major cause of ocular infection, particularly in the Middle East. Serotypes A, B, and C are associated with trachoma, while serotypes D through K cause neonatal and adult inclusion conjunctivitis. *Microsporida* are another group of obligate intracellular parasites that may cause conjunctivitis, keratitis, or keratoconjunctivitis, particularly in patients with acquired immunodeficiency syndrome (AIDS). Exfoliative cytology of conjunctival or corneal epithelium (Giemsa stain) may be useful in demonstrating these intracellular organisms (Fig V-6).

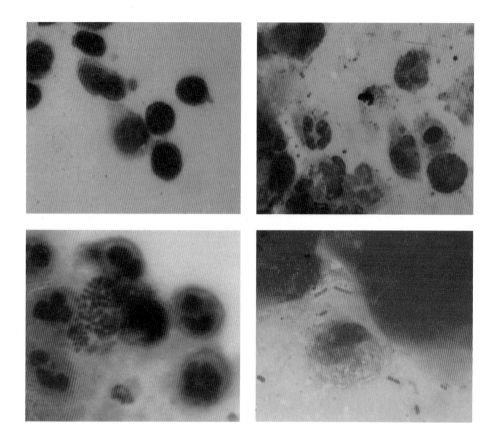

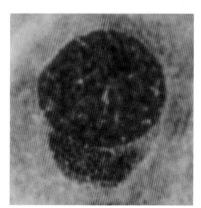

FIG V-6—Exfoliative conjunctival cytology. *Upper left,* Lymphocytes predominate in viral conjunctivitis. *Upper right,* A mixture of polymorphonuclear leukocytes and eosinophils is typical of vernal conjunctivitis. *Middle left,* Gram's stain reveals the polymorphonuclear leukocyte response to gonococcal conjunctivitis. Note the intracellular, gram-negative diplococci. *Middle right,* A case of *Moraxella lacunata* angular conjunctivitis demonstrating the bacilli, which often are found in pairs. *Bottom left, Chlamydia,* conjunctival scraping, Giemsa stain. The inclusion body, composed of multiple chlamydial organisms, can be seen capping the nucleus. A distinct space separates the inclusion body from the nuclear chromatin. Occasionally, crushing of the cells during specimen preparation may cause chromatin to stream through a defect in the nuclear membrane, resulting in an appearance similar to a chlamydial inclusion body.

Noninfectious Conjunctivitis

Sarcoidosis may involve any of a number of ocular tissues, including the conjunctiva. It manifests as small, tan nodules primarily within the forniceal conjunctiva. Conjunctival biopsy can be a simple, expedient way of providing pathologic correlation in this systemic disease. Histopathologically, granulomas (aggregates of epithelioid histiocytes) are present within the conjunctival stroma with a variable, but usually minimal, cuff of lymphocytes and plasma cells. Multinucleated giant cells may or may not be present within the granuloma. Central necrosis is not characteristic and, if present, should suggest other causes of granulomatous inflammation, such as infection with mycobacteria, fungi, spirochetes, or parasites. Bacteria such as *Francisella tularensis* (tularemia) and *Bartonella henselae* (cat-scratch disease) are other considerations. In fact, the diagnosis of sarcoidosis is tenable only when supported by clinical findings and after other causes of granulomatous inflammation have been excluded by histochemical stains and/or culture. BCSC Section 9, *Intraocular Inflammation and Uveitis,* discusses sarcoidosis in greater detail. See also chapter VII in this volume.

Granulomatous conjunctivitis in association with preauricular lymphadenopathy is known as *Parinaud oculoglandular syndrome.* This condition is discussed in BCSC Section 6, *Pediatric Ophthalmology and Strabismus;* and Section 8, *External Disease and Cornea.*

As an exposed surface, the conjunctiva is vulnerable to contact with foreign bodies. Some may be transient and/or inert, while others may become embedded and incite a foreign body reaction, identifiable as a granuloma surrounding the foreign object. Multinucleated giant cells are common. Viewing the slide under polarized light may be helpful in identifying the type of offending foreign material.

Degenerations

Pinguecula and Pterygium

A *pinguecula* is a small yellowish gray nodule, often bilateral, situated at the nasal or temporal limbus (Fig V-7). It is seen in individuals with prolonged exposure to sunlight and is therefore more common with advancing years. The overlying epithelium is often thinned but may be hyperplastic or dysplastic. The stromal collagen shows fragmentation and basophilic degeneration called *elastotic degeneration* because the degenerated collagen will stain positively with a histochemical stain for elastic fibers, such as the Verhoeff–van Gieson stain. However, pretreatment of the slide with elastase does not diminish the staining.

A *pterygium* has a similar etiology, location, and histologic features, but it encroaches onto the cornea in a winglike fashion (Fig V-8). Because they can interfere with vision, pterygia are excised when they threaten the visual axis. The destruction of Bowman's layer by the advancing fibrovascular tissue results in a corneal scar. So-called recurrent pterygia lack the histopathologic feature of elastotic degeneration and are more accurately classified as an exuberant granulation tissue response.

Gans LA. Surgical treatment of pterygium. In: *Focal Points: Clinical Modules for Ophthalmologists.* San Francisco: American Academy of Ophthalmology; 1996: vol 14, no 12.

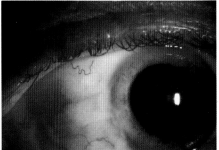

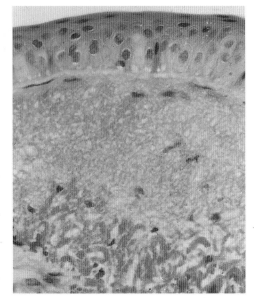

FIG V-7—*Left,* Pinguecula forms a dome-shaped yellow nodule adjacent to the limbus. *Right,* Pinguecula showing the basophilic hue of elastotic degeneration, a type of collagen degeneration caused by ultraviolet light. A pterygium specimen would be similar except that a portion of Bowman's layer could be represented in the section.

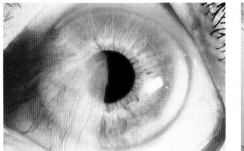

FIG V-8—*Left,* Pterygium is so named because of its winglike configuration across the corneal surface. *Right,* Histologically, pterygium differs from pinguecula only in the encroachment onto the cornea and destruction of Bowman's layer.

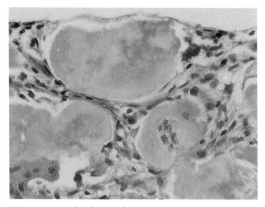

FIG V-9—Amyloidosis characterized by extracellular amorphous eosinophilic material in the substantia propria of the conjunctiva.

Amyloid Deposits

Amyloid deposition in the conjunctiva is most commonly a primary localized process seen in healthy young and middle-aged adults. Less often, it occurs secondary to preexisting, long-standing inflammation, such as with trachoma; or as an ocular manifestation of a systemic disease such as multiple myeloma. Deposits within the stroma cause a waxy, rubbery nodular or diffuse thickening of any portion of the conjunctiva (Fig V-9). Amyloid is an eosinophilic, extracellular, hyaline-appearing substance within the stroma, often in a perivascular distribution. Congo red stain tints amyloid an orange-red, but amyloid deposits viewed with polarized light and a rotating analyzer polarization filter also exhibit dichroism; that is, they change from orange-red to green-yellow as the analyzer is rotated. Other useful staining methods include crystal violet and thioflavin T. When describing amyloid deposits involving the eyelid, the physician should specify the location of the deposit: amyloid deposits affecting the skin of the eyelid usually reflect a sytemic condition, while amyloid deposits affecting the palpebral conjunctiva usually indicate localized pathology.

Neoplasia

Epithelial Lesions

Squamous papillomas are exophytic, pink-red, strawberry-like papillary growths with a biphasic age distribution, growth pattern, and site of involvement (Fig V-10). In children they are most commonly multiple and pedunculated, involving the fornix, caruncle, or eyelid margin. In adults they are usually single and sessile, occurring at the limbus. Limbal papillomas cannot be clinically distinguished from precancerous dysplasia or invasive squamous cell carcinoma; they require excision for histopathologic diagnosis.

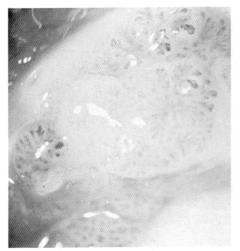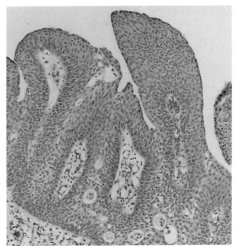

FIG V-10—Squamous papilloma. *Left,* The focal red highlights correspond with the fibrovascular cores of this proliferative lesion. The papilloma may be pedunculated or sessile. *Right,* The epithelium is acanthotic and draped over fibrovascular cores.

Human papilloma virus (HPV) has been detected in both pediatric and adult papillomas: HPV subtype 6 in the former, and subtype 16 in the latter. The histopathologic examination of papillomas demonstrates papillary fibrovascular fronds covered by acanthotic squamous epithelium. Pediatric papillomas often have an admixture of goblet cells and neutrophils within the epithelium. A chronic inflammatory infiltrate may occupy the stroma. Adult papillomas may exhibit various degrees of epithelial dysplasia, characterized by nuclear enlargement, increased nuclear-to-cytoplasmic ratio, loss of architectural maturation toward the epithelial surface, and mitotic figures above the basal epithelial layer.

Dysplasia of the conjunctival epithelium also occurs in other clinical settings. *Dysplasias* are generally classified as focal and well circumscribed or diffuse and poorly demarcated (Fig V-11). As mentioned previously, dysplasia may arise in the epithelium covering areas of solar elastosis, similar to actinic keratoses of the skin. The dysplasia is focal and well delineated in this situation, often showing a white, flaky appearance (leukoplakia) caused by surface keratinization. When diffuse dysplasias occur in regions of the conjunctiva not exposed to the sun, the clinical appearance is more gelatinous and less well defined. HPV subtype 16 has been demonstrated within some cases of dysplasia as well.

Dysplasia is graded as mild, moderate, or severe, according to the degree of involvement of the epithelium. Mild dysplasia, or *conjunctival intraepithelial neoplasia (CIN)*, grade I, is defined as dysplasia confined to the lower third of the conjunctival epithelial thickness. Moderate dysplasia (CIN II) extends into the middle third, and severe dysplasia (CIN III) the upper third. The risk of invasive carcinoma developing from conjunctival dysplasia appears to be lower than in its counterpart in the uterine cervix. Excision of affected epithelium with cryotherapy of the margins

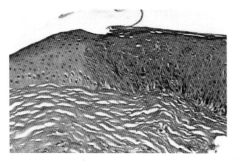

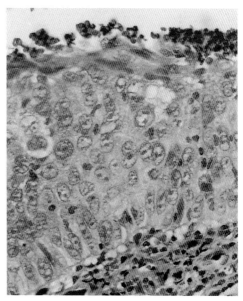

FIG V-11—Conjunctival dysplasia. *Left,* Note the sharp demarcation between normal and abnormal epithelium. The abnormality is almost but not quite to the surface. *Right,* This is carcinoma in situ, showing full-thickness abnormalities. Because of the difficulties in distinguishing between partial- and full-thickness abnormalities, the term *conjunctival intraepithelial neoplasia (CIN)* is used to describe the spectrum of abnormalities in these conditions.

is the standard treatment. Topical mitomycin-C has been proposed as an alternative therapy in select cases.

Invasive *squamous cell carcinoma* of the conjunctiva is an uncommon sequela to preexisting dysplasia (Fig V-12). It occurs in older individuals, usually beginning at the limbus, then superficially invading the conjunctival stroma and spreading onto the corneal surface. Deep invasion of the cornea or sclera and intraocular spread are uncommon complications. Histopathologic examination demonstrates infiltrating nests that have penetrated the epithelial basement membrane and spread into the conjunctival stroma. Tumor cells may be well differentiated and easily recognizable as squamous, moderately differentiated, or poorly differentiated and difficult to distinguish from other malignancies such as sebaceous carcinoma. Although regional lymph node metastasis is not common, dissemination and death is possible.

Mucoepidermoid carcinoma and *spindle cell carcinoma,* entities even rarer than squamous cell carcinoma, are more aggressive neoplasms with higher rates of recurrence and intraocular spread.

Subepithelial Lesions

Clinically, both benign and malignant lymphoid lesions of the conjunctiva usually show a salmon pink appearance, are relatively flat with a smooth surface, and have a soft consistency (Fig V-13). Most conjunctival lymphoid lesions are localized and *not* associated with systemic disease; however, nearly two thirds of lymphomas arising in the preseptal skin eventually show evidence of systemic involvement.

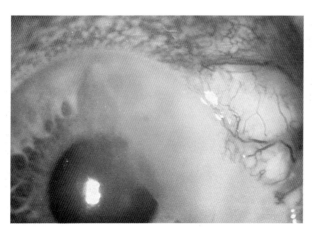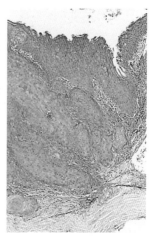

FIG V-12—Squamous cell carcinoma. *Left,* Squamous cell carcinoma of the conjunctiva is commonly centered about the limbus and may spread to involve the corneal epithelium. *Right,* The tumor has massively replaced the conjunctival substantia propria. The thick bundle of eosinophilic material at the bottom of the photograph is sclera. It is unusual for squamous cell carcinoma of the conjunctiva to penetrate the sclera into the eye.

Prediction of biologic behavior based on clinical, histopathologic, and even immunophenotypic features is not always clear-cut in pathologic diagnosis of lymphoproliferative disorders of the conjunctiva. See also chapter XIV on lymphoid lesions of the orbit.

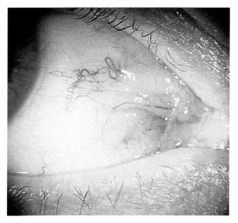

FIG V-13—Benign reactive lymphoid hyperplasia of the conjunctiva. *Left,* Clinical photograph (note the salmon patch). *Right,* Note the irregularly shaped germinal centers in the conjunctival substantia propria.

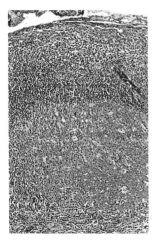

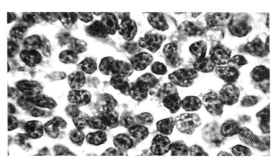

FIG V-14—Note the large germinal center in this case of benign reactive lymphoid hyperplasia of the conjunctiva.

FIG V-15—Lymphoma composed of sheets of atypical lymphocytes.

Histopathologic features favoring a diagnosis of *reactive lymphoid hyperplasia* include the presence of lymphoid follicles with germinal centers and an admixture of plasma cells and mature small lymphocytes in the surrounding stroma (Fig V-14). Russell bodies, eosinophilic spherules representing inspissated immunoglobulin, may be present either within plasma cell cytoplasm or extruded into the extracellular milieu. A diffuse sheet of monotonous small round or cleaved lymphocytes is more characteristic of a *low-grade malignant lymphoma* (Fig V-15). *High-grade lymphomas* are readily recognized as malignant by virtue of their nuclear features and high mitotic rate.

As expected, a diagnostically indeterminate gray zone separates reactive hyperplasia from low-grade lymphoma, and ancillary studies may be helpful in classifying proliferations as benign or malignant. Immunophenotypic analysis, either by flow cytometry of fresh, unfixed tissue or by immunoperoxidase staining, may demonstrate B-cell monoclonality by revealing either κ or λ light chain predominance (Fig V-16). More sophisticated molecular techniques may show monoclonality by revealing immunoglobulin gene rearrangements within tumor cells. However, although these advanced techniques are helpful, they are not definitive: not all lesions demonstrating monoclonality will behave in a malignant fashion resulting in systemic disease. Other factors, such as host immune response, are important in determining clinical behavior of the lesion.

Albert DM, Jakobiec FA, eds. *Principles and Practice of Ophthalmology.* 2nd ed. Philadelphia: Saunders; 1994:3328–3343.

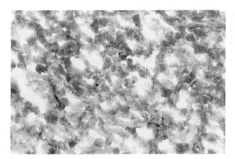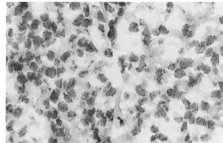

FIG V-16—Conjunctival lymphoma. *Left,* This is an immunoperoxidase stain for λ light chains. Note the diffuse staining. *Right,* This is an immunoperoxidase stain for κ light chains. The stain is negative. The fact that only λ light chains were demonstrated in this tumor indicates that this is a monoclonal proliferation, consistent with the histologic impression of malignant lymphoma.

Melanocytic Lesions

As with hemangiomas, melanocytic nevi are classified by some authors as hamartomas and by others as neoplasms (Table V-1). *Conjunctival melanocytic nevi* usually appear on the bulbar conjunctiva in childhood. Analogous to cutaneous melanocytic nevi, conjunctival nevi undergo evolutionary changes. In the initial junctional phase nevus cells are confined to nests *(theques)* at the interface between the epithelium and the substantia propria. As the nevus evolves, the nests "drop off" into the substantia propria, eventually losing connection with the epithelium and existing solely in the substantia propria. Nevi with both junctional and subepithelial components are designated as *compound nevi;* those without junctional activity are termed *subepithelial* or *stromal nevi.* Subcategories of nevi (e.g., Spitz nevus, halo nevus) and other types of nevi (e.g., blue nevi) also exist. Epithelial cysts may be

TABLE V-1

CLINICAL COMPARISON OF CONJUNCTIVAL PIGMENTARY LESIONS

LESION	ONSET	AREA	LOCATION	MALIGNANT POTENTIAL
Freckle	Youth	Small	Conjunctiva	No
Benign acquired melanosis	Adulthood	Patchy or diffuse	Conjunctiva	No
Conjunctival nevus	Youth	Small	Conjunctiva	Low (conjunctival melanoma)
Ocular and oculodermal melanocytosis	Congenital	Patchy or diffuse	Under conjunctiva	Yes (uveal melanoma)
Primary acquired melanosis	Middle age	Diffuse	Conjunctiva	Yes (conjunctival melanoma)

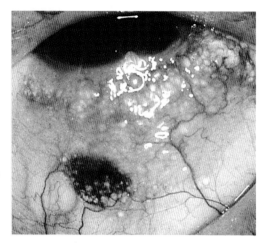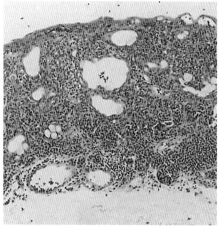

FIG V-17—*Left,* Compound nevus of the conjunctiva. Note the characteristic cysts. *Right,* Histology of a compound conjunctival nevus. Note the epithelial inclusions within the lesion, corresponding with the clinically observed cysts.

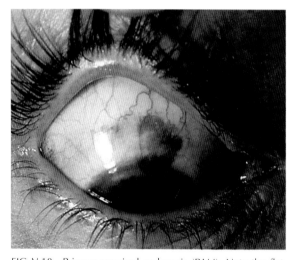

FIG V-18—Primary acquired melanosis (PAM). Note the flat, patchy pigmentation of the conjunctiva. When examining this patient clinically, the physician should evert the eyelids to exclude involvement of the palpebral conjunctiva.

encountered within compound and subepithelial nevi (Fig V-17). Nevi occur only rarely in the palpebral conjunctiva; pigmented lesions in this area are more likely to be primary acquired melanosis or melanoma.

Primary acquired melanosis (PAM) appears as a unilateral flat patch, or patches, of golden brown pigmentation with an irregular margin (Fig V-18). It is most com-

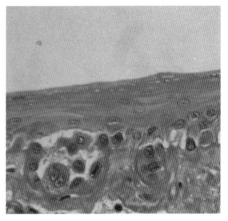

FIG V-19—*Left,* PAM without atypia. The basilar layer of the conjunctival epithelium is pigmented. There is no histologic evidence of melanocytic atypia. Note that in the term *PAM without atypia* the word *atypia* refers to histologic findings, not the clinical presentation. *Right,* PAM with atypia. Highly atypical epithelioid melanocytes are present within the epithelium. The patient is at high risk for progression to melanoma.

mon in middle-aged persons. The lesions may wax and wane or grow slowly without remission over a period of 10 or more years. It is not possible to predict in which patient PAM is likely to progress to malignant melanoma on clinical grounds alone. However, histologic criteria have been developed to identify patients at high risk for malignancy. *PAM without atypia* denotes hyperplasia of melanocytes without atypical cytologic or architectural features (Fig V-19, left). PAM without atypia does not progress to melanoma. *PAM with atypia* will progress to invasive melanoma in approximately 46% of patients (Fig V-19, right).

Atypia in PAM is defined according to both cytomorphologic and architectural features. Atypical melanocytes show nuclear enlargement as compared to adjacent basal epithelial cells and may be spindled, polygonal, or epithelioid. Architectural features of atypia include lentiginous hyperplasia, intraepidermal migration of individual cells or nests *(pagetoid spread),* or complete replacement of the epithelium, mimicking carcinoma in situ. Pagetoid spread by epithelioid melanocytes and full-thickness replacement of the epithelium are the most important of these features as predictors of subsequent invasive melanoma (75%–90% of cases). PAM with atypia should be treated by excision if the area is small or by cryotherapy for more extensive areas. Mitomycin-C has been shown to cause complete regression in a case of primary acquired melanosis with atypia; the efficacy of this treatment remains to be proven in a larger series.

Helm CJ. Melanoma and other pigmented lesions of the ocular surface. In: *Focal Points: Clinical Modules for Ophthalmologists.* San Francisco: American Academy of Ophthalmology; 1996: vol 14, no 11.

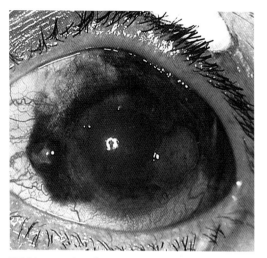 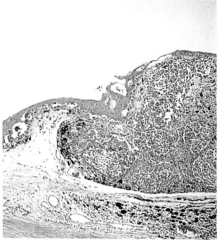

FIG V-20—*Left*, Melanoma with PAM. Note the melanoma nodule at the 2 o'clock position at the limbus that has appeared on a background of PAM (diffuse flat, brown pigmentation). *Right*, Melanoma with PAM, histologic appearance. Intraepithelial atypical melanocytes (PAM) are present just to the left of the nodule of invasive melanoma.

Approximately two thirds of cases of *conjunctival melanoma* arise from PAM with atypia (Fig V-20, left), while the remainder develop either from a preexisting nevus or de novo. Tumors are usually nodular growths that may involve any portion of the conjunctiva; those not on the bulbar surface appear to behave more aggressively. Histopathologically, melanomas have diverse cellular morphology from pleomorphic, large, bizarre cells with prominent nucleoli to small polygonal cells with mild anaplasia to spindle cells without identifiable melanin pigment. Immunohistochemical stains for S-100 protein and HMB-45 may help to identify problematic cases as melanocytic (Fig V-20, right). Conjunctival melanomas are more akin to cutaneous melanoma than uveal melanoma in behavior.

The overall mortality of conjunctival melanoma is 25%. Typically, metastases first develop in parotid or submandibular lymph nodes. Unfavorable prognostic factors, in addition to conjunctival site as mentioned above, include

☐ Orbital or scleral invasion

☐ Histopathologic identification of pagetoid or full-thickness intraepithelial spread

☐ Involvement of the eyelid skin margin

Tumor thickness can be measured objectively using a calibrated microscope; tumors greater than 1.8 mm thick carry a greater risk for dissemination and death than thinner melanomas. However, even lesions less than 0.8 mm thick have resulted in patient mortality. The treatment for conjunctival melanoma is complete surgical removal.

Albert DM, Jakobiec FA, eds. *Principles and Practice of Ophthalmology.* 2nd ed. Philadelphia: Saunders; 1994:286–289, 2132–2134.

CHAPTER VI

Cornea

Topography

The normal cornea is composed of five layers: epithelium, Bowman's layer, stroma, Descemet's membrane, and endothelium (Fig VI-1). The average adult cornea has a horizontal diameter of 11–12 mm, a vertical diameter of 9–11 mm, and a thickness ranging between 0.52 mm centrally and 0.65 mm peripherally. The cornea is embryologically derived from surface ectoderm and neural crest. BCSC Section 8, *External Disease and Cornea*, discusses the structures and disorders of the cornea in depth.

The normal external surface of the cornea is composed of a stratified squamous, nonkeratinizing *epithelium* ranging between five and seven cell layers in thickness. The one to two most superficial layers consist of flattened cells that are continually exfoliated and replaced by the underlying cells. The deepest epithelial layer is composed of basal cells, where mitotic activity is greatest. The basal cells are attached to the underlying basement membrane by means of hemidesmosomes and filaments that are visible through transmission electron microscopy. The epithelial basement membrane is thin and is best seen with the use of periodic acid–Schiff (PAS) stain.

Bowman's layer is immediately subjacent to the epithelial basement membrane. This layer is composed of acellular collagen and measures 8–14 nm in thickness. The posterior aspect of Bowman's layer blends imperceptibly with the underlying corneal stroma.

The corneal *stroma* makes up 90% of the total corneal thickness. The elongated collagenous lamellae are arranged in a precise orientation to allow for the orderly passage of light through the cornea. The ground substance, consisting of mucoprotein and glycoprotein, coats each collagen fibril and is responsible for the exact spacing required for corneal clarity.

The next layer, *Descemet's membrane,* is the basement membrane elaborated by the corneal endothelium. The production of Descemet's membrane begins during fetal development and continues throughout adulthood; therefore, the thickness of Descemet's membrane continually increases with age. Descemet's membrane is a true basement membrane composed primarily of type IV collagen and is strongly PAS positive.

The corneal *endothelium* is a single layer derived from the neural crest. The primary function of the endothelium is to maintain corneal clarity by pumping water from the corneal stroma. The number of endothelial cells gradually decreases over time. As the endothelial cell number declines, the remaining cells flatten and elongate to provide coverage of the posterior corneal surface.

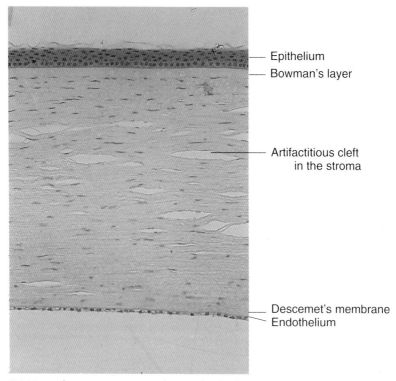

Epithelium
Bowman's layer

Artifactitious cleft
in the stroma

Descemet's membrane
Endothelium

FIG VI-1—The cornea is composed primarily of collagen. Because of dehydration of the tissue during processing for paraffin embedding, multiple areas of separation of the stromal lamellae are evident. If the lamellar separations are absent, corneal edema is suspected. This is an example of a meaningful artifact.

Congenital Anomalies

Congenital Hereditary Endothelial Dystrophy (CHED)

Two forms of this condition causing bilateral congenital corneal edema are described: one autosomal recessive and one autosomal dominant. The more common autosomal recessive form is present at birth, remains stationary, and is accompanied by nystagmus. Clinically, the cornea appears bluish white, is two to three times the normal thickness, and has a ground-glass appearance. The autosomal dominant form of CHED becomes apparent in the first or second year of life and exhibits slowly increasing edema of the corneal stroma. In these patients the cornea has the same diffuse, blue-white appearance as in the autosomal recessive form, and they may experience pain and photophobia (Fig VI-2A). Nystagmus, however, does not develop.

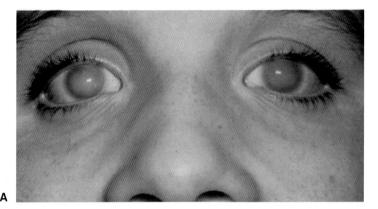

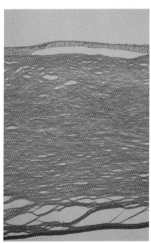

FIG VI-2—Congenital hereditary endothelial dystrophy. *A,* Clinical appearance. *B,* Note diffuse edema of corneal epithelium and stroma. Descemet's membrane is diffusely thickened.

Despite the distinct clinical differences between autosomal recessive and autosomal dominant CHED, the two forms appear similar histologically. The corneal stroma is diffusely edematous, accounting for the marked increase in thickness observed clinically. Descemet's membrane appears thickened, but guttata are not present (Fig VI-2B). The endothelium appears atrophic or may be focally absent. The primary abnormality is thought to be a degeneration of endothelial cells during or after the fifth month of gestation. CHED may be considered part of the spectrum of anterior segment dysgenesis abnormalities caused by abnormal differentiation of the neural crest ectoderm that forms the corneal endothelium. No systemic abnormalities are consistently associated with CHED.

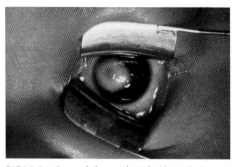

FIG VI-3—Corneal dermoid. *Left,* Clinical photograph shows elevated tan smooth lesion on corneal surface. *Right,* Histopathology shows keratinizing stratified epithelium overlying fibrous stroma containing scattered adnexal structures.

Dermoid

This type of choristoma, which may involve the cornea, is discussed in chapter V, Conjunctiva (Fig VI-3).

Posterior Keratoconus

A localized central or paracentral indentation of the posterior cornea without protrusion of the anterior surface is referred to as *posterior keratoconus,* also known as *internal ulcer of von Hippel.* The stroma may be thinned significantly, approaching one third normal corneal thickness, and often appears hazy. Descemet's membrane and endothelium are usually preserved in the area of the defect (Fig VI-4). Most cases occur in females and are unilateral, nonprogressive, and sporadic. Astigmatism and amblyopia may occur.

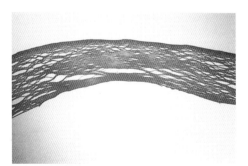

FIG VI-4—Posterior keratoconus. *Left,* Anterior bowing of the posterior corneal surface accompanies corneal thinning. *Right,* Descemet's membrane is thickened at the edge of the posterior concavity.

Sclerocornea

This nonprogressive, noninflammatory scleralization of the cornea may be limited to the corneal periphery or may involve the entire cornea. The limbus is usually poorly defined, and superficial vessels that are extensions of normal scleral, episcleral, and conjunctival vessels cross the cornea. Both sexes are affected equally, and 90% of cases are bilateral. Half of the cases are sporadic; the remainder are either autosomal dominant or recessive, the latter form being more severe. The most common ocular association is cornea plana, found in 80% of cases.

Histologically, the stromal lamellae of the cornea are irregularly thickened, without differentiation between sclera and cornea. The small- to medium-sized vessels observed clinically are seen in the superficial stroma. No evidence of inflammation appears.

Congenital Corneal Staphyloma

This condition is characterized by varying degrees of ectasia of the central, peripheral, or entire cornea. The posterior surface of the ectatic cornea is covered by remnants of anteriorly displaced iris. These findings may represent a severe expression of Peters anomaly or posterior keratoconus and may result from intrauterine trauma, maternal alcohol ingestion, or inflammation causing perforation.

Histologically, the scarred corneal and limbal tissues are thinned. Vascularization of the posterior aspects of the scar is often present in the area of the iris remnants. The anterior chamber is occluded by iris adhesions, and scattered collections of chronic inflammatory cells may be present.

Inflammations

Infectious Inflammation

The cornea may be involved by infectious processes caused by a number of different microbial agents. Acute corneal inflammation is commonly characterized by edema and infiltration by inflammatory cells. Limbal hyperemia and iritis may be present. Severe inflammation can lead to corneal necrosis, ulceration, or corneal perforation.

Bacteria Corneal infections caused by bacterial agents often follow a disruption in the corneal epithelial integrity prompted by

- Contact lens wear
- Trauma
- Contaminated ocular medications
- Alteration in immunologic defenses (e.g., use of topical or systemic immunosuppressives)
- Antecedent corneal disease
- Malposition of the eyelids

Some common bacterial organisms involved in corneal infections include *Staphylococcus aureus, Streptococcus pneumoniae, Pseudomonas aeruginosa,* and Enterobacteriaceae.

Scrapings obtained from infected corneas demonstrate collections of neutrophils admixed with necrotic debris. The presence of organisms may be demonstrated using tissue Gram stains such as the Brown & Hopps (B&H) or Brown & Brenn (B&B) stains. However, growing the organism in culture remains the only method of obtaining accurate identification of specific organisms.

Herpes simplex virus keratitis This is usually a self-limited corneal epithelial disease characterized by a linear arborizing pattern of opacification and swelling of epithelial cells called a *dendrite*. Corneal scrapings obtained from a dendrite and prepared using the Giemsa stain will reveal the presence of intranuclear viral inclusions. Infected epithelial cells may coalesce to form multinucleated giant cells. Chronic stromal keratitis may accompany or follow epithelial infection, leading to ulceration and scarring. With full-thickness stromal involvement, a granulomatous reaction can be seen, most often at the level of Descemet's membrane (Fig VI-5).

Fungal keratitis Mycotic keratitis is often a complication of trauma or of corticosteroid use. Unlike most bacteria, fungi are able to penetrate the cornea and extend through Descemet's membrane into the anterior chamber. The most common organisms include *Aspergillus, Candida,* and *Fusarium.* Many fungi can be seen in tissue sections using special stains such as Grocott-Gomori methenamine–silver nitrate (GMS), PAS, or Giemsa (Fig VI-6). Other fungal organisms, including *Candida* and organisms causing mucormycosis, are visible with routine H&E preparations.

Acanthamoeba keratitis *Acanthamoeba* protozoa most commonly cause infection in soft contact lens wearers who do not take appropriate precautions in cleaning and sterilizing their lenses. The most frequently involved species are *A castellani* and *A polyphagia.* Patients presenting with *Acanthamoeba* keratitis usually have severe eye pain. Clinically, the cornea may show a ring infiltrate.

Biopsy specimens or scrapings from infected areas may demonstrate cysts and trophozoites that are discernable in H&E sections (Fig VI-7). Other techniques, such as use of monoclonal antibodies, may enhance the recognition of cysts and troph-

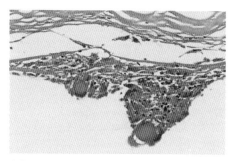

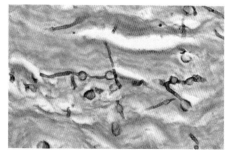

FIG VI-5—Herpes simplex virus keratitis. Note the granulomatous response to Descemet's membrane. Herpesvirus antigen has been detected in this area.

FIG VI-6—*Fusarium* keratitis, Grocott-Gomori methamine–silver nitrate stain.

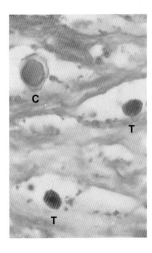

FIG VI-7—*Acanthamoeba* keratitis. Note the cyst (C) and trophozoite (T) forms.

ozoites in tissue sections. Special culture techniques and media, including non-nutrient blood agar layered with *E coli,* are required to grow *Acanthamoeba.* The pathologic findings in corneal buttons removed because of this infection are quite variable, spanning the spectrum from no inflammation to a marked granulomatous reaction.

Noninfectious Inflammation

Corneal inflammation can also be caused by noninfectious agents. For example, foreign bodies may be retained in the cornea as a result of accidental or surgical trauma. Often, a localized granulomatous reaction can be seen surrounding the foreign material. Foreign bodies are often birefringent and can be demonstrated on examination of tissue sections with polarized light.

Degenerations and Dystrophies

Degenerations

Corneal degenerations are secondary changes that occur in previously normal tissue. They are often associated with aging, are not inherited, and are not necessarily bilateral.

Band keratopathy   Seen clinically as calcific plaques in the interpalpebral zone, band keratopathy is characterized by the deposition of calcium in the epithelial basement membrane, Bowman's layer, and the anterior stroma (Fig VI-8). The calcium deposits appear as basophilic granules in H&E sections; the presence of calcium can be further confirmed by use of special stains such as alizarin red or the von Kossa stain. Band keratopathy may develop in any chronic local corneal disease, in association with systemic hypercalcemic states, and in eyes with prolonged chronic inflammation.

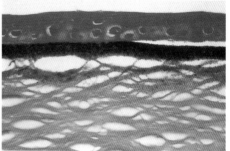

FIG VI-8—Band keratopathy. *Left,* Clinical appearance shows white calcium deposition in the interpalpebral region of cornea. *Right,* Calcium deposition in Bowman's layer is shown with von Kossa stain.

Actinic keratopathy   Also known as *spheroidal degeneration* or *Labrador keratopathy,* actinic keratopathy involves damage to corneal collagen similar to that seen in pingueculae and pterygia and solar elastosis of the skin. The actinic damage usually occurs within the palpebral fissure, similar to the pattern seen in band keratopathy. Upon clinical examination, translucent, golden-brown spheroidal deposits are visible in the superficial cornea. H&E-stained sections show basophilic globules in the superficial stroma, immediately subjacent to the epithelium. No associated inflammatory changes are present (Fig VI-9).

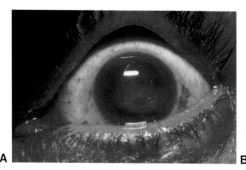
A

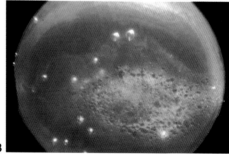
B

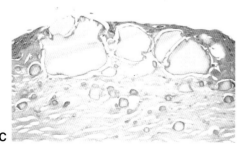
C

FIG VI-9—Actinic keratopathy (spheroidal degeneration). *A,* Clinical appearance shows golden brown spheroidal deposits in the cornea. *B,* Gross appearance of corneal button. The air bubbles are artifacts. *C,* Histopathology shows lightly staining basophilic globules in the epithelium and superficial stroma.

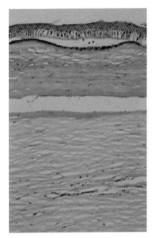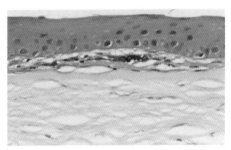

FIG VI-10—Pannus. *Left,* This is degenerative pannus: fibrous connective tissue is interposed between the epithelium and Bowman's layer (note the basophilic stippling superficially in degenerative pannus, indicative of calcification). *Right,* This is fibrovascular pannus, which may be accompanied by inflammatory cells with destruction of Bowman's layer (a condition sometimes called *inflammatory pannus*).

Pannus   Corneal pannus is the growth of tissue between the epithelium and Bowman's layer. This subepithelial fibrous tissue may have a significant vascular component, in which case the term *subepithelial fibrovascular pannus* is employed. Bowman's layer may be disrupted (Fig VI-10). Pannus is frequently seen in cases of chronic corneal edema or prolonged corneal inflammation.

Bullous keratopathy   The end result of persistent stromal edema, this condition is most frequently caused by the failure of the corneal endothelial cell layer to perform its normal pump function (Fig VI-11). The pumping failure can occur either because the cells themselves do not function normally or because the absolute number of endothelial cells has decreased below a critical level necessary to maintain corneal clarity. The condition is mainly seen following cataract surgery.

   In corneal buttons varying degrees of diffuse corneal edema are present. The epithelium is separated from the underlying Bowman's layer, creating microcysts or coalescing to form bullae. The epithelial basement membrane may be thickened and redundant, and intraepithelial basement membrane material similar to that seen in map-dot-fingerprint dystrophy is often observed. There is a paucity of endothelial cells, and those cells remaining are flattened and attenuated. Descemet's membrane is preserved intact.

Keratoconus   This noninflammatory condition is characterized by a bilateral central ectasia of the cornea with anterior protrusion of the cornea. Although bilateral, one eye may be more severely affected than its fellow. The alteration in the normal corneal contour produces myopia and irregular astigmatism. Keratoconus can occur as an isolated finding, or it may be associated with other ocular disorders or with systemic conditions including atopy, Down syndrome, and Marfan syndrome.

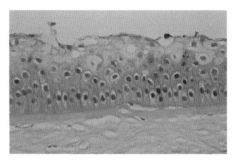

FIG VI-11—Bullous keratopathy. Note the swelling of the corneal epithelial cells (hydropic degeneration) and the subepithelial bulla.

The earliest histologic changes are focal disruptions of the epithelial basement membrane and Bowman's layer. Central stromal thinning and anterior stromal scarring are usually present. Iron deposition in the basal epithelial layers *(Fleischer ring)* can often be demonstrated using the Prussian blue stain or Perls' test. Spontaneous breaks in Descemet's membrane can lead to acute stromal edema, or *hydrops* (Fig VI-12). Other causes of spontaneous breaks in Descemet's membrane include ob-

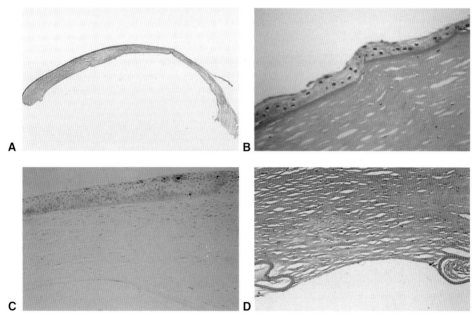

FIG VI-12—Keratoconus. *A,* Low-magnification view shows corneal stromal thinning. *B,* Masson trichrome stain demonstrates focal disruption of Bowman's layer. *C,* Intraepithelial iron deposition (Fleischer ring). *D,* Rupture of Descemet's membrane with rolled edges of Descemet's membrane at the edge of the rupture site.

stectric forceps injury, congenital glaucoma (Haab's striae), Terrien marginal degeneration, and pellucid marginal degeneration.

Dystrophies

Dystrophies of the cornea are primary, inherited, bilateral disorders, categorized by the layer of the cornea most involved. Keratoconus, which is discussed above under Degenerations, is often considered a dystrophy. Only the most common corneal dystrophies are discussed below.

Epithelial dystrophy   Also called *map-dot-fingerprint, Cogan microcystic,* or *anterior basement membrane dystrophy,* epithelial dystrophy may be the most common of the corneal dystrophies seen by the comprehensive ophthalmologist (Fig VI-13).

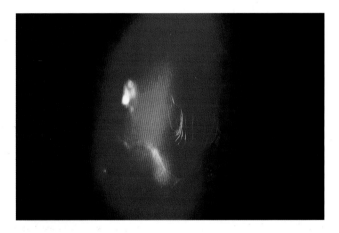

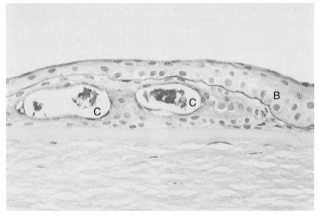

FIG VI-13—Epithelial dystrophy (map-dot-fingerprint dystrophy). *Top,* Clinical appearance of cornea using retroillumination to demonstrate numerous wavy lines and dotlike lesions. *Bottom,* The changes in primary map-dot-fingerprint dystrophy are almost identical to those seen in cases of chronic corneal epithelial edema. Note the intraepithelial basement membrane (B) and the degenerating intraepithelial cells trapped within cystic spaces (C).

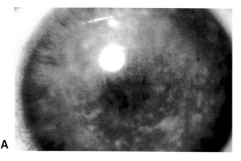

A

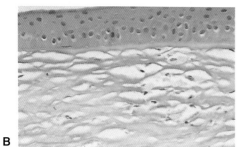

B

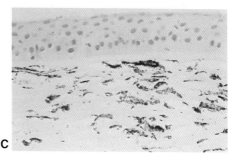

C

FIG VI-14—Macular dystrophy. *A*, Clinical appearance. *B*, H&E stain. Note the clear spaces surrounding the keratocytes and in the stroma. *C*, Colloidal iron stain for mucopolysaccharides.

In this condition the basement membrane is thickened and may extend into the epithelium. Additionally, abnormal epithelial cells with microcysts are present. A deposition of fibrillar material forms between the basement membrane and Bowman's layer. Patients with epithelial dystrophy will often present with symptoms of recurrent erosion syndrome.

Macular dystrophy This autosomal recessive stromal dystrophy involves the entire cornea to the limbus. Clinically, it is characterized by poorly defined stromal lesions with hazy intervening stroma. Mucopolysaccharide material is deposited both intracellularly and extracellularly in the corneal stroma. This material stains blue with the alcian blue and colloidal iron stains (Fig VI-14). Corneal thinning may occur as well. Two types of macular dystrophy have been described depending on the specific abnormality in the keratan sulfate and dermatan sulfate–proteoglycan metabolism. The genes for macular dystrophy and one variant, the North Carolina type, have been identified on chromosomes 6p and 6q, respectively.

Granular dystrophy This autosomal dominant stromal dystrophy involves the central cornea and has sharply defined lesions with clear intervening stroma (Fig VI-15). Histologically, irregularly shaped, well-circumscribed depositions of hyaline material are visible in the stroma. This material stains bright red with the Masson trichrome stain.

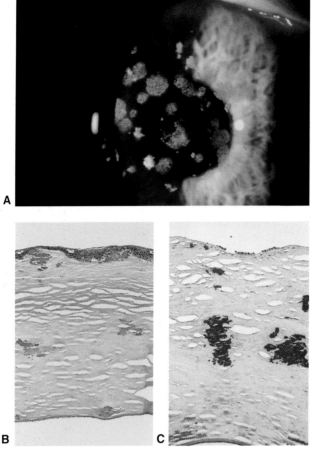

FIG VI-15—Granular dystrophy. *A*, Clinical appearance; note the clear intervening stroma. *B*, H&E stain. Note the chunky stromal deposits at all levels of the cornea. *C*, Trichrome stain. The corneal stroma stains blue, and the granular deposits stain brilliant red.

Lattice dystrophy This autosomal dominant condition involves the central cornea and is characterized by refractile lines with hazy intervening stroma (Fig VI-16). The disorder is a primary localized corneal amyloidosis, in which the amyloid deposits may result from epithelial cells and keratocytes. Histologically, the amyloid deposits are concentrated most heavily in the anterior stroma, but they may also occur in the subepithelial area. The amyloid material stains positive with the Congo red stain and demonstrates metachromasia with crystal violet stain. The amyloid material is bi-refringent, appearing apple green under polarized light. Recurrence of amyloid deposits in the corneal graft following penetrating keratoplasty occurs more frequently than after grafting for granular or macular dystrophy.

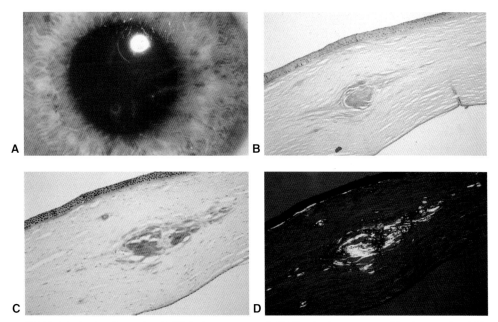

FIG VI-16—Lattice dystrophy. *A,* Clinical appearance. *B,* H&E stain shows scattered fusiform eosinophilic material deposited at all levels of the stroma. *C,* Congo red stain demonstrates that the fusiform deposits are amyloid. *D,* Examination of Congo red stain with polarized light shows birefringence of amyloid deposits.

Avellino dystrophy   Features of both granular and lattice dystrophy appear in this condition, first described in patients tracing their ancestry to Avellino, Italy. Histologically, both hyaline deposits (typical of granular dystrophy) and amyloid deposits (characteristic of lattice dystrophy) are present within the corneal stroma. This dystrophy, like granular and lattice dystrophy, has been mapped to chromosome 5q.

Fuchs dystrophy   This dystrophy has a variable inheritance pattern and occurs more commonly in women. It is one of the leading causes of bullous keratopathy. This condition can be recognized clinically before corneal decompensation occurs by the appearance of guttata in Descemet's membrane. In corneal buttons Descemet's membrane appears diffusely thickened. Focal, anvil-shaped excrescences of basement membrane material are seen protruding into the anterior chamber or buried within the thickened Descemet's membrane. The endothelial cells are usually sparse to absent. As in bullous keratopathy from other causes, there are varying degrees of secondary epithelial basement membrane changes and subepithelial fibrosis (Fig VI-17).

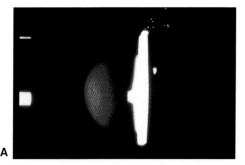

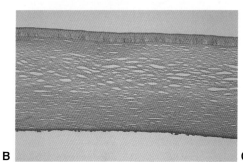

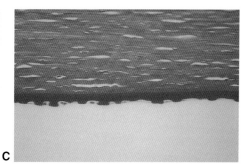

FIG VI-17—Fuchs dystrophy. *A,* Retroillumination of cornea shows "beaten bronze" appearance. *B,* Histology shows diffuse edema of corneal epithelium and stroma. *C,* Higher magnification of Descemet's membrane and posterior corneal stroma using PAS stain shows numerous focal areas of thickening of Descemet's membrane (guttata).

Pigment Deposits

Krukenberg spindle occurs in the pigment dispersion syndrome. The melanin pigment is primarily located within the endothelial cells but is also free on the posterior corneal surface (Fig VI-18).

FIG VI-18—Pigment dispersion syndrome. Krukenberg spindle. Melanin is found within the endothelial cells.

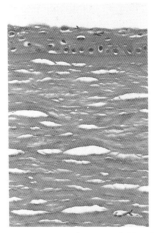

FIG VI-19—*Left*, Corneal blood staining. H&E stain. The orange particles represent hemoglobin in the corneal stroma. *Right*, An iron stain demonstrates iron confined to the stromal keratocytes.

Blood staining of the cornea may complicate hyphema when the IOP is very high; however, if the endothelium is compromised, blood staining can occur even at normal or low IOP. In acute blood staining, hemoglobin is demonstrated in the corneal stroma. Later, iron may be demonstrated in the keratocytes (Fig VI-19).

Iron lines result from pooling of tears in areas where the corneal surface is irregular. Histologically, iron is found within the basal epithelial cells and can be demonstrated using the Prussian blue stain or Perls' test. Some of the named iron lines include the following:

☐ Hudson-Stähli

☐ Fleischer (in keratoconus)

☐ Stocker (at the advancing edge of a pterygium)

☐ Ferry (anterior to a filtering bleb)

The *Kayser-Fleischer ring* is a brown ring seen in the periphery of the cornea in Wilson disease. It corresponds to copper deposition in Descemet's membrane.

Neoplasia

Primary conjunctival intraepithelial neoplasia may extend from the limbus and involve the corneal epithelium. *Dysplasia* of the corneal epithelium refers to abnormal maturation of the epithelium as it differentiates from the basal layer to the superficial layers. This condition has been described further in chapter V, Conjunctiva. Rarely, primary intraepithelial neoplasia may arise in the clear cornea.

Carcinoma in situ describes full-thickness dysplastic involvement of the epithelium. Bowman's layer normally acts as a natural barrier against invasion by neoplasia; therefore, invasive squamous cell carcinoma involving the corneal stroma is seen only if the disease is very advanced, or if Bowman's layer is compromised.

CHAPTER VII

Anterior Chamber and Trabecular Meshwork

Topography

The anterior chamber is bounded anteriorly by the corneal endothelium, posteriorly by the anterior surface of the iris–ciliary body and pupillary portion of the lens, and peripherally by the trabecular meshwork (Fig VII-1). The depth of the anterior chamber is about 3.4–3.7 mm. The trabecular meshwork is derived from the neural crest.

Trabecular Beams and Endothelium

The outermost corneoscleral meshwork is composed of multiple layers of collagenous sheets that are lined by very thin endothelium. This endothelium forms bridges between the sheets. The uveal meshwork, the innermost portion of trabecular meshwork, is composed of two to three layers of intersecting trabecular beams that course meridionally from the ciliary body and iris root to the zone between the corneoscleral and trabecular endothelium. These beams, or cords, are covered by a slightly thicker layer of endothelium. Trabecular beams are thicker in primary infantile glau-

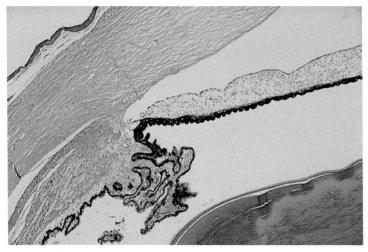

FIG VII-1—The normal anterior chamber angle, the site of drainage for the major portion of the aqueous humor flow, is defined by the anterior border of the iris, the face of the ciliary body, the internal surface of the trabecular meshwork, and the posterior surface of the cornea.

FIG VII-2—Light micrograph of anterior chamber angle demonstrates Schlemm's canal adjacent to the trabecular meshwork and the external collector vessels.

coma than in normal individuals. Schlemm's canal encircles the trabecular meshwork and is joined to the corneoscleral meshwork by the internal collector channel (Fig VII-2).

Congenital Anomalies

Schwalbe's line varies in prominence depending upon the number and thickness of inserted cords at the zone of transition between the corneal and trabecular endothelium. Thickening of Schwalbe's line is known as *posterior embryotoxon* (Fig VII-3).

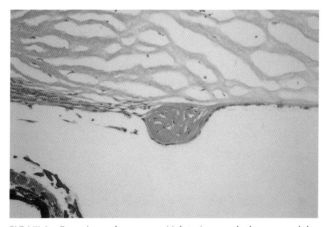

FIG VII-3—Posterior embryotoxon. Light micrograph shows a nodular prominence at the termination of Descemet's membrane.

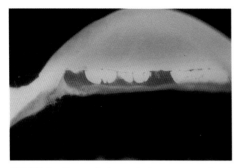 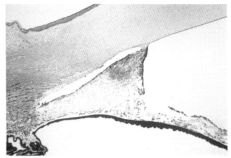

FIG VII-4—Gross photograph shows a prominent Schwalbe's line and the anterior insertion of iris strands (Axenfeld anomaly). (Photograph courtesy of Robert Y. Foos, MD.)

FIG VII-5—Light micrograph shows iris strands that insert anteriorly on Schwalbe's line. (Reproduced from Yanoff M, Fine BS. *Ocular Pathology: A Color Atlas.* New York: Gower; 1988. Photograph courtesy of Robert Y. Foos, MD.)

Axenfeld-Rieger syndrome has recently been chosen as the name for a spectrum of congenital anterior segment defects previously called by the term mesodermal dysgenesis and a variety of eponyms. All the conditions discussed below are now subsumed under the single name Axenfeld-Rieger syndrome.

Axenfeld anomaly is a congenital anomaly in which Schwalbe's line is anteriorly displaced and iris bands extend to the cornea (Figs VII-4, VII-5). If the development of the meshwork is defective and glaucoma is present, the condition is called *Axenfeld syndrome.*

Rieger anomaly is the term used to described iris pupillary abnormalities in combination with the findings of Axenfeld anomaly. Rieger anomaly is associated with the later onset of glaucoma. If Rieger anomaly is associated with dental and skeletal abnormalities, the condition is called *Rieger syndrome.*

Degenerations

Iridocorneal Endothelial Syndrome

The iridocorneal endothelial (ICE) syndrome refers to a spectrum of acquired abnormalities affecting the cornea, anterior chamber angle, and iris. Abnormal proliferation of corneal endothelium is a constant feature of all forms of the ICE syndrome. When these cells cover the angle, secondary open-angle glaucoma develops. Over time peripheral anterior synechiae may form, closing the angle (Fig VII-6). Three different clinical presentations are known:

☐ Iris nevus (Cogan-Reese) syndrome

☐ Chandler syndrome

☐ Essential iris atrophy

The first letter for each type forms the mnemonic ICE. Most patients are young to middle-aged adults who are affected unilaterally. See also BCSC Section 10, *Glaucoma,* which discusses secondary angle-closure glaucoma as well as the issues covered throughout this chapter in depth.

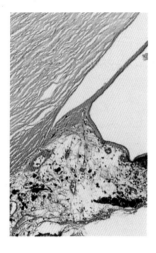

FIG VII-6—ICE syndrome. Descemet's membrane lines the anterior surface of the iris. The iris is apposed to the cornea (peripheral anterior synechiae).

Albert DM, Jakobiec FA, eds. *Principles and Practice of Ophthalmology.* 2nd ed. Philadelphia: Saunders; 1994:1448–1454.

Secondary Glaucoma with Material in the Trabecular Meshwork

Pseudoexfoliation of the lens is a condition that is characterized by deposits of PAS-positive material on the lens capsule, zonular fibers, iris, and elsewhere in the eye. These deposits distinguish pseudoexfoliation from the rare *true exfoliation,* which is the splitting of the lens capsule induced by infrared radiation. (Other volumes of the BCSC series use the term *exfoliation syndrome.*) Pseudoexfoliation may be unilateral or bilateral and usually affects persons over 50 years of age. Recent evidence suggests that it is a systemic process involving the deposition of a substance that contains fibrillin and is coated with the glycosaminoglycan hyalouran acid. This material, produced in the iris, ciliary body, lens endothelium, conjunctiva, skin, and viscera, accumulates on the surface of intraocular structures (Figs VII-7, VII-8).

The trabecular meshwork in pseudoexfoliation also contains an excessive amount of pigment, but its distribution is more uneven than in pigmentary glaucoma (see p 87). Transillumination defects and circumferential ridges are prominent in the posterior iris. When glaucoma develops in eyes with pseudoexfoliation, it is often referred to as *capsular glaucoma.*

Albert DM, Jakobiec FA, eds. *Principles and Practice of Ophthalmology.* 2nd ed. Philadelphia: Saunders; 1994:1400–1425.

Ritch R. Exfoliation syndrome. In: *Focal Points: Clinical Modules for Ophthalmologists.* San Francisco: American Academy of Ophthalmology; 1994: vol 12, no 9.

The condition known as *phacolytic glaucoma* occurs when denatured lens protein leaks from a hypermature cataract and occludes the trabecular meshwork. Although some controversy persists regarding the pathogenesis of phacolytic glaucoma, evidence suggests that the abnormal lens protein leaking into the anterior

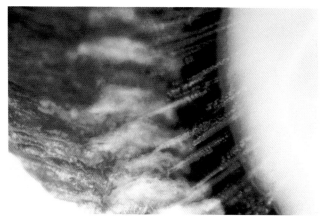

FIG VII-7—Gross photograph shows fibrillar deposits on the lens zonule in pseudoexfoliation.

chamber may be directly responsible for the increased resistance to outflow. Macrophages, containing numerous vacuoles, may be present (Fig VII-9). BCSC Section 9, *Intraocular Inflammation and Uveitis,* discusses lens-induced uveitis in more detail.

Trauma Following an intraocular hemorrhage, blood breakdown products may accumulate in the trabecular meshwork. Hemolyzed erythrocytes may obstruct aqueous outflow and lead to a secondary open-angle glaucoma known as *ghost cell glaucoma.* These ghost erythrocytes are tan in color, spherical in shape, and rigid. Their rigidity makes it difficult for the cells to escape through the trabecular meshwork (Fig VII-10).

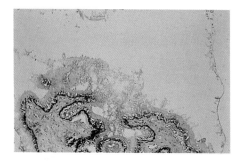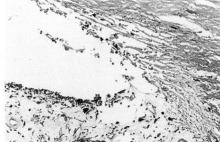

FIG VII-8—Pseudoexfoliation, or exfoliation syndrome. *Left,* Abnormal material appears on ciliary processes, resembling iron filings on the edge of a magnet. *Right,* Note the intense pigmentation in the angle.

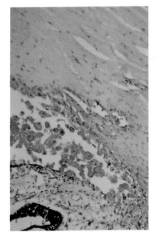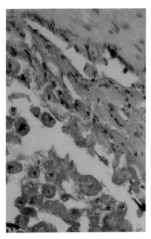

FIG VII-9—Phacolytic glaucoma. *Left,* Low magnification of macrophages filled with degenerated lens cortical material in the angle. *Right,* Higher magnification.

In some cases of secondary open-angle glaucoma associated with chronic intraocular hemorrhage, histologic examination has revealed hemosiderin within endothelial cells of the trabecular meshwork and within macrophages. The effect of hemosiderin on the trabecular meshwork and on the pathogenesis of glaucoma is not known. The iron stored in the cells may be an enzyme toxin that damages trabecular function in hemosiderosis oculi. Alternatively, the hemosiderin may be a sign of damage that has occurred during oxidation of hemoglobin. Iron deposition in

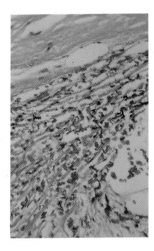

FIG VII-10—Degenerating red blood cells can clog the trabecular meshwork in patients with hyphema.

hemosiderosis oculi can be demonstrated within many ocular epithelial structures by means of the Prussian blue reaction.

In other cases of hemorrhage-associated glaucoma, macrophages in the anterior chamber are noted to contain phagocytosed erythrocytes. In *hemolytic glaucoma* hemoglobin-laden macrophages block the trabecular outflow channels. It is possible that macrophages are a sign of trabecular obstruction rather than the actual cause.

Blunt injury to the globe may be associated with traumatic hyphema and with recession of the angle, the most common manifestation of this type of trauma. The probability that glaucoma will develop as a late sequela of hyphema depends, in part, on the amount of angle recession. Between 5% and 10% of patients having greater than 180° of angle recession eventually develop chronic glaucoma.

Histologically, angle recession represents a tear in the ciliary body between the longitudinal and circular muscles (Fig VII-11). If the longitudinal muscle is detached from the scleral spur, the tear is referred to as a *cyclodialysis*. Tears in the root of the iris *(iridodialysis)* may also occur with blunt trauma (Fig VII-12).

Although recession of the angle provides evidence of past blunt trauma, it does not necessarily mean that the trauma is the direct cause of glaucoma. Since glaucoma usually takes years to develop following angle recession, progressive degenerative changes in the remaining trabecular meshwork may be an important factor in the pathogenesis of postcontusion glaucoma.

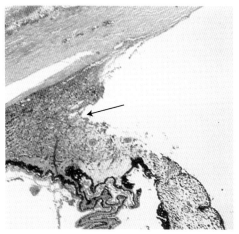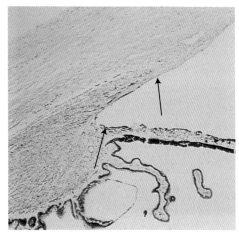

FIG VII-11—*Left,* Contusion injury to the ciliary body. There is a rupture in the face of the ciliary body in the plane between the external longitudinal muscle fibers of the ciliary body and the internal circular and oblique fibers (arrow). Concurrent injury to the trabecular meshwork often occurs. *Right,* Contusion angle deformity. The iris root (lower arrow) is displaced posteriorly in relation to the longitudinal muscle bundle and its insertion into the scleral spur (upper arrow). In the region of the injury, the anterior chamber may be deep. Although clinically and histologically unapparent, injury to the drainage structures can be significant.

FIG VII-12—Blunt trauma to eye may cause rupture of the iris at its base, a point of relative weakness, resulting in iridodialysis.

Pigment dispersion associations   Pigment dispersion may be associated with a variety of other conditions in which pigment epithelium or uveal melanocytes are injured, such as uveitis (uveitic glaucoma) or uveal melanoma. These conditions are characterized by pigment within the trabecular meshwork and in macrophages littering the angle (Fig VII-13).

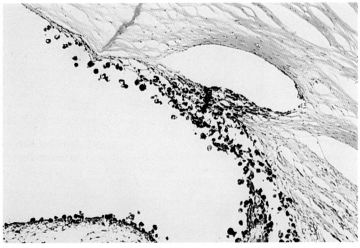

FIG VII-13—Secondary open-angle glaucoma. Trabecular meshwork obstructed by macrophages that have ingested pigment from a necrotic intraocular melanoma (melanomalytic glaucoma).

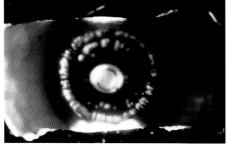 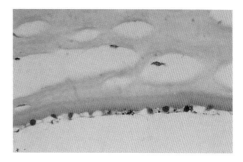

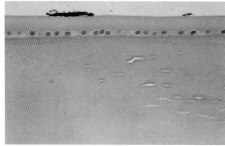 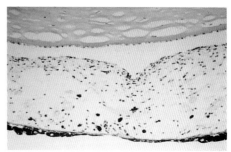

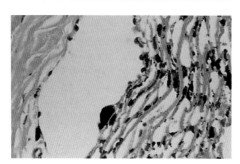

FIG VII-14—Pigment dispersion syndrome. *Top left,* Gross photograph, demonstrating radially oriented transillumination defects in the iris. *Top right,* Krukenberg spindle. Melanin is present within the corneal endothelial cells. *Middle left,* Scheie stripe. Melanin is present on the anterior surface of the lens. *Middle right,* Note the focal loss of iris pigment epithelium. Chafing of the zonules against the epithelium may release the pigment that is dispersed in this condition. *Bottom left,* Note the accumulation of pigment in the trabecular meshwork.

Secondary open-angle glaucoma can occur as a result of the *pigment dispersion syndrome* (Fig VII-14). This type of glaucoma is characterized by radially oriented defects in the midperipheral iris and pigment in the trabecular meshwork, the corneal endothelium (Krukenberg spindle), and other anterior segment structures such as the lens capsule. The dispersed pigment is presumed to be iris pigment epithelium mechanically rubbed off by contact with lens zonular fibers. Histologic studies of eyes with pigmentary glaucoma show large accumulations of pigment granules and cellular debris in the trabecular meshwork and phagocytosed pigment in and on endothelial cells of the cornea. Pigment is present both intracellularly and extracellularly in the trabecular meshwork.

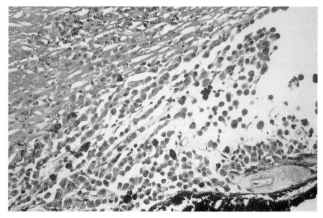

FIG VII-15—Photomicrograph shows malignant melanoma cells filling the anterior chamber angle and obstructing the trabecular meshwork.

Neoplasia

Melanocytic nevi and melanomas that arise in the iris or extend to the iris from the ciliary body may obstruct the trabecular meshwork (Fig VII-15). See also chapter XVII. In addition, pigment elaborated from the melanomas may be shed into the trabecular meshwork and produce secondary glaucoma.

CHAPTER VIII

Sclera

Topography

The sclera is the white, nearly opaque portion of the outer wall of the eye, covering from four fifths to five sixths of the eye's circumference. It is continuous anteriorly at the limbus with the corneal stroma. Posteriorly, the outer two thirds of the sclera merge with the dura of the optic nerve sheath; the inner one third continues as the lamina cribrosa, through which pass the axonal fibers of the optic nerve. The diameter of the scleral shell averages 22.0 mm, and its thickness varies from 1.0 mm posteriorly to 0.3 mm just posterior to the insertions of the four rectus muscles (Fig VIII-1). Histologically, the sclera is divided into three layers (from outermost inward): episclera, stroma, and lamina fusca. The sclera is derived from the neural crest.

Episclera

This thin fibrovascular layer covers the outer surface of the scleral stroma. It is thickest anterior to the rectus muscle insertions and immediately surrounding the optic nerve, and thinnest at the limbus and posterior to the rectus muscle insertions at the equator of the eye. The episclera is composed of loosely arranged collagen fibers and a vascular plexus.

FIG VIII-1—Normal sclera at the equator demonstrating thinning just posterior to the insertion of the rectus muscle.

FIG VIII-2—An emissarial channel through the sclera for the nerve loop of Axenfeld is present overlying the pars plana (trichrome stain).

Stroma

The bulk of the sclera is made up of sparsely vascularized, dense type I collagen fibers whose diameters range from 28 nm to more than 300 nm; the thicker fibers are more centrifugally located. In general, collagen fibers in the stroma course parallel to the external surface of the scleral shell, but individual fibers are randomly arranged and may branch and curl. In comparison to the corneal stroma, scleral collagen fibers are thicker and more variable in thickness and orientation. Transmural emissarial channels provide outlets within the stroma in the following fashion (Fig VIII-2):

☐ Posterior region for posterior ciliary arteries and nerves

☐ Equatorial region for vortex veins

☐ Anterior regions for anterior ciliary arteries, veins, and nerves

Lamina Fusca

This thin network of bridging collagen fibers loosely binds the uvea to the sclera. Sclerouveal attachments are strongest along major emissarial canals and the anterior supraciliary zone. The lamina fusca contains variable numbers of melanocytes.

Congenital Anomalies

Choristomas

Limbal dermoids have been discussed earlier in chapter V, Conjunctiva. See pp 45–46 and Figure VI-3.

Episcleral osseous choristoma is found most commonly in the superotemporal quadrant of the epibulbar surface, 0.5–1.0 cm posterior to the limbus. The clinical appearance is that of a single stationary hard white plaque, round to oval in shape and measuring up to 1.0 cm in diameter, beneath the conjunctiva. No other congenital anomalies are associated. The histopathologic appearance demonstrates mature lamellar bone trabeculae; rarely, hematopoietic elements occupy the marrow space.

Nanophthalmos

An eye that is uniformly reduced in size except for the lens, which is normal or slightly enlarged, results in severe hyperopia. Nanophthalmos is usually bilateral. The sclera is abnormally thick, which is thought to predispose to uveal effusion because of reduced protein permeability and impaired venous outflow through the vortex veins. Glaucoma, which is common in nanophthalmic eyes, may be caused by a variety of mechanisms including angle closure, pupillary block, and open angle with elevated episcleral venous pressure.

Inflammations

Episcleritis

Simple episcleritis most commonly presents as a tender, movable, sectoral red macule involving the anterior episclera. It affects males and females equally, predominantly in the fifth decade, and usually has no association with antecedent injury or systemic illness. Histopathologic examination shows vascular congestion and stromal edema associated with a chronic inflammatory infiltrate, composed primarily of lymphocytes, in a perivascular distribution. Granulomatous inflammation and necrosis are not present. The diagnosis is made on clinical findings, and complete resolution is the rule, with or without topical corticosteroid therapy. The condition may be recurrent, however, and can ultimately cause fibrosis and scar formation.

In contrast to simple episcleritis, *nodular episcleritis* more often affects females and patients who have rheumatoid arthritis. It is characterized by tender, elevated, rounded pink-red nodules on the anterior episclera. Histopathologically, the nodules are composed of necrobiotic granulomatous inflammation, a palisading arrangement of epithelioid histiocytes around a central core of necrotic collagen. This light microscopic pattern is the same as that seen in rheumatoid nodules in subcutaneous tissue. Spontaneous resolution is the expected outcome, and topical corticosteroids or nonsteroidal anti-inflammatory agents (NSAIDs) may reduce symptoms. See also BCSC Section 8, *External Disease and Cornea,* for further discussion of this condition and those covered below.

Scleritis

Scleritis is a painful, often progressive, ocular disease with potentially serious sequelae. There is a high association with systemic autoimmune vasculitic connective tissue diseases such as

- Rheumatoid arthritis
- Systemic lupus erythematosus
- Polyarteritis nodosa
- Wegener granulomatosis
- Relapsing polychondritis
- Reiter syndrome

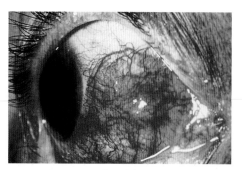

FIG VIII-3—A sectoral nodular anterior scleritis is present in this patient with severe ocular pain and photophobia.

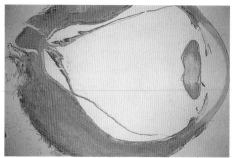

FIG VIII-4—Diffuse posterior scleritis (brawny scleritis) demonstrates marked thickening of the posterior sclera.

The inflammation may be localized to the anterior or the posterior sclera, or it may affect other ocular tissues, particularly the cornea and uvea. *Anterior scleritis* is usually a severely painful sectoral inflammation of episclera and sclera with intense photophobia (Fig VIII-3). The disease is bilateral in approximately 50% of cases. *Posterior scleritis* is marked by a different constellation of signs and symptoms: patients present with unilateral proptosis, retrobulbar pain, gaze restriction, and visual field loss. Contiguous spread of inflammation may result in optic neuritis or retinal and choroidal detachments; it may even give the mistaken impression of an intraocular neoplasm.

Histopathologic examination of scleritis reveals two main categories: necrotizing and nonnecrotizing inflammation. Either type may occur anteriorly or posteriorly. *Necrotizing inflammation* may be nodular or diffuse (so-called brawny scleritis, Fig VIII-4). Both patterns demonstrate a palisading arrangement of epithelioid histiocytes and multinucleated giant cells surrounding sequestered areas of necrosis (Fig VIII-5). Peripheral to the histiocytes is a rim of lymphocytes and plasma cells. Multiple foci may show different stages of evolution. In the course of healing, the necrotic stroma is resorbed, leaving in its wake a thinned scleral remnant prone to staphyloma formation (Fig VIII-6). Complete destruction of the scleral shell predisposes to herniation of uveal tissue through the defect, a condition known as *scleromalacia perforans*.

Nonnecrotizing inflammation is characterized by a perivascular lymphocytic and plasma cell infiltrate without a granulomatous inflammatory component. Vasculitis may be present in the form of fibrinoid necrosis of vessel walls. Treatment with NSAIDs usually leads to resolution without significant weakening of the scleral shell.

Dubord PJ, Chambers A. Scleritis and episcleritis: diagnosis and management. In: *Focal Points: Clinical Modules for Ophthalmologists*. San Francisco: American Academy of Ophthalmology; 1995: vol 13, no 9.

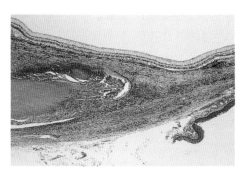

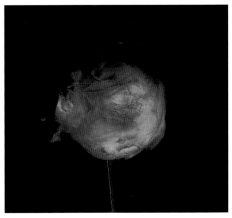

FIG VIII-5—Area of necrosis is sequestered by a zonal inflammatory reaction of histiocytes, lymphocytes, and plasma cells in this necrotizing granulomatous scleritis.

FIG VIII-6—A posterior staphyloma is present in this eye as a sequela of scleritis.

Degenerations

Senile calcific plaques occur commonly in elderly persons as flat, firm, gray rectangular to oval patches that appear bilaterally and measure less than 1.0 cm in greatest dimension. They are located anterior to the insertions of the medial and lateral rectus muscles (Fig VIII-7). On histologic sections the calcium appears within the midportion of the scleral stroma. It initially occurs as a finely granular deposition but may progress to involve both superficial and deep layers as a confluent plaque. Senile calcific plaque may be highlighted by special stains such as that of von Kossa. The etiology is unknown; dehydration and actinic damage have been proposed but not proved.

Corneal staphylomas have been discussed in chapter VI. *Scleral staphylomas* are ectasias lined by uveal tissue that may occur at points of weakness in the scleral shell, either in inherently thin areas (such as posterior to the rectus muscle insertions) or in areas weakened by tissue destruction (as in scleritis associated with rheumatoid arthritis; see Figure VIII-6). In children staphylomas may occur as a result of long-standing increased IOP or axial myopia, owing to the relative distensibility of the sclera in younger, as compared to older, individuals. Age at onset and location, therefore, vary according to the underlying etiology. Staphylomas appear as variably sized and shaped patches of blue-purple discoloration of the sclera caused by increased visibility of the underlying uveal pigment and vasculature. Histopathologic examination invariably reveals thinned sclera, with or without fibrosis and scarring, again depending on the cause.

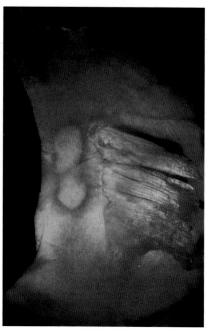

FIG VIII-7—A calcific plaque within the sclera just anterior to the insertion of a rectus muscle is present in this postmortem specimen.

Neoplasia

Neoplasms of the sclera are rare. Reported examples include fibrous histiocytoma, reticulohistiocytoma, and melanocytoma. Nodular fasciitis is included in this discussion, although it is a reactive proliferative process.

Fibrous histiocytoma is a benign neoplasm formed by a proliferation of spindle cells, characteristically in a matlike *(storiform)* pattern. Intermixed histiocytes, often lipid-laden, are a variable finding. Nuclear pleomorphism and mitotic activity are minimal. Hyalinized collagen may be present in older lesions. Infiltrative margins of the neoplasm are associated with increased risk of locally aggressive behavior and recurrence. Malignant fibrous histiocytoma has not been reported in the sclera, although it has been described in the conjunctiva.

Nodular fasciitis is a reactive process that may cause a tumor in the episclera. Antecedent trauma has been implicated as an etiologic factor for the development of nodular fasciitis in other body sites, but no such association has been identified in the sclera. It usually affects young adults as a rapidly growing, round to oval, firm white-gray nodule measuring 0.5–1.5 cm and appearing at the limbus or anterior to a rectus muscle insertion. Although self-limited, it is usually excised because of its rapid growth. Histopathologic examination reveals a circumscribed spindle cell pro-liferation in which individual cells are likened to the appearance of fibroblasts grow-ing in tissue culture. These spindle cells aggregate in whorling fascicles, admixed with a chronic inflammatory infiltrate and lipid-laden histiocytes, in a myxoid back-ground. Older lesions may show foci of dense collagen deposition. Although mitotic figures may be present, atypical (e.g., tripolar) mitotic figures are absent. The cellu-lar nature of these proliferations and the presence of mitotic figures may lead to the histologic misinterpetation that they represent a malignant process, a pitfall to avoid.

CHAPTER IX

Lens

Topography

The crystalline lens is a soft, elastic, avascular biconvex structure that in the adult measures 9–10 mm in diameter and 3.5 mm in anteroposterior thickness (Fig IX-1). The lens is derived from surface ectoderm. BCSC Section 11, *Lens and Cataract*, discusses in depth the structure, embryology, and pathology of the lens.

Capsule

The lens capsule is composed of a thick basement membrane that surrounds the entire lens and is elaborated by the lens epithelial cells. It is thickest anteriorly (12–21 μm) and peripherally near the equator, and thinnest posteriorly (2–9 μm). The capsule provides insertions for the zonular fibers and plays an important part in molding the lens shape in accommodation.

Epithelium

The lens epithelium is derived from the cells of the original lens vesicle that did not differentiate into primary fibers. Although epithelial cells located centrally do not usually undergo mitosis, those located peripherally in the equatorial zone actively divide. The anterior or axial cells form a single layer of cuboidal cells with their

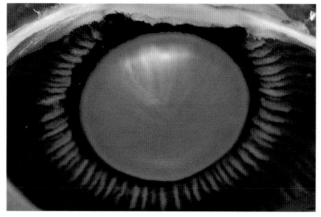

FIG IX-1—Posterior aspect of the crystalline lens depicting its relationship to the peripheral iris and ciliary body.

FIG IX-2—Zonular fibers attached to the anterior and posterior aspect of the lens capsule. (Reproduced with permission from Wilson DJ, Jaeger MJ, Green WR. Effects of extracapsular cataract extraction on the lens zonules. *Ophthalmology.* 1987; 94:467–470.)

basilar surface toward the anterior lens capsule, while the cells nearer the equator appear more elongated as they differentiate into lens fibers.

Cortex and Nucleus

New lens fibers are continuously laid down from the outside as the lens epithelial cells differentiate. The oldest fibers, the embryonic and fetal lens nucleus, were produced in embryonic life, have lost their nuclei, and persist in the center of the lens. The outermost fibers, which are the most recently formed, make up the cortex of the lens composed of fibers derived from the differentiated lens epithelial cells.

Zonular Fibers

The lens is supported by the zonular fibers that attach to the anterior and posterior lens capsule in the midperiphery (Fig IX-2). These fibers hold the lens in place through their attachments to the ciliary body processes.

Congenital Anomalies

Ectopia Lentis

The lens may be partially dislocated *(subluxation)* or totally dislocated *(luxation)* (Fig IX-3). Congenital ectopia lentis may occur as an isolated phenomenon (simple ectopia lentis) or as part of an inherited syndrome that has systemic manifestations.

   Marfan syndrome is a disorder of connective tissue with ocular, musculoskeletal, and cardiovascular manifestations. The lens is usually displaced upward or in a superotemporal direction, and axial myopia is often present. Marfan syndrome is caused by mutations in the fibrillin gene on chromosome 15.

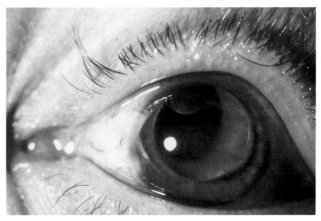

FIG IX-3—Anterior dislocation of the lens. The entire lens is present in the anterior chamber.

In patients with *homocystinuria* the lens is displaced inferonasally, or it may luxate into the anterior chamber or posterior segment. This autosomal recessive trait is caused by a defect in cystathionine β–synthase. Other conditions associated with ectopia lentis are listed in Table IX-1.

Congenital Cataract

Lens opacities present at birth or developing during the first year of life are called *congenital cataracts*. The term *infantile cataracts* is also used for those not seen at birth. Congenital cataracts may be unilateral or bilateral. In general, about one third of these cataracts are associated with other disease syndromes, one third occur as an inherited trait, and one third result from undetermined causes. See also BCSC Section 6, *Pediatric Ophthalmology and Strabismus.*

Rubella cataract This congenital cataract occurs in the fetus if the mother is exposed to the rubella virus during the first or second trimester of the pregnancy. The lens opacity is but one of several birth anomalies associated with in utero rubella exposure. Histologically, the lens is microspherophakic, and retained lens fiber nuclei are present. Rubella virus may be cultured from surgically removed lenses.

Inflammations

Phacoantigenic Endophthalmitis

Also known as *lens-induced granulomatous endophthalmitis* or *phacoanaphylactic endophthalmitis,* this type of lens-induced intraocular inflammation is mediated by IgG immunoglobulins directed against lens protein. The inflammation may follow accidental or surgical trauma to the lens. Histologically, lens-induced granulomatous endophthalmitis consists of a central nidus of degenerating lens material sur-

TABLE IX-1

With systemic abnormalities

    Marfan syndrome—lens dislocated up

    Homocystinuria—lens dislocated down

    Weill-Marchesani syndrome—superotemporal or temporal displacement of
                    spherophakic lens

    Others—hyperlysinemia, Ehlers-Danlos syndrome, Crouzon disease, and oxycephaly

With other congenital ocular abnormalities

    Aniridia

    Uveal coloboma

    Buphthalmos

    Megalocornea

    High myopia

    Corectopia

    Peters anomaly

rounded by concentric layers of imflammatory cells (zonal granuloma). Multi-nucleated giant cells and neutrophils are present within the inner layer adjacent to the degenerating lens material. Lymphocytes and histiocytes make up the intermediate mantle of cells. These cells may be surrounded by fibrous connective tissue and collagen, depending on the duration of the inflammatory response (Figs IX-4, IX-5). See also BCSC Section 9, *Intraocular Inflammation and Uveitis*.

Phacolytic Glaucoma

In a hypermature cataract the liquefied cortical material may leak through the capsule and gain access to the anterior chamber. This material incites a marked non-granulomatous inflammatory response in which numerous macrophages phago-cytize the lens protein material. Collections of these protein-laden macrophages, as well as extracellular lens protein, may obstruct the trabecular meshwork and thereby cause a type of secondary glaucoma known as *phacolytic glaucoma*, which has also been discussed in chapter VII. Cytologic examination of aqueous humor from patients with phacolytic glaucoma reveals collections of macrophages containing eosinophilic lens protein and extracellular proteinaceous material (see Figure VII-9, p 84). The treatment for phacolytic glaucoma is surgical removal of the lens and irrigation of the anterior chamber.

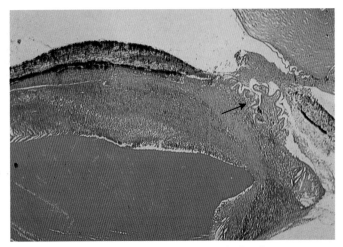

FIG IX-4—Phacoantigenic endophthalmitis, in which inflammatory reaction surrounds the lens (lower left). The torn capsule can be observed in the pupillary region (arrow). Also note corneal scar (upper right) representing the site of ocular penetration.

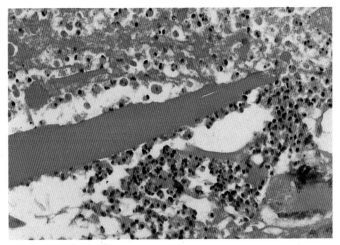

FIG IX-5—Phacoantigenic endophthalmitis. Granulomatous inflammation including giant cells (lower right) surrounds inciting lens fibers.

P acnes *Endophthalmitis*

Chronic postoperative endophthalmitis secondary to *Propionibacterium acnes* may develop following cataract surgery, usually 2 months to 2 years later. It may be characterized by granulomatous keratic precipitates, a small hypopyon, vitritis, and a white plaque containing *P acnes* and residual lens material sequestered within the capsular bag (Figs IX-6, IX-7). Onset of the inflammation may follow Nd:YAG laser capsulotomy that allows release of the sequestered organisms.

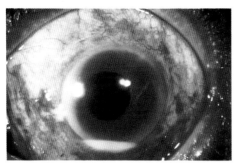

FIG IX-6—Clinical photograph of eye with *P acnes* endophthalmitis. Note injection of the conjunctiva and small hypopyon. (Photograph courtesy of William C. Lloyd III, MD, and Ralph C. Eagle Jr, MD.)

FIG IX-7—Histopathology of lens capsule from case of *P acnes* endophthalmitis. (Photograph courtesy of William C. Lloyd III, MD, and Ralph C. Eagle Jr, MD.)

Degenerations

Cataract and Other Abnormalities

Capsule Mild thickening of the lens capsule can be associated with pathologic proliferation of lens epithelium or with chronic inflammation of the anterior segment. Focal, internally directed excrescences of the lens capsule are seen in several conditions, including aniridia and Lowe syndrome.

Coronary, or *cerulean, cataracts* consist of wartlike excrescences on the capsule. With time these excrescences are replaced by clumps of epithelium, resulting in granular debris in the peripheral cortex.

In *posterior lenticonus* the lens capsule is abnormally thin, and the lens bulges into the anterior aspect of the vitreous (Fig IX-8). The outermost layers of the adult nucleus and cortex in the region of the bulge become opacified. *Anterior lenticonus* is much rarer and shows more extensive cytoarchitectural abnormalities.

Pseudoexfoliation, or *exfoliation syndrome,* is not an abnormality of the lens capsule per se but is the result of the deposition of a fibrillary proteinlike material on the anterior lens capsule. The material is also deposited on other intraocular structures. Histologically, the eosinophilic deposits appear sprinkled on the surface of the capsule like iron filings standing upright on the surface of a magnet (Fig IX-9). See also chapter VII, Anterior Chamber and Trabecular Meshwork.

Epithelium Severe elevation of IOP causes injury to the lens epithelial cells, leading to degeneration of the cells. Clinically, patches of white flecks *(glaukomflecken)* are seen beneath the lens capsule. Histology shows focal areas of necrotic lens epithelial cells beneath the anterior lens capsule. Associated degenerated subepithelial cortical material is also present.

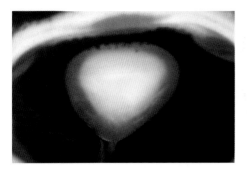

FIG IX-8—Posterior lenticonus.

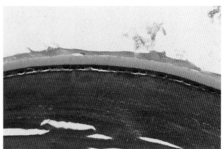

FIG IX-9—Pseudoexfoliation, or exfoliation syndrome. Abnormal material appears on the anterior lens capsule like iron filings on the edge of a magnet.

Chronic iritis may cause degeneration and necrosis, as well as proliferation of anterior lens epithelium. Epithelial hyperplasia may be associated with the formation of subcapsular fibrous plaques (Fig IX-10). In this situation the epithelial cells have undergone metaplastic transformation into cells capable of producing collagen. These functionally transformed epithelial cells arise in response to a variety of stimuli, including chronic inflammation or trauma. Following resolution of the inciting stimulus, the lens epithelium may produce another capsule, thereby totally surrounding the fibrous plaque and producing a duplication cataract.

Retention of iron-containing metallic foreign bodies in the lens may lead to lens epithelial degeneration and necrosis secondary to *siderosis*. The presence of iron within the epithelial cells can be nicely demonstrated by the use of the Prussian blue stain or Perls' test.

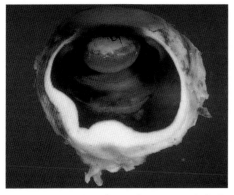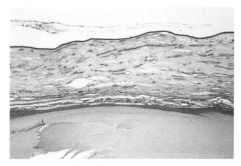

FIG IX-10—Anterior subcapsular cataract. *Left,* Gross appearance. *Right,* Fibrous plaque is present anterior to the original anterior capsule.

FIG IX-11—Posterior subcapsular cataract with bladder cells (Wedl cells).

Posterior subcapsular cataract may be the most common abnormality involving the lens epithelium. This condition is often associated with cortical degeneration and nuclear sclerosis. The process begins with epithelial disarray at the equator, followed by posterior migration of the lens epithelium. As the cells migrate posteriorly, they enlarge and swell to five to six times their normal size. These swollen cells, referred to as *bladder cells* or *Wedl cells,* can cause significant visual impairment if they involve the axial portion of the lens (Fig IX-11). Conditions often associated with posterior subcapsular cataracts include chronic vitreal inflammation, ionizing radiation, and prolonged use of corticosteroids.

Disruption of the lens capsule will often result in proliferation of the lens epithelial cells. Following extracapsular cataract extraction, for example, remaining epithelial cells can proliferate and cover the inner surface of the posterior capsule. These collections of proliferating epithelial cells may form partially transparent globular masses called *Elschnig pearls* (Fig IX-12). Sequestration of proliferating lens

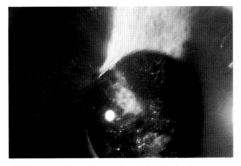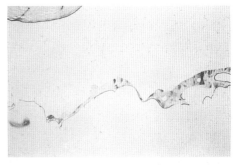

FIG IX-12—Elschnig pearls. *Left,* Clinical appearance of opacities on posterior capsule. *Right,* Histology depicting proliferating lens epithelium on posterior capsule.

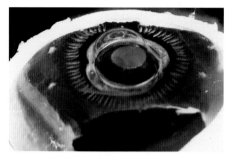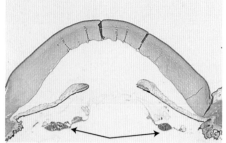

FIG IX-13—Soemmerring's ring cataract. *Left,* A ring cataract found adjacent to a posterior chamber intraocular lens. *Right,* Ring cataract, photomicrograph (arrow).

fibers in the equatorial region, often as a result of incomplete cortical removal during cataract surgery, may create a doughnut-shaped configuration referred to as a *Soemmerring's ring* (Fig IX-13).

Cortex Opacities of the cortical lens fibers are most often associated with nuclear sclerosis or posterior subcapsular cataracts. Clinically, cortical degenerative changes fall into two broad categories:

☐ Generalized discolorations with loss of transparency

☐ Focal opacifications

Generalized loss of transparency cannot be diagnosed histologically with reliability, as histologic stains that are used to colorize the lens after it is processed prevent the assessment of lens clarity. The earliest sign of focal cortical degeneration is hydropic swelling of the lens fibers with decreased intensity of the eosinophilic staining. Focal cortical opacities become more apparent when fiber degeneration is advanced enough to cause liquefactive change. Light microscopy shows the accumulation of eosinophilic globules (morgagnian globules) in slitlike spaces between the lens fibers, which is a reliable histologic sign of cortical degeneration (Fig IX-14). As focal cortical lesions progress, the slitlike spaces become confluent, forming globular collections of lens protein. Ultimately, the entire cortex can become liquefied, allowing the nucleus to sink downward and the capsule to wrinkle *(Morgagnian cataract)* (Fig IX-15).

Denatured lens protein can escape through an intact capsule and provoke an anterior chamber inflammatory reaction composed predominantly of macrophages. This condition, sometimes known as phacolytic glaucoma, has been discussed earlier in this chapter and in chapter VII (see pp 82–84, 99).

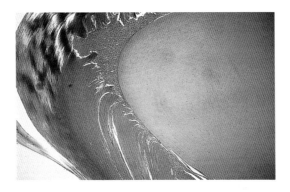

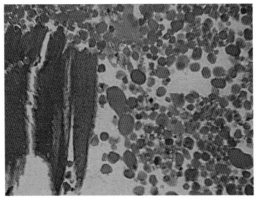

FIG IX-14—Cataract. *Top,* Extensive cortical changes are present. *Bottom,* Cortical degeneration. Lens cells (fibers) have swollen and fragmented to form morgagnian globules. The lenticular fragments are opaque and will increase osmotic pressure within the capsule.

Nucleus The continued production of lens fibers subjects the nucleus in the adult lens to the lifelong stress of mechanical compression. This compression causes hardening of the lens nucleus. Aging is also associated with alterations in the chemical composition of the nuclear fibers that may cause them to accumulate urochrome pigment. These changes in the nucleus increase the index of refraction, inducing a myopic shift of the refractive error.

The pathogenesis of nuclear discoloration is poorly understood and probably involves more than one mechanism. Clinically, the lens nucleus may appear yellow, brunescent, or deep brown. The histologic appearance, however, will not necessarily correlate to the clinical appearance because of the absorption of eosin dye (Fig IX-16).

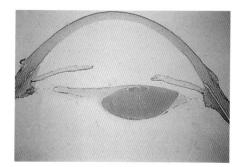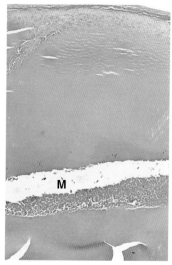

FIG IX-15—Morgagnian cataract. *Left,* The lens cortex is liquefied, leaving lens nucleus floating free within the capsular bag. *Right,* Note the artifactitious (sharply angulated) clefts in this nuclear sclerotic cataract. A zone of morgagnian globules (M) is identified.

Nuclear cataracts are difficult to assess histologically because they take on a subtle homogeneous eosinophilic appearance. The loss of cellular laminations probably correlates better with the nucleus firmness than it does with the optical opacification clinically. The more homogeneous the nucleus becomes, the less likely it is to artifactitiously fracture during sectioning.

Occasionally, crystalline deposits identified as calcium oxalate crystals may be identified within a nuclear cataract. The examiner can identify these crystals by viewing sections under polarized light.

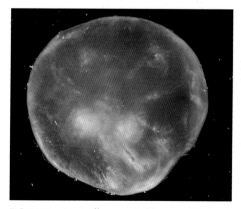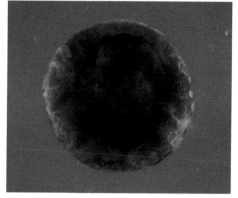

FIG IX-16—Surgically extracted lens nuclei showing varying degrees of brunescence and opacification.

Neoplasia and Associations with Systemic Disorders

There are no reported examples of neoplasms arising in the human lens. Premature opacification of the lens has been noted in many disorders, including the following:

☐ Diabetes mellitus

☐ Galactosemia

☐ Hypercupremia

☐ Fabry disease

Exogenous agents, such as electric shock and radiation, may also play causative roles in the formation of cataracts. Retained intralenticular foreign bodies, especially those containing iron, may lead to cataract formation.

Intraocular Lenses

Placement of an intraocular lens (IOL) following removal of a cataract has become standard in most cases of cataract surgery. The selection of the type of IOL depends on a host of factors including

☐ Type of cataract procedure used

☐ Anatomy of the anterior chamber

☐ Presence of underlying ocular disease

☐ The ophthalmic surgeon's proclivities

If the capsular bag is intact after removal of the lens nucleus and cortical material, most surgeons will place a posterior chamber lens within the remaining capsular bag. The haptics are supported by the capsule, thereby maintaining centration of the optic (Fig IX-17). In the absence of adequate capsular support, an anterior chamber

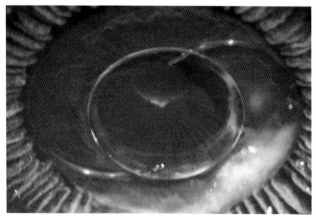

FIG IX-17—Posterior view of posterior intraocular lens that is positioned within the capsular bag.

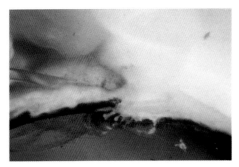 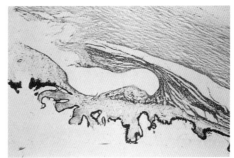

FIG IX-18—Anterior chamber intraocular lens. *Left,* Gross appearance of iris root and ciliary body with lens haptic. *Right,* Microscopic appearance of anterior chamber. The IOL has been removed during tissue processing; the site where the haptic has partially eroded through the iris root can be seen. (Reproduced with permission from Champion R, McDonnell PJ, Green WR. Intraocular lenses: histopathologic characteristics of a large series of autopsy eyes. *Surv Ophthalmol.* 1985; 30:1–32. Photographs courtesy of W. Richard Green, MD.)

lens may be inserted. In this case the entire lens is placed anterior to the iris, and the iris root supports the lens haptics (Fig IX-18).

Stamper RL, Sugar A, Ripkin DJ. *Intraocular Lenses: Basic and Clinical Applications.* Ophthalmology Monograph 7. San Francisco: American Academy of Ophthalmology; 1993.

CHAPTER X

Vitreous

Topography

The vitreous humor makes up most of the volume of the globe and is important in many diseases that affect the eye. BCSC Section 12, *Retina and Vitreous,* discusses the vitreous in detail.

The average volume of the adult vitreous is 4 cc. The vitreous is composed of 99% water and several macromolecules, including

- Types II and IX collagen
- Glycosaminoglycans
- Soluble proteins
- Glycoproteins

The outer portion of the vitreous has a greater number of collagen fibrils and is termed the *vitreous cortex.* The outer surface of the cortex is known as the *hyaloid face.*

The vitreous is bordered anteriorly by the lens, where its attachment to the lens capsule is called the *hyaloideocapsular ligament.* This attachment is firm in young patients and becomes increasingly tenuous with age. The vitreous is attached to the internal limiting membrane (ILM) of the retina by the insertion of the cortical collagen into the basement membrane structure that comprises the basal lamina of the ciliary epithelium and the ILM.

The vitreous attaches most firmly to the vitreous base, a 360° band that straddles the ora serrata and varies in width from 2 mm to 6 mm. The vitreous base extends more posteriorly with advancing age. Other relatively firm attachments of the vitreous are

- At the margins of the optic nerve head
- Along the course of major retinal vessels
- In a circular area around the fovea
- At the edges of areas of vitreoretinal degeneration such as lattice degeneration

The strength of the vitreoretinal attachment is important in the pathogenesis of retinal tears and detachment, macular hole formation, and vitreous hemorrhage from neovascularization.

The embryologic development of the vitreous is generally divided into three stages:

- Primary vitreous
- Secondary vitreous
- Tertiary vitreous

The *primary vitreous* consists of fibrillar material; mesenchymal cells; and vascular components: the hyaloid artery, vasa hyaloidea propria, and tunica vasculosa lentis. The *secondary vitreous* begins to form at approximately the ninth week of gestation and is destined to become the main portion of the vitreous in the postnatal and adult eye. The primary vitreous atrophies with formation of the secondary vitreous, leaving only Cloquet's canal and occasionally Bergmeister's papilla and Mittendorf's dot as vestigeal remnants. The secondary vitreous is relatively acellular and completely avascular. The cells present in the secondary vitreous are called *hyalocytes,* and they exhibit features distinguishing them from macrophages and glial cells. The zonular fibers represent the *tertiary vitreous.*

Congenital Anomalies

Persistent Hyperplasia of the Primary Vitreous (PHPV) or Persistent Fetal Vasculature (PFV)

PHPV is characterized by persistence of variable components of the primary vitreous. In most cases of clinically significant PHPV a fibrovascular plaque in the retrolental space extends laterally to involve the ciliary processes, which may be pulled centripetally by traction from the fibrovascular tissue. The clinical and gross appearance of elongated ciliary processes results. The anterior fibrovascular plaque is generally contiguous posteriorly with a remnant of the hyaloid artery that may attach to the optic nerve head (Fig X-1). Involvement of the posterior structures may be more extensive, with tractional detachment of the peripapillary retina resulting from traction from preretinal membranes. The lens is often cataractous, and nonocular tissues such as adipose tissue and cartilage may be present in the retrolental mass. Eyes affected by PHPV are often microphthalmic.

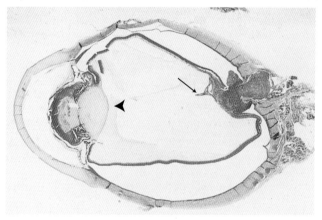

FIG X-1—PHPV. There is a prominent anterior fibrovascular plaque (arrowhead). The posterior remnant of the persistent hyaloid is evident at the optic nerve head (arrow).

Bergmeister's Papilla

Persistence of a small part of the posterior portion of the hyaloid artery is referred to as *Bergmeister's papilla*. This anomaly generally takes the form of a veil-like structure overlying the optic nerve head.

Mittendorf's Dot

The hyaloid artery attaches to the tunica vasculosa lentis just inferior and nasal to the center of the lens. With regression of these vascular structures it is not uncommon to see a focal lens opacity at this site, which is referred to as *Mittendorf's dot.*

Inflammations

As a relatively acellular and completely avascular structure, the vitreous is not an active participant in inflammatory disorders. It does become involved secondarily in inflammatory conditions of adjacent tissues, however. The most notable involvement of the vitreous is in infectious endophthalmitis secondary to bacterial or fungal agents. The vitreous may also become involved secondarily with the inflammatory response associated with the following:

- Toxocariasis
- Toxoplasmosis
- Acute retinal necrosis (ARN)
- Cytomegalovirus (CMV) retinitis
- Sarcoidosis
- Other forms of noninfectious retinitis

See also BCSC Section 9, *Intraocular Inflammation and Uveitis.*

Inflammatory conditions cause predictable changes to develop in the vitreous. Marked neutrophil infiltration of the vitreous occurs in acute inflammatory conditions such as bacterial endophthalmitis (Fig X-2). This infiltration leads to liquefac-

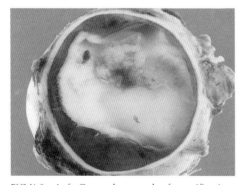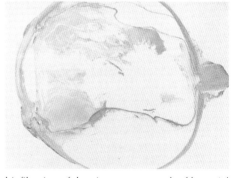

FIG X-2—*Left,* Gross photograph of opacification and infiltration of the vitreous as a result of bacterial endophthalmitis. *Right,* Section shows cellular infiltration of vitreous in endophthalmitis (retinal detachment is artifactitious).

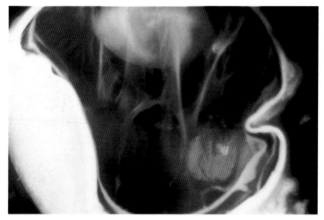

FIG X-3—Gross photograph of vitreous condensations outlining syneretic cavities.

tion of the vitreous with subsequent detachment of the posterior vitreous. Severe cases may be accompanied by formation of fibrocellular membranes, which typically form in the retrolental space and may exert traction on the peripheral retina. Chronic inflammatory conditions such as pars planitis (intermediate uveitis) and sarcoidosis may lead to infiltration of the vitreous with chronic inflammatory cells as well as neovascularization of the anterior or posterior vitreous.

Degenerations

Syneresis and Aging

Syneresis of the vitreous is defined as liquefaction of the gel. Syneresis of the central vitreous is an almost universal consequence of aging. It also occurs as a consequence of vitreous inflammation and hemorrhage. The prominent lamellae and strands that develop in aging and following inflammation or hemorrhage are the result of abnormally aggregated vitreous fibers around syneretic areas (Fig X-3). Syneresis is one of the contributing factors that leads to vitreous detachment.

Hemorrhage

A constellation of histopathologic findings may develop in the vitreous following vitreous hemorrhage. After 3–10 days red blood cell clots undergo fibrinolysis, and red blood cells may diffuse throughout the vitreous cavity. At this time breakdown of the red blood cells also occurs. Loss of hemoglobin from the red cells produces ghost cells (Fig X-4) and hemoglobin spherules (Fig X-5). Obstruction of the trabecular meshwork by these cells may lead to *ghost cell glaucoma*. (See Figure VII-10 and BCSC Section 10, *Glaucoma*.)

The process of red cell dissolution attracts macrophages, which phagocytose the effete red cells. The hemoglobin is broken down to hemosiderin, then removed

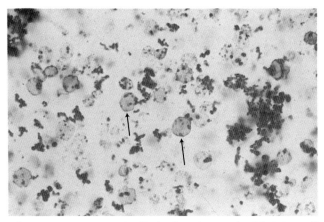

FIG X-4—Ghost cells (arrows) represent red cells that have lost much of their intracellular hemoglobin.

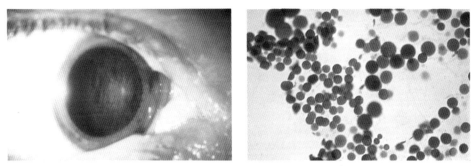

FIG X-5—*Left,* Clinical photograph of retrolental hemoglobin spherules. *Right,* Cytologic preparation of hemoglobin spherules removed from the vitreous cavity. (Reproduced with permission from Spraul CW, Grossniklaus HE. Vitreous hemorrhage. *Surv Ophthalmol.* 1997; 42:3–39.)

from the eye. In massive hemorrhages cholesterol crystals caused by breakdown of red blood cell membranes may be present, often surrounded by a foreign body giant cell reaction. Cholesterol appears clinically as refractile intravitreal crystals. As mentioned above, syneresis of the vitreous and posterior vitreous detachment is common after vitreous hemorrhage.

Asteroid Hyalosis

Asteroid hyalosis is a condition with a spectacular clinical appearance but little clinical significance. Asteroid bodies are rounded structures measuring 10–100 nm that stain positively with alcian blue, stains for neutral fats, phospholipids, and calcium (Fig X-6). The bodies stain metachromatically and exhibit birefringence. Occasional

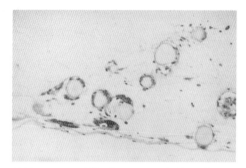

FIG X-6—Asteroid bodies surrounded by a foreign body reaction.

asteroid bodies will be surrounded by a foreign body giant cell, but the condition is not generally associated with an inflammatory reaction. The exact mechanism of formation of asteroid bodies is not known.

Vitreous Amyloidosis

The term *amyloidosis* refers to a group of diseases that lead to extracellular deposition of amyloid. Amyloid is composed of various proteins that have a characteristic ultrastructural appearance of nonbranching fibrils with variable length and a diameter of 75–100 Å (Fig X-7). The proteins forming amyloid also have in common the ability to form a tertiary structure characterized as a β pleated sheet, which then enables the proteins to bind Congo red stain and show birefringence in polarized light (Fig X-8).

Amyloid may be derived from various types of protein, and the protein of origin is characteristic for different forms of amyloidosis. Amyloid deposits occur in the vit-

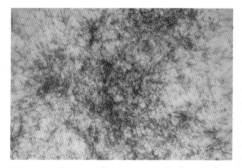

FIG X-7—Electron photomicrograph shows characteristic amyloid fibrils.

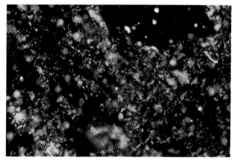

FIG X-8—Polarized light photomicrograph of the Congo red–stained vitreous from a patient with familial amyloid polyneuropathy.

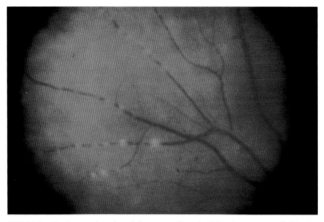

FIG X-9—Perivascular sheathing associated with vitreous amyloidosis.

reous when the protein forming the amyloid is *transthyretin,* previously known as *prealbumin.* Multiple genetic mutations have been described resulting in various amino acid substitutions in the transthyretin protein. The most common mutations were originally described based on their clinical findings as *familial amyloid poly- neuropathy (FAP)* types I and II. Systemic manifestations in patients with this type of amyloidosis include vitreous opacities and perivascular infiltrates (Fig X-9), pe- ripheral neuropathy, cardiomyopathy, and carpal tunnel syndrome.

The mechanism by which the vitreous becomes involved is not known with certainty. As there is deposition of amyloid within the walls of retinal vessels and in the RPE, amyloid may gain access to the vitreous through these tissues. Also since transthyretin is a blood protein, it may gain access to the vitreous by crossing the blood–aqueous barrier at the ciliary body.

Posterior Vitreous Detachment

Posterior vitreous detachment (PVD) occurs when a dehiscence in the vitreous cor- tex permits fluid from a syneretic cavity to gain access to the potential subhyaloid space, causing the remaining cortex to be stripped from the ILM (Fig X-10). As fluid drains out of the syneretic cavities under the newly formed posterior hyaloid, the vitreous body collapses anteriorly. Vitreous detachment generally occurs rapidly, so that over a course of a few hours to days the vitreous has collapsed anteriorly and remains attached only at its base.

A weakening of the adherence of the cortical vitreous to the ILM with age also plays a role in PVDs. The reported incidence of PVD varies between 31% and 65% at age 65 and is increased by intraocular inflammation, aphakia or pseudophakia, trauma, and vitreoretinal disease. PVD is important in the pathogenesis of many conditions including retinal tears and detachment, vitreous hemorrhage, and macu- lar hole formation. Chapter XI discusses the retina in greater detail.

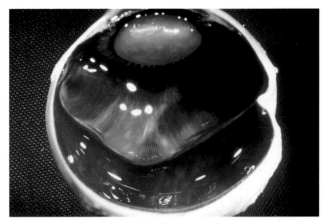

FIG X-10—Gross photograph of posterior vitreous detachment.

Rhegmatogenous Retinal Detachment and Proliferative Vitreoretinopathy

Retinal tears form from vitreous traction on the retina during or after PVD or secondary to ocular trauma. Tears are most likely to occur at sites of greatest vitreoretinal adhesion, such as the vitreous base or at the margin of lattice degeneration (Fig X-11). The histopathology of retinal tears reveals that the vitreous is adherent to the retina along the flap of the tear. There is loss of the photoreceptors in the area of retina separated from the underlying retinal pigment epithelium (RPE).

Retinal detachment occurs when vitreous traction and fluid currents resulting from eye movements combine to overcome the forces maintaining retinal adhesion

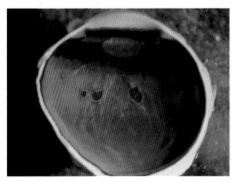 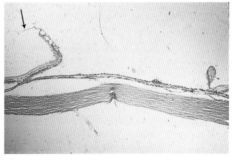

FIG X-11—*Left,* Gross photograph of retinal tears at vitreous base. *Right,* Photomicrograph shows vitreous (arrow) attached to anterior flap of retinal tear.

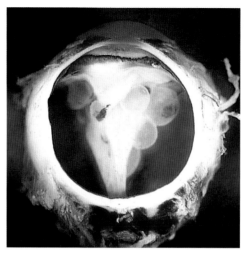

FIG X-12—Long-standing total retinal detachment with macrocystic degeneration of the retina.

to the RPE. The principle histopathologic findings in retinal detachment consist of the following:

□ Degeneration of the outer segments of the photoreceptors

□ Eventual loss of photoreceptor cells as a result of apoptosis, or programmed cell death

□ Migration of Müller cells

□ Proliferation and migration of RPE cells

Small cystic spaces develop in the detached retina, and in chronic detachment these cysts may coalesce into large macrocysts (Fig X-12).

With rhegmatogenous retinal detachment, cellular membranes may form on either surface of the retina (Fig X-13). Clinically, this process is referred to as *proliferative vitreoretinopathy (PVR)*. Membrane formation can occur posteriorly or anteriorly. Membranes form as a result of proliferation of RPE cells and contain other cellular elements including glial cells, macrophages, fibroblasts, and possibly hyalocytes. The cell biology of membrane formation in the vitreous is complex and involves interaction of various growth factors, integrins, and cellular proliferation.

Macular Holes

It is very likely that idiopathic macular holes form as the result of degenerative changes in the vitreous. The most widely held theory of pathogenesis for macular holes is that degenerative changes in the vitreous lead to tangential traction on the macula, eventually bringing about the formation of a small macular hole. Intraoperative observations have supported this theory in that most full-thickness macular holes occur in eyes with an attached posterior vitreous cortex. Histologically, full-thickness macular holes are similar to holes in other locations. A full-thickness retinal defect with rounded tissue margins is accompanied by loss of the photoreceptor

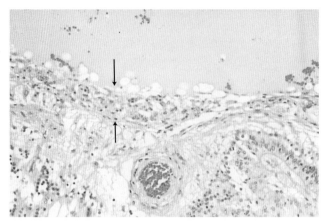

FIG X-13—Preretinal membrane (between arrows) on surface of the retina, secondary to proliferative vitreoretinopathy.

outer segments in adjacent retina that is separated from the RPE by subretinal fluid. Following surgical repair of macular holes, closer apposition of the remaining photoreceptors and variable glial scarring close the macular defect.

Neoplasia

Intraocular Lymphoma

Primary neoplastic involvement of the vitreous is predictably uncommon because of the relatively acellular nature of the vitreous. However, the vitreous can be the site of primary involvement in cases of B-cell lymphoma. In the past this type of lymphoma has been referred to as *reticulum cell sarcoma*, but immunohistochemical and molecular genetic studies have confirmed that this entity is a B-cell lymphoma. Rare cases of vitreous involvement may occur in T-cell lymphomas.

The most common presentation of intraocular lymphoma is as a posterior uveitis. Some patients will have sub-RPE infiltrates (Fig X-14), but these are present in the minority of the patients with intraocular lymphoma. Approximately 50% of patients presenting with ocular findings will have concomitant involvement of the central nervous system.

The diagnosis of intraocular lymphoma is made by cytologic analysis of vitrectomy specimens. Immunohistochemical study of cell markers, flow cytometry, and/or gene amplification studies can be performed on vitreous specimens, although the standard method of diagnosis is cytology.

Cytologically, the vitreous infiltrate in intraocular lymphoma is heterogeneous. The atypical cells are large lymphoid cells, frequently with a convoluted nuclear membrane and small multiple nucleoli. An accompanying infiltrate of small lymphocytes almost always appears, and the normal cells may obscure the neoplastic

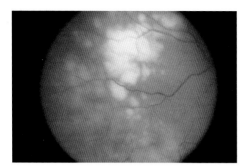

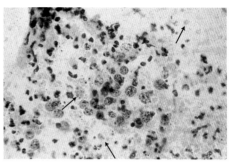

FIG X-14—Sub-RPE infiltrates in a patient with vit-reous lymphoma.

FIG X-15—Cytologic preparation of vitreous lymphoma. There are many atypical cells with large nuclei and multiple nucleoli. Cell ghosts (arrows) are also present.

cell population. These small round lymphocytes are largely reactive T cells. Numerous cell ghosts are usually present, and this feature is very suggestive of a diagnosis of intraocular lymphoma (Fig X-15). Immunohistochemically, the viable tumor cells label as a monoclonal population of B cells. Demonstration of a monoclonal population is aided through the use of flow cytometry.

The subretinal infiltrates are composed of atypical lymphoid cells. With or without treatment the subretinal infiltrates tend to resolve, leaving a focal area of RPE atrophy. Optic nerve and retinal infiltration may also be present. Infiltrates in these locations tend to be perivascular and may lead to ischemic retinal or optic nerve damage.

CHAPTER XI

Retina

Topography

The retina and retinal pigment epithelium (RPE) make up two distinct layers that together line the inner two thirds of the globe:

□ The RPE is a pigmented layer derived from the outer layer of the optic cup

□ The neurosensory retina is a delicate, transparent layer derived from the inner layer of the optic cup

Anteriorly, the RPE becomes continuous with the pigmented epithelium of the ciliary body, and the retina becomes continuous with the nonpigmented ciliary body epithelium. Posteriorly, the RPE terminates at the optic nerve, just prior to the termination of Bruch's membrane. The nuclear, photoreceptor, and synaptic layers of the retina gradually taper at the optic nerve head, and only the nerve fiber layer continues on to form the optic nerve. BCSC Section 12, *Retina and Vitreous,* discusses the anatomy of the retina as well as other topics covered in this chapter in depth.

RPE

The RPE consists of a monolayer of hexagon-shaped cells with apical microvilli and a basement membrane at the base of the cells. This monolayer has the following specialized functions:

□ Vitamin A metabolism

□ Maintenance of the outer blood–retinal barrier

□ Phagocytosis of the photoreceptor outer segments

□ Absorption of light

□ Heat exchange

□ Formation of the basal lamina of the inner portion of Bruch's membrane

□ Production of the mucopolysaccharide matrix that surrounds the photoreceptor outer segments

□ Active transport of materials into and out of the subretinal space

Compared to the retina, the topographic variation of the RPE is subtle. In the macula the RPE is taller, narrower, and more heavily pigmented, and it forms a regular hexagonal array. In the equatorial and midperipheral area the RPE cells are larger in diameter and thinner. Variability in the diameter of the RPE cells increases in the peripheral area. The amount of cytoplasmic pigment, primarily lipofuscin, increases with age, particularly within the RPE present in the macular region.

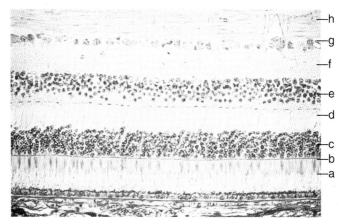

FIG XI-1—Normal retinal layers. From choroid to vitreous: *a*—photoreceptors of rods and cones, *b*—external limiting membrane, *c*—outer nuclear layer, *d*—outer plexiform layer, *e*—inner nuclear layer, *f*—inner plexiform layer, *g*—ganglion cell layer, and *h*—nerve fiber layer. The ILM is not shown in this figure.

Retina

The topographic variation in the structures of the retina is striking, with regional variation in the neural structures as well as the retinal vasculature. The neurosensory retina has nine layers (Fig XI-1). Beginning on the choroidal side and progressing to the vitreous side they are

- Photoreceptors of the rods and cones
- External limiting membrane—not a true basement membrane but rather an apparent membrane caused by a series of tight junctions between Müller cells and photoreceptors
- Outer nuclear layer (nuclei of the photoreceptors)
- Outer plexiform layer
- Inner nuclear layer
- Inner plexiform layer
- Ganglion cell layer
- Nerve fiber layer (NFL)
- Internal limiting membrane (ILM)—a true basement membrane synthesized by Müller cells

The arrangement of the retina is vertical from outer to inner layers, except for the NFL, where the axons run horizontally toward the optic nerve head. Consequently, deposits and hemorrhages in the deep retinal layers have a round appearance clinically when viewed on edge, while those in the NFL have a feathery appearance.

The blood supply of the retina comes from two sources, with the watershed inside the inner nuclear layer. The *retinal blood vessels* supply the NFL, ganglion cell layer, inner plexiform layer, and inner third of the inner nuclear layer. The *cho-*

roidal vasculature supplies the outer two thirds of the inner nuclear layer, outer plexiform layer, outer nuclear layer, photoreceptors, and RPE. Because of this division of the blood supply to the retina, ischemic choroidal vascular lesions and ischemic lesions attributed to the retinal vasculature produce different histologic pictures. Ischemic retinal injury produces inner ischemic atrophy of the retina, and choroidal ischemia produces outer ischemic retinal atrophy.

Macula   Histologically, the term *macula* refers to that area of the retina where the ganglion cell layer is thicker than a single cell (Fig XI-2). Clinically, this area corresponds approximately with the area of the retina bound by the inferior and superior vascular arcades. The macula is subdivided into the *foveola,* the *fovea,* the *parafovea,* and the *perifovea.* Only photoreceptor cells appear in the central foveola; the ganglion cells, other nucleated cells (including Müller cells), and blood vessels are not present. The concentration of cones is greater in the macula than in the peripheral retina, and in the fovea there are no rods, only cones.

Nerve fibers in the outer plexiform layer (Henle's layer) of the macula run obliquely (compare Figures XI-1 and XI-2). This morphologic feature results in the flower-petal appearance of cystoid macular edema (CME) seen on fluorescein angiography and the star-shaped configuration of hard exudates seen ophthalmoscopically in states causing macular edema. Xanthophyll pigment gives the macula its yellow appearance clinically and grossly (macula lutea), but the xanthophyll dissolves during tissue processing and is not present in histologic sections.

Congenital Anomalies

Albinism

Albinism is a general term that refers to a congenital dilution of the pigment of the skin, the eyes and the skin, or just the eyes. True albinism has been subdivided into oculocutaneous and ocular albinism. This distinction is somewhat helpful clinically, but in reality all cases of ocular albinism have some degree of mild cutaneous involvement. There is pathophysiologic difference between the two types of albinism: in oculocutaneous albinism the amount of melanin in each melanosome is reduced, whereas in ocular albinism the number of melanosomes is reduced.

Many different types of oculocutaneous and ocular albinism have been described, but the ocular involvement always conforms to one of two clinical patterns:

- Congenitally subnormal visual acuity and nystagmus
- Normal or minimally reduced visual acuity and no nystagmus, a clinical pattern termed *albinoidism* because the visual consequences are much milder

Both patterns share clinical features such as photophobia, iris transillumination, and hypopigmented fundi as a result of the reduction in melanin content of the RPE and choroid. These two patterns also differ: albinism is accompanied by foveal hypoplasia, whereas albinoidism shows normal or nearly normal foveal architecture.

Two types of ocular albinism have important systemic associations:

- *Hermansky-Pudlak syndrome:* albinism is associated with a hemorrhagic disorder characterized by easy bruising
- *Chédiak-Higashi syndrome:* an abnormality of neutrophils results in an increased susceptibility for infection

BCSC Section 6, *Pediatric Ophthalmology and Strabismus,* discusses albinism in greater detail.

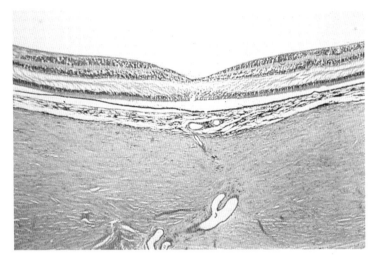

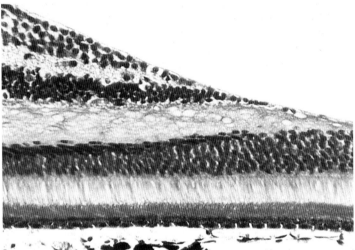

FIG XI-2—*Top,* The normal macula is identified histologically by a multicellular thick ganglion cell layer and an area of focal thinning, the foveola. Clinically, the macula lies between the inferior and superior vascular arcades. *Bottom,* In the region of the foveola, the inner cellular layers are absent, with an increased density of pigment in the RPE. The incident light falls directly on the photoreceptor outer segments, reducing the potential for distortion of light by overlying tissue elements.

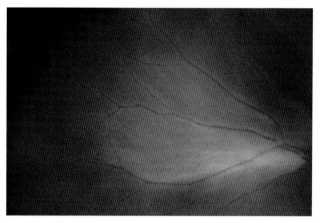

FIG XI-3—Myelinated nerve fibers.

Myelinated (Medullated) Nerve Fibers

Generally, myelination of the optic pathways terminates at the optic nerve head. However, myelination of the nerve fibers in the nerve fiber layer can occur and produce a striking clinical appearance (Fig XI-3). The area of myelination is usually contiguous with the optic nerve head, but myelination may occur isolated from the optic nerve head as well. The area of myelination is typically small, but large areas can produce a clinically significant scotoma. The myelin is produced by oligodendroglial cells within the nerve fiber layer. Myelinated nerve fibers have been associated with myopia, amblyopia, strabismus, and nystagmus.

Vascular Anomalies

The numerous congenital anomalies of the retinal vasculature include

- Capillary (hemangioblastoma) and cavernous hemangiomas
- Proliferative retinopathy associated with anencephaly
- Parafoveal telangiectasias
- Leber miliary aneurysm
- Coats disease

Of these, the latter three diseases may represent a continuum of vascular anomalies that produce varying degrees of exudative retinopathy.

One histopathologic study of parafoveal telangiectasia revealed focal endothelial degeneration, accumulation of lipid within the walls of vessels, and extensive degeneration of pericytes. These findings were more pronounced in the area of clinically abnormal vessels but were also present diffusely in the retinal vasculature. In that study no dilated or telangiectatic vessels were present.

Leber miliary aneurysm shows varying degrees of retinal capillary nonperfusion and aneurysmal dilation of retinal vessels. The changes in Leber miliary aneurysm

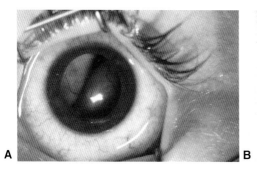

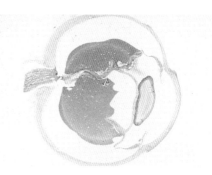

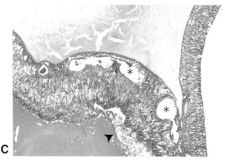

FIG XI-4—*A,* Leukocoria as a result of Coats disease. *B,* Total exudative retinal detachment in Coats disease. *C,* Telangiectatic vessels (asterisks) and "foamy" macrophages (arrowhead) typical of Coats disease.

are similar to those present to a greater degree in Coats disease. In Coats disease exudative retinal detachment occurs as a result of leakage from abnormalities in the peripheral retina including telangiectatic vessels, microaneurysms, and saccular dilations of retinal vessels (Fig XI-4). These changes are most often unilateral but may be bilateral. Histologically, retinal detachments secondary to Coats disease are characterized by the presence of "foamy" macrophages in the subretinal space.

Congenital Hypertrophy of the RPE (CHRPE)

This relatively common congenital lesion is characterized clinically by a flat dark black lesion varying in size from a few to 10 mm in diameter (Fig XI-5). Frequently, central lacunae and a peripheral zone of less dense pigmentation appear within the lesion. This lesion is histopathologically characterized by enlarged RPE cells with densely packed and larger-than-normal, spherical melanin granules. This benign congenital condition can generally be distinguished from choroidal nevi and malignant melanoma on the basis of ophthalmoscopic features.

In addition, CHRPE may be present in Gardner syndrome, or familial adenomatous polyposis. In this syndrome bilateral or multiple (greater than four) areas of RPE hypertrophy are a marker for the presence of the phenotype in members of pedigrees affected with Gardner syndrome. Four different types of RPE hypertrophy have been described in Gardner syndrome, and one of these types is similar to that present in CHRPE.

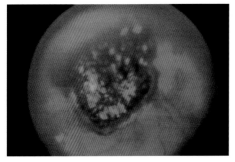
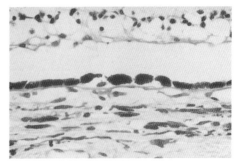

FIG XI-5—*Left*, Congenital hypertrophy of the RPE (CHRPE) with nonpigmented "lacunae." *Right*, In CHRPE the RPE cells are larger than normal and contain more densely packed melanin granules.

Inflammations

Infectious

Viral Multiple viruses may cause retinal infections including rubella, measles, human immunodeficiency virus (HIV), herpes simplex, herpes zoster, and cytomegalovirus (CMV). Two of the clinically most important entities are discussed here: the acute retinal necrosis syndrome (ARN) and CMV infection.

 Acute retinal necrosis is a clinically descriptive term that has been applied to the findings in patients with acute retinal infection caused by herpes simplex virus types 1 and 2 and herpes zoster. In at least one case CMV has also been reported as a causative agent. The histopathologic findings are diffuse uveitis, vitritis, retinal vasculitis, and necrotizing retinitis (Fig XI-6). Electron microscopy has demonstrated

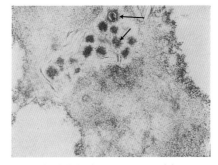

FIG XI-6—*Left*, Acute retinal necrosis (ARN) is characterized by full-thickness necrosis of the retina (between arrowheads). *Right*, Electron microscopy demonstrates viral particles (arrows) within retinal cells.

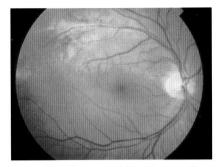 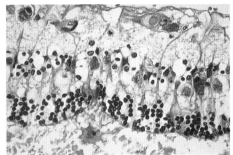

FIG XI-7—*Left,* CMV retinitis. There are intraretinal hemorrhages and areas of opaque retina along the superotemporal retinal vessels. *Right,* Histopathologically, intranuclear and/or intracytoplasmic inclusions (arrowhead) are present. (Reproduced with permission from Grossniklaus HE, Frank KE, Tomsak RL. Cytomegalovirus retinitis and optic neuritis in acquired immune deficiency syndrome: report of a case. *Ophthalmology.* 1987;94:1602.)

viral inclusions in retinal cells. The involvement of the viruses named above in ARN has been demonstrated by culture, polymerase chain reaction, and immunohistochemistry.

CMV *infection* of the retina occurs as an opportunistic infection in approximately 37% of patients with AIDS and less commonly in patients immunosuppressed for other reasons (Fig XI-7). This infection is histopathologically characterized by retinal necrosis, which leads to a thin fibroglial scar with healing. Acute lesions show large neurons (20–30 μm) that contain large eosinophilic intranuclear or intracytoplasmic inclusion bodies. At the cellular level CMV may infect vascular endothelial cells, retinal neurons, and macrophages.

Bacterial See discussion of endophthalmitis in chapter X. See also BCSC Section 9, *Intraocular Inflammation and Uveitis.*

Fungal Fungal infections of the retina are uncommon, occurring almost exclusively in immunosuppressed patients as a result of fungemia. These infections usually begin as single or multiple foci of choroidal and retinal infection (Fig XI-8). The most common causative fungi are *Candida* species. Less common agents include *Aspergillus* species and *Cryptococcus neoformans.*

Histopathologically, fungal infections are typified by necrotizing granulomatous inflammation. A central zone of necrosis is typically surrounded by granulomatous inflammation, and a surrounding infiltrate of lymphocytes is common. With treatment the lesions heal with a fibrous scar. The causative agent can usually be identified by culture or by the specific features of the fungal hyphae in histopathologic material.

Toxoplasmosis Most cases of toxoplasmosis represent reactivation of a transplacentally acquired retinal infection. Less commonly, toxoplasmic retinitis occurs as an acquired retinal infection in immunosuppressed patients. Microscopic examination of active toxoplasmic retinitis reveals necrosis of the retina, a prominent infil-

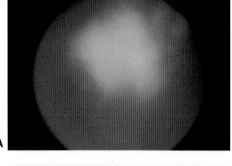

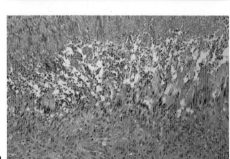

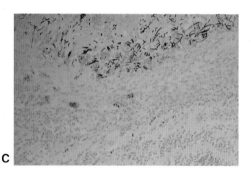

FIG XI-8—*A*, Vitreous, retinal, and choroidal infiltrate in a patient with fungal chorioretinitis. *B*, Granulomatous infiltration surrounding central area of necrosis. *C*, Gomori's methenamine silver stain of section parallel to B shows numerous fungal hyphae.

A

B

C

trate of neutrophils and lymphocytes, and toxoplasma organisms in the form of cysts and tachyzoites (Fig XI-9). There is generally a prominent lymphocytic infiltrate of the vitreous and the anterior segment. Healing brings resolution of the inflammatory cell infiltrate with encystation of the organisms in the retina adjacent to the chorioretinal scar.

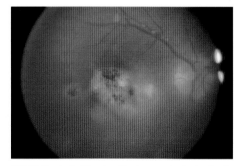

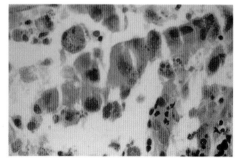

FIG XI-9—*Left*, Chorioretinal scars typical of prior infection with toxoplasmosis. *Right*, Tachyzoites in active toxoplasmosis.

Noninfectious

Noninfectious inflammatory retinal conditions include birdshot retinochoroidopathy, pars planitis, Eales disease, and cancer-associated retinopathy (CAR). See BCSC Section 9, *Intraocular Inflammation and Uveitis,* and Section 12, *Retina and Vitreous,* for discussion of these conditions.

Sarcoidosis This systemic inflammatory process is characterized by granulomatous inflammation without a demonstrable infectious cause (see Figure XII-7). Sarcoidosis can affect virtually any tissue within the eye, and the retina is no exception. Retinal involvement is characterized histopathologically by the presence of noncaseating granulomas. These are generally small, but when they are large, exudative retinal detachment may be present. Associated retinal findings include retinal periphlebitis, which corresponds to the clinical *taches de bougie,* or candle wax drippings; cystoid macular edema; retinal vascular occlusive disease; and retinal and optic nerve head neovascularization.

Degenerations

Typical and Reticular Peripheral Cystoid Degeneration

Typical peripheral cystoid degeneration (TPCD) is a universal finding in eyes of people over the age of 20. In TPCD cystic spaces develop in the outer plexiform layer. *Reticular peripheral cystoid degeneration (RPCD)* is less common. In RPCD the cystic spaces are present in the nerve fiber layer. When present, RPCD occurs posterior to areas of TPCD (Fig XI-10).

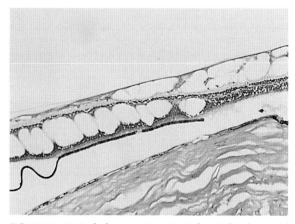

FIG XI-10—Retinal degeneration. Typical peripheral cystoid degeneration consists of cystoid spaces in the outer plexiform layer on the lower left. In the upper right, reticular peripheral cystoid degeneration is present.

Typical and Reticular Degenerative Retinoschisis

Coalescence of the cystic spaces of TPCD forms typical degenerative retinoschisis. *Retinoschisis* is said to be present when the fluid-filled space in the outer plexiform layer is 1.5 mm or greater in diameter. *Typical degenerative retinoschisis* is present in approximately 1% of adults and is usually inferotemporal in location. *Reticular degenerative retinoschisis* is present in 1.6% of adults. In reticular degenerative retinoschisis the splitting of retinal layers occurs in the nerve fiber layer, so the inner layer of the schisis cavity is thinner than in typical degenerative retinoschisis. Reticular degenerative retinoschisis tends to be more bullous than typical degenerative retinoschisis and is more likely to be associated with outer layer breaks and a more posterior location.

Lattice Degeneration

Lattice degeneration may be a familial condition (Fig XI-11). It is found in 8%–10% of the general population, but only a small number of affected persons develop retinal detachment. In contrast, lattice degeneration is seen in 20%–40% of all rhegmatogenous detachments. The most important histopathologic features of lattice degeneration include

- Discontinuity of the inner limiting membrane of the retina
- An overlying pocket of liquefied vitreous
- Sclerosis of the retinal vessels, which remain physiologically patent
- Condensation and adherence of vitreous at the margins of the lesion
- Variable degrees of atrophy of the inner layers of the retina

Although atrophic holes often develop in the center of the lattice lesion, they are rarely the cause of retinal detachment because the vitreous is liquefied over the surface of the lattice, and thus no vitreous traction occurs.

Radial perivascular lattice degeneration is a special type that has the same histopathologic features as typical lattice degeneration but occurs posteriorly along the course of retinal vessels. Radial perivascular lattice degeneration is more common in hereditary vitreoretinal degenerations such as Stickler syndrome and can be associated with severe forms of retinal detachment.

Paving-Stone Degeneration

In contrast to retinal vascular occlusion, which leads to inner retinal ischemia, occlusion of the choriocapillaris can lead to loss of the outer retinal layers and RPE. This type of atrophy, called *cobblestone,* or *paving-stone, degeneration,* is very common in the retinal periphery. The well-demarcated flat pale lesions seen clinically correspond to circumscribed areas of retinal and RPE atrophy in which the inner nuclear layer is adherent to Bruch's membrane (Fig XI-12).

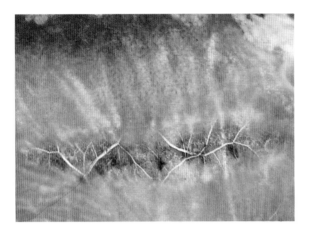

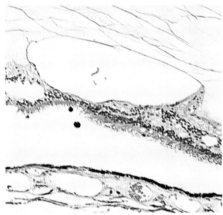

FIG XI-11—Retinal lattice degeneration. *Top,* Lattice degeneration may present as prominent sclerotic vessels in a wicker or lattice pattern. The clinical presentation has many variations. *Left,* The vitreous directly over lattice degeneration is liquefied, but formed vitreous remains adherent at the margins of the degenerated area. The inner limiting membrane is discontinuous, and the inner retinal layers are atrophic.

Ischemia

The causes of retinal ischemia are multiple, including

□ Diabetes

□ Retinal artery and vein occlusion

□ Radiation retinopathy

□ Retinopathy of prematurity

□ Sickle cell retinopathy

The specific aspects of these diseases are discussed subsequently. However, certain histopathologic findings are common among all the disorders that result in retinal ischemia. The retinal changes that occur with ischemia can be grouped into cellular responses and vascular responses.

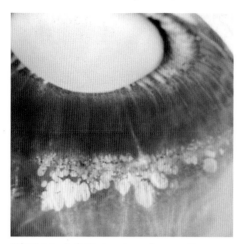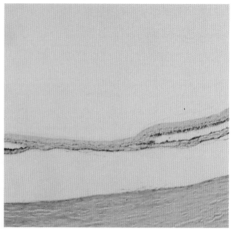

FIG XI-12—*Left,* Paving-stone degeneration appears as areas of depigmentation in the periphery of the retina. *Right,* Histopathologically, paving-stone degeneration consists of atrophy of the outer retinal elements and chorioretinal adhesion to the remaining inner retinal elements. There is a sharp boundary between normal and atrophic retina, corresponding with the clinical appearance of paving-stone degeneration.

Cellular responses   The neurons in the retina are highly active metabolically, producing nearly all of their adenosine triphosphate (ATP) by glycolytic metabolism (see also BCSC Section 2, *Fundamentals and Principles of Ophthalmology,* Part 4, Biochemistry and Metabolism). This makes them highly sensitive to interruption of their oxygen supply. With prolonged oxygen deprivation (greater than 90 minutes in experimental studies) the neuronal cells become pyknotic, and they are subsequently phagocytosed and disappear. The extent and location of the area of atrophic retina resulting from ischemia is dependent on the size of the occluded vessel and whether it is a retinal or choroidal blood vessel. As described earlier, the retinal circulation supplies the inner retina, and the choroidal circulation supplies the outer retina and RPE. Infarctions of the retinal circulation lead to *inner ischemic retinal atrophy* (Fig XI-13), and infarctions of the choroidal circulation lead to *outer ischemic retinal atrophy* (Fig XI-14).

The neuronal cells of the retina have no capacity for regeneration after ischemic damage. Following ischemic damage of the nerve fibers of the ganglion cells, *cystoid bodies* (swollen axons) become apparent histopathologically (Fig XI-15). These are localized accumulations of axoplasmic material that are present in ischemic infarcts of the nerve fiber layer. *Cotton-wool spots* are the clinical correlate of ischemic infarcts of the nerve fiber layer that resolve over 4–12 weeks, leaving an area of inner ischemic atrophy.

Glial cells degenerate as well as the axons in areas of infarction. Proliferation of the glial cells may occur adjacent to local areas of infarction or in areas of ischemia without infarction, resulting in a glial scar.

Microglial cells are actually tissue macrophages rather than true glial cells. These cells are involved with the phagocytosis of necrotic cells as well as extracel-

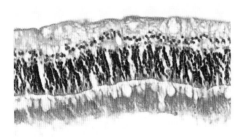

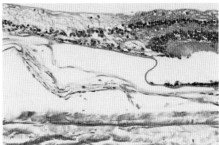

FIG XI-13—Inner retinal ischemia. The photoreceptor nuclei (outer nuclear layer) and the outer portion of the inner nuclear layer are identifiable. The inner portion of the inner nuclear layer is absent. There are no ganglion cells, and the nerve fiber layer is absent. This pattern of ischemia corresponds to the supply of the retinal arteriolar circulation.

FIG XI-14—Begin at the right edge of the photograph and trace the ganglion cell nuclei and the inner nuclear layer toward the left. In this case there is loss of the nuclei of the photoreceptor layer (outer nuclear layer), the photoreceptor inner and outer segments, and the RPE. This is the pattern of outer retinal atrophy, secondary to interruption in the choroidal vascular blood supply. Compare with Figure XI-13.

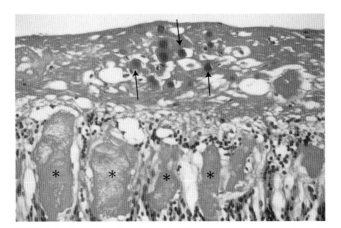

FIG XI-15—Cytoid bodies (arrows) within nerve fiber layer. Cystoid spaces (asterisks) are filled with proteinaceous fluid.

lular material, such as lipid and blood, that accumulates in areas of ischemia. Microglial cells are fairly resistant to ischemia.

Vascular changes   In addition to the vascular changes secondary to ischemia itself, vascular changes may also be caused by the specific disease process responsible for the ischemia. Edema and hemorrhages are common with acute retinal ischemia. Retinal capillary closure, microaneurysms, lipid exudates, and neovascularization may develop with chronic retinal ischemia.

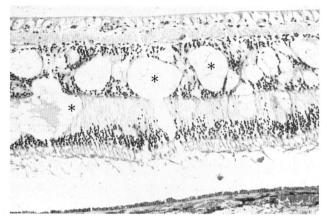

FIG XI-16—Cystoid spaces in inner nuclear and outer plexiform layers (asterisks).

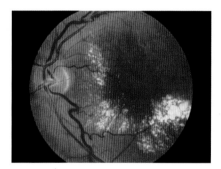

FIG XI-17—Intraretinal lipid deposits, or hard exudates.

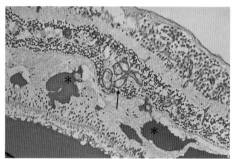

FIG XI-18—Intraretinal exudates (asterisks) surrounding intraretinal microvascular abnormalities (IRMA, arrow).

Edema, one of the earliest manifestations of retinal ischemia, is a result of transudation across the inner blood–retinal barrier (Fig XI-16). Fluid and serum components accumulate in the extracellular space, and the fluid pockets are delimited by the surrounding neurons and glial cells. Exudate accumulating in the outer plexiform layer of the macula (Henle's layer) produces a star figure because of the orientation of the nerve fibers in this layer (Fig XI-17). In cases of chronic edema the extracellular deposits will become richer in protein and lipids, as the water component of the exudate is more efficiently removed, resulting in "hard exudates." Histologically, retinal exudates appear as eosinophilic, sharply circumscribed spaces within the retina (Fig XI-18). Chronic edema may result in intraretinal lipid deposits that are contained within the microglial cells.

Retinal hemorrhages also develop as a result of ischemic damage to the inner blood retinal barrier. As with edema and exudates, the shape of the hemorrhage conforms to the surrounding retinal tissue. Consequently, hemorrhages in the nerve fiber

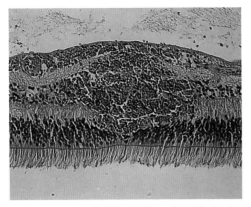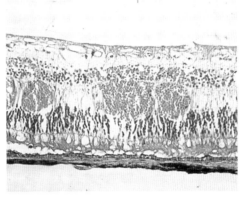

FIG XI-19—Intraretinal hemorrhage. *Left,* The horizontal orientation of the nerve fibers in the inner retina allows lateral displacement of extravasated blood. By ophthalmoscopy, this type of hemorrhage appears flame-shaped or feathered. *Right,* Outer plexiform nerve fibers restrict the lateral displacement of extravasated blood in the deep retinal layers. By ophthalmoscopy, this type of hemorrhage has a dot-and-blot appearance.

are "flame-shaped" and those in the nuclear or inner plexiform layers are circular, or "dot and blot" (Fig XI-19). Subhyaloid and sub-ILM hemorrhages have a "boat-shaped" configuration. White-centered hemorrhages (Roth spots) may be present in a number of conditions. The white centers of the hemorrhages can have a number of causes including aggregates of white blood cells, platelets, and fibrin; or they may be due to retinal light reflexes. Hemorrhages clear over a period of time ranging from days to months.

Architectural changes in the retinal vessels occur with disorders leading to chronic retinal ischemia. In an area of vascular occlusion the capillary bed becomes acellular. Adjacent to acellular areas, dilated irregular vascular channels known as *intraretinal microvascular abnormalities (IRMA)* and microaneurysms often appear (Figs XI-20, XI-21). Microaneurysms are fusiform or saccular outpouchings of the

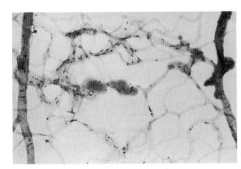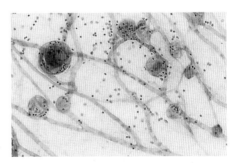

FIG XI-20—Trypsin digest preparation illustrating acellular capillaries adjacent to dilated irregular vascular channels (IRMA).

FIG XI-21—Retinal trypsin digest preparation, showing diabetic microaneurysms.

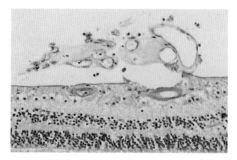

FIG XI-22—Retinal neovascularization. The new blood vessels have broken through the internal limiting membrane.

retinal capillaries best seen clinically with fluorescein angiography and histologically with PAS-stained trypsin digest preparations. Microaneurysms and IRMA frequently have a variable density of the endothelial cells lining the vessels. Microaneurysms evolve from thin-walled hypercellular microaneurysms to hyalinized, hypocellular microaneurysms.

In some cases of retinal ischemia, neovascularization of the retina and the vitreous may occur, most commonly in diabetes and branch retinal vein occlusion (BRVO). Retinal neovascularization generally consists of growth of new vessels on the vitreous side of the ILM (Fig XI-22), and only rarely does neovascularization occur within the retina itself. Hemorrhage may develop from retinal neovascularization as the associated vitreous exerts traction on the fragile new vessels. Retinal neovascularization should be distinguished from retinal collaterals and arteriovenous shunts that represent dilation and increased flow in existing retinal vessels.

Specific Ischemic Retinal Disorders

Central and branch retinal artery and vein occlusions   *Central retinal artery occlusions (CRAO) result from*

☐ Localized arteriosclerotic changes

☐ An embolic event

☐ Rarely, vasculitis as in temporal arteritis

As the retina becomes ischemic, it swells and loses its transparency. This swelling is best appreciated clinically and histopathologically in the posterior pole where the NFL and the ganglion cell layer are the thickest. Because the ganglion cell layer and the NFL are thickest in the macula but absent in the fovea, the normal color of the choroid shows through in the fovea and produces a cherry-red spot, ophthalmoscopically suggesting CRAO. The retinal swelling eventually clears and leaves the classic histologic picture of inner ischemic atrophy (see Figure XI-13). Scarring and neovascularization are rare.

Branch retinal artery occlusions (BRAO) are usually the result of emboli, most frequently the ones that lodge at the bifurcation of a retinal arteriole. Hollenhorst plaques are cholesterol emboli within retinal arterioles that seldom occlude the vessel. Emboli may be the first or most important clue to a significant systemic disorder such as carotid vascular disease (cholesterol emboli, or Hollenhorst plaques), cardiac valvular disease (calcific emboli), or platelet-fibrin emboli (thromboembolism).

The histology of the acute phase of BRAO is characterized by swelling of the inner retinal layers with death of all nuclei. As the edema resolves, a classic picture emerges of inner ischemic atrophy in the distribution of the retina supplied by the occluded arteriole. The NFL, the ganglion cell layer, the inner plexiform layer, and the inner nuclear layer are affected (see Figure XI-13). Arteriolar occlusions result in infarcts with complete postnecrotic atrophy of the affected layers.

Central retinal vein occlusion (CRVO) is occlusion of the central retinal vein at the level of the lamina cribrosa. The pathophysiology of CRVO is the same as hemiretinal vein occlusion but different from branch retinal vein occlusion (see below). What has previously been called *papillophlebitis* represents a CRVO in a patient with good collateral circulation. Central retinal vein occlusions develop as a result of structural changes in the central retinal artery and the lamina cribrosa that lead to compression of the central retinal vein. This compression creates turbulent flow in the vein and predisposes to thrombosis. These structural changes occur in arteriosclerosis, hypertension, diabetes, and glaucoma.

CRVOs are recognized clinically by the presence of retinal hemorrhages in all four quadrants. Usually, prominent edema of the optic nerve head occurs along with dilation of the retinal veins and variable amounts of cotton-wool spots and macular edema. CRVOs occur in two forms: a milder perfused type and a more severe nonperfused type.

Nonperfused CRVO was defined in the CRVO study as a CRVO in which greater than 10 disc areas showed nonperfusion on fluorescein angiography. Nonperfused CRVOs typically have extensive retinal edema and hemorrhage. Marked venular dilation and a variable number of cotton-wool spots are found.

Central Vein Occlusion Study Group. Baseline and early natural history report. The central vein occlusion study. *Arch Ophthalmol.* 1993;111:1087–1095.

Acute ischemic CRVO is characterized histologically by the following:

- Marked retinal edema
- Focal retinal necrosis
- Subretinal, intraretinal, and preretinal hemorrhage

Vein occlusions can produce ischemia, allowing glial cells to survive and respond to the insult by replication and intracellular deposition of filaments (gliosis). Hemorrhage, hemosiderosis, disorganization of the retinal architecture, and gliosis are found, distinguishing the final histologic picture from that seen in CRAO (Fig XI-23). Numerous microaneurysms are present in the retinal capillaries following CRVO, and acellular capillary beds are present to a variable degree. With time dilated collateral vessels develop at the optic nerve head. Neovascularization of the iris is common following CRVO.

Branch retinal vein occlusion (BRVO) is occlusion of a tributary retinal vein. These occlusions occur almost universally at the site of an arteriovenous crossing. At the crossing of a branch retinal artery and vein, the two vessels share a common

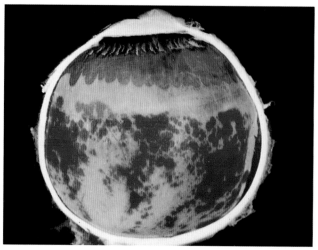

FIG XI-23—Diffuse retinal hemorrhage following central retinal vein occlusion. The damaged retina will be replaced by gliosis.

adventitial sheath. With arteriosclerotic changes in the arteriole, the retinal venule may become compressed, leading to turbulent flow that predisposes to thrombosis. This condition is more common in patients with arteriosclerosis and hypertension.

BRVO occurs most commonly in the superotemporal quadrant (63% of cases). The occlusion results in retinal hemorrhages and cotton-wool spots. Because BRVO does not always result in total inner retinal ischemia and death of all tissue, neovascularization of the optic nerve and retina may develop. Overall, 50%–60% of patients with BRVO will maintain a visual acuity of 20/40 or better after 1 year. Findings in eyes with permanent visual loss from BRVO include

- CME
- Pigmentary macular disturbance
- Macular edema with hard lipid exudates
- Subretinal fibrosis
- Epiretinal membrane formation

Photocoagulation therapy is considered for chronic macular edema and neovascularization.

The histologic picture of BRVO resembles that seen in CRVO but is localized to the area of the retina in the distribution of the occluded vein (Fig XI-24). Numerous microaneurysms and dilated collateral vessels may be present. Acellular retinal capillaries are present to a variable degree, correlating with retinal capillary nonperfusion on fluorescein angiography.

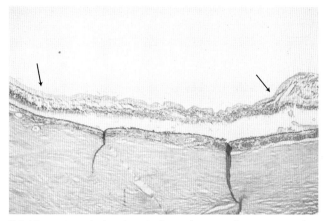

FIG XI-24—Inner ischemic retinal atrophy secondary to BRVO (between arrows).

Diabetic Retinopathy

Diabetic retinopathy is one of the four most frequent causes of new blindness in the United States and the leading cause among 20- to 64-year-olds. Early in the course of diabetic retinopathy, certain physiologic abnormalities occur:

□ Impaired autoregulation of the retinal vasculature

□ Alterations in retinal blood flow

□ Breakdown of the blood–retinal barrier

Histologically, the primary changes are in the retinal microcirculation:

□ Thickening of the retinal capillary basement membrane

□ Selective loss of pericytes compared to retinal capillary endothelial cells

□ Microaneurysm formation (see Figure XI-21)

□ Retinal capillary closure (see Figure XI-20) (histologically recognized as acellular capillary beds)

Dilated intraretinal telangiectatic vessels may develop IRMA, as shown in Figure XI-20, and finally neovascularization may develop (see Figure XI-22).

Secondary to these primary retinal vascular changes intraretinal edema, hemorrhages, exudates, and microinfarcts of the inner retina develop. Acutely, microinfarcts of the inner retina are characterized clinically as cotton-wool spots (see Figure XI-15). Subsequently, focal inner ischemic atrophy appears (see Figure XI-13).

Stages of diabetic retinopathy   The Early Treatment Diabetic Retinopathy Study (ETDRS) has classified diabetic retinopathy into clinical stages useful for purposes of treatment and prognosis.

Nonproliferative diabetic retinopathy (NPDR) is characterized by microaneurysms, dilated capillaries, dot-and-blot hemorrhages, hard exudates, and retinal edema. CME is the leading cause of decreased vision in diabetic retinopathy.

Preproliferative diabetic retinopathy is characterized by widespread capillary closure with resultant formation of cotton-wool spots, IRMA, venous beading, and large-blot retinal hemorrhages (see Figure XI-19).

Proliferative diabetic retinopathy (PDR) is characterized by neovascularization. Fibrovascular tissue has a tendency both to bleed, because of the delicate nature of the capillaries formed, and to cause retinal traction. In addition, partial posterior vitreous detachment (PVD) frequently develops in eyes with fibrovascular proliferation. PVD may result in elevation of the new vessels, vitreous hemorrhages, and tractional complications such as retinal detachment and macular heterotopia. Neovascularization of the vitreous base is classified as anterior hyaloidal fibrovascular proliferation. Neovascularization of the iris with secondary angle-closure glaucoma and phthisis may be the endstage result of PDR.

Other histologic changes in diabetes   The corneal epithelial basement membrane is thickened. This change is associated with poor adherence of the epithelium to the underlying Bowman's layer, predisposing diabetic patients to corneal abrasions and poor corneal epithelial healing. Lacy vacuolation of the iris pigment epithelium occurs in association with hyperglycemia; histologically, the intraepithelial vacuoles contain glycogen (PAS-positive and diastase-sensitive). Histopathologically, thickening of the ciliary epithelial basement membrane is almost universally present in diabetic eyes. There is an increased incidence of cataract formation.

Laser photocoagulation has frequently been used in eyes with diabetic retinopathy. Argon laser photocoagulation, the type most frequently employed, results in variable destruction of the outer retina, destruction of the RPE, and occlusion of the choriocapillaris (Fig XI-25). These lesions heal by proliferation of the adjacent RPE and glial scarring.

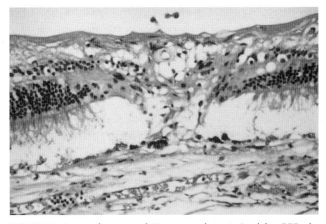

FIG XI-25—Laser photocoagulation scar characterized by RPE absence centrally with peripheral RPE hyperplasia and loss of the photoreceptors, outer nuclear layer, and a portion of the inner nuclear layer.

Retinopathy of Prematurity

Retinal ischemia also plays a role in retinopathy of prematurity. This ischemia does not develop because of the occlusion of existing vessels but rather because of the absence of retinal vessels in the incompletely developed retinal periphery. A decrease in retinal blood flow from oxygen-induced vasoconstriction may also be a contributing factor.

The clinical and histologic features of this disorder are somewhat different from those present in other retinal ischemic states. Retinal edema and exudates do not develop. Retinal hemorrhages and retinal vascular dilation develop only in the most severe cases (Plus or Rush disease). Neovascularization of the retina and vitreous may develop as a result of proliferation of new vessels at the border of the vascularized and avascular peripheral retina. Fibrovascular proliferation into the vitreous at this site may lead to traction retinal detachment, macular heterotopia, and high myopia.

The retinopathy of prematurity study (CRYO-ROP Study) has defined the clinical indications for peripheral retinal ablation to prevent severe vision loss in eyes affected with severe ROP. BCSC Section 6, *Pediatric Ophthalmology and Strabismus,* discusses ROP in detail.

Cryotherapy for Retinopathy of Prematurity Cooperative Group. Multicenter trial of cryotherapy for retinopathy of prematurity: Snellen visual acuity and structural outcome at 5½ years after randomization. *Arch Ophthalmol.* 1996;114:417–424.

Age-Related Macular Degeneration

Age-related macular degeneration (AMD) is the leading cause of new blindness in the United States. The precise pathogenesis of this disorder is not known, but it undoubtedly is a disorder in which genetic predisposition plays an important role. It is likely that this disease is a general phenotype resulting from a variety of genetic mutations.

Several characteristic changes in the retina, RPE, Bruch's membrane, and choroid occur in AMD. Perhaps the first detectable pathologic change is the appearance of deposits between the basement membrane of the RPE and the elastic portion of Bruch's membrane (basal linear deposits) and similar deposits between the plasma membrane of the RPE and the basement membrane of the RPE (basal laminar deposits). These deposits are not clinically visible and may require electron microscopy to be distinguished. In advanced cases these deposits may become confluent, in which case they have been described as *diffuse drusen* and can be seen at the light microscopic level (Fig XI-26). There is no exact clinical correlate for diffuse drusen.

The first clinically detectable feature of AMD is the appearance of drusen. The clinical term *drusen* has been correlated pathologically to large PAS-positive deposits between the RPE and Bruch's membrane. In many cases, and especially in the case of soft drusen, clinically apparent drusen are present in eyes that are shown to have basal laminar and/or basal linear deposits and diffuse drusen on histopatho-

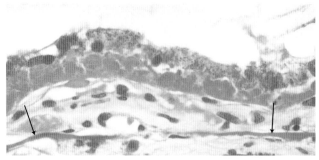

FIG XI-26—Diffuse drusen. There is diffuse deposition of eosinophilic material beneath the RPE. CNV is present between the diffuse drusen and the elastic portion of Bruch's membrane (arrows).

FIG XI-27—Hard drusen. (Reproduced with permission from Spraul CW, Grossniklaus HE. Characteristics of drusen and Bruch's membrane changes in postmortem eyes with age-related macular degeneration. *Arch Ophthalmol.* 1997;115:267–273. © 1997, American Medical Association.)

logic analysis. Drusen, which may be transient, have been classified clinically as follows:

☐ Hard (hyaline) drusen: the typical discrete yellowish lesions that are PAS-positive nodules composed of hyalin material between the RPE and Bruch's membrane (Fig XI-27)

☐ Soft drusen: drusen with amorphous poorly demarcated boundaries, usually >63 μm in size; histologically represent cleavage of the RPE and basal laminar or linear deposit from Bruch's membrane (Fig XI-28)

☐ Small drusen: <64 μm

☐ Large drusen: >64 μm

☐ Basal laminar or cuticular drusen: diffuse, small, regular, and nodular deposits of drusenlike material in the macula

☐ Calcific drusen: sharply demarcated, glistening, refractile lesions usually associated with RPE atrophy

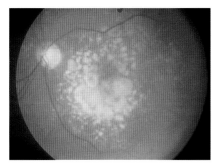 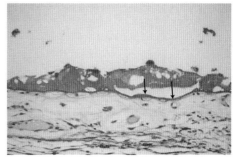

FIG XI-28—*Left,* Clinical photograph of multiple confluent drusen. *Right,* Thick eosinophilic deposits (arrows) between the RPE and the elastic portion of Bruch's membrane. (Reproduced with permission from Spraul CW, Grossniklaus HE. Characteristics of drusen and Bruch's membrane changes in postmortem eyes with age-related macular degeneration. *Arch Ophthalmol.* 1997;115:267–273. © 1997, American Medical Association.)

Photoreceptor atrophy occurs to a variable degree in macular degeneration. It is not clear if this atrophy is a primary abnormality of the photoreceptors or if it is secondary to the underlying changes in the RPE and Bruch's membrane. In addition to photoreceptor atrophy, large zones of atrophy may appear in the RPE. When this occurs centrally, it has been termed *central areolar atrophy of the RPE* (Fig XI-29). Drusen, photoreceptor atrophy, and RPE atrophy may all be present to varying degrees in *dry,* or *nonexudative, AMD.*

Eyes with choroidal neovascularization (*wet,* or *exudative, AMD*) associated with AMD have fibrovascular tissue present between the inner and outer layers of

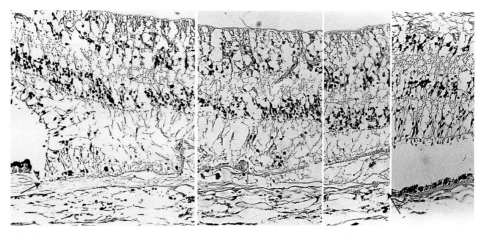

FIG XI-29—Central areolar atrophy (between arrows). There is loss of the RPE and the photoreceptor cells in the area of areolar atrophy.

143

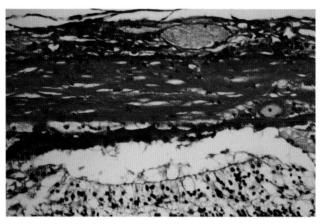

FIG XI-30—CNV. Fibrovascular tissue is present between the retinal pigment epithelium and the elastic portion of Bruch's membrane.

Bruch's membrane, beneath the RPE, or in the subretinal space (Fig XI-30). This neovascular tissue is the cause of the exudative consequences of wet AMD. Choroidal neovascularization is associated with the presence of basal laminar deposits and diffuse drusen. The new blood vessels leak fluid, producing serous retinal detachments, and they are prone to hemorrhage, leading to subretinal and intraretinal hemorrhages.

Subretinal neovascular membranes have been classified as type 1 or type 2 based on their pathologic and clinical features. Type 1 neovascularization is characterized by neovascularization within Bruch's membrane in the sub-RPE space. This type of neovascularization generally features a broad expanse of the inner portion of Bruch's membrane in which the RPE is abnormally oriented or absent. Type 2 neovascularization occurs in the subretinal space and generally features only a small defect where there is abnormal orientation or absence of the RPE. Type 1 neovascularization is more characteristic of AMD, while type 2 neovascularization is more characteristic of ocular histoplasmosis.

Grossniklaus HE, Gass JD. Clinicopathologic correlations of surgically excised type 1 and type 2 submacular neovascular membranes. *Am J Ophthalmol.* 1998;126:59–69.

Surgically excised choroidal neovascular membranes are composed of vascular channels, RPE, and various other components of the RPE–Bruch's membrane complex. These latter may include photoreceptor outer segments, basal laminar and linear deposits, hyperplastic RPE, and inflammatory cells.

Generalized Chorioretinal Degeneration

The term *retinitis pigmentosa* is a misnomer, because clearly evidence of inflammation is lacking. Retinitis pigmentosa can be inherited primarily by a variety of modes or can occur in a sporadic manner. The specific genetic abnormality has been identified in some types.

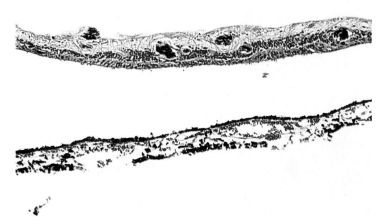

FIG XI-31—Retinitis pigmentosa with marked loss of photoreceptor cells. RPE pigment has migrated through the retina and collected around blood vessels, corresponding to the bone-spicule–like pattern seen clinically. The retina is arti-factitiously detached.

Grossly, pigment is arranged in a bone-spicule–like configuration around the arterioles. Microscopically, photoreceptor cell loss occurs as well as RPE hyperplasia with migration into the retina around retinal vessels (Fig XI-31). The arterioles, while narrowed clinically, show no histologic abnormality initially. Later, a thickening and hyalinization of the vessel walls appears. The optic nerve may show diffuse or sectoral atrophy with gliosis as a late change.

Neoplasia

Retinoblastoma

Retinoblastoma is the most common primary intraocular malignancy in childhood, occurring in 1 in 14,000–20,000 live births; the incidence varies slightly from country to country. Chapter XIX in Part 2 of this volume, Intraocular Tumors: Clinical Aspects, also discusses retinoblastoma at length, from a more clinical point of view. Several other volumes of the BCSC series cover various aspects of this topic as well; consult the *Master Index.*

Pathogenesis   Although retinoblastoma was once considered to be of glial origin (lesions clinically simulating retinoblastoma were formerly called *pseudogliomas*), the neuroblastic origin of this tumor from the nucleated layers of the retina has now been established. Immunohistochemical studies have demonstrated that tumor cells stain positive for neuron-specific enolase, rod–outer segment photoreceptor–specific S antigen, and rhodopsin. Tumor cells also secrete an extracellular substance known as *interphotoreceptor retinoid-binding protein,* a product of normal photoreceptors.

Recently, retinoblastoma tumor cells grown in culture have been shown to express a red and a green photopigment gene as well as cone cell alpha subunits of transducin. These findings further support the concept that retinoblastoma may be a neoplasm of cone cell lineage. Continuing immunohistochemical and molecular studies are adding data that complicate the hypothesis that a single cell type is the progenitor of retinoblastoma, however. The presence of small amounts of glial tissue within retinoblastoma suggests that tumor cells may possess the ability to differentiate into astroglia, or that the resident glial cells proliferate in response to primary neoplastic cells.

The so-called retinoblastoma gene, localized to the long arm of chromosome 13, is deceptively named as it does not actively cause retinoblastoma. The normal gene *suppresses* the development of retinoblastoma (and possibly other tumors, such as osteosarcoma). Retinoblastoma develops when both homologous loci of the suppressor gene become nonfunctional by either a deletion error or by mutation. Although one normal gene is sufficient to suppress the development of retinoblastoma, the presence of one normal gene and one abnormal gene is apparently an unstable situation that may lead to mutation in the normal gene and the loss of tumor suppression, thus allowing retinoblastoma to develop.

Dryja TP, Cavenee W, White R, et al. Homozygosity of chromosome 13 in retinoblastoma. *N Engl J Med.* 1984;310:550–553.

Histologic features   Histologically, retinoblastoma consists of cells with round, oval, or spindle-shaped nuclei that are approximately twice the size of a lymphocyte (Fig XI-32). Nuclei are hyperchromatic and surrounded by an almost imperceptible amount of cytoplasm. Mitotic activity is usually high, although pyknotic nuclei may make this difficult to assess. As tumors grow into the vitreous or subretinal space, they frequently outgrow their blood supply, creating a characteristic pattern of ne-

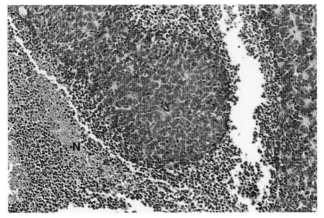

FIG XI-32—Retinoblastoma. Note the viable tumor, aggregated around a blood vessel, and the alternating zones of necrosis (N).

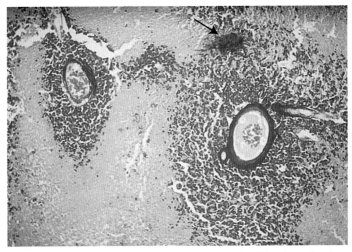

FIG XI-33—Zones of viable tumor (usually surrounding blood vessels) alternate with zones of tumor necrosis. Calcium (arrow) is present in the necrotic area. The basophilic material surrounding the blood vessels is DNA, presumably liberated from the necrotic tumor.

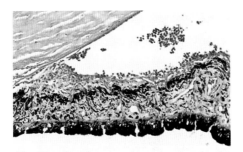

FIG XI-34—Retinoblastoma. Note the thick iris neovascular membrane in this patient with retinoblastoma and the free-floating tumor cells in the anterior chamber.

crosis; calcification is a common finding in areas of necrosis (Fig XI-33). Cuffs of viable cells course along blood vessels with regions of ischemic necrosis beginning 90–120 μm from nutrient vessels. DNA released from necrotic cells may be detected within tumor vessels and within blood vessels in tissues remote from the tumor such as the iris. Neovascularization of the iris can complicate retinoblastoma (Fig XI-34).

Cells shed from retinoblastoma tumors remain viable in the vitreous and subretinal space, and they may eventually give rise to implants throughout the eye. It may be difficult to determine histologically if multiple intraocular foci of tumor represent multiple primary tumors, implying a systemic distribution of the abnormal gene, or tumor seeds (see Figure XIX-5).

The formation of highly organized *Flexner-Wintersteiner rosettes* is a characteristic feature of retinoblastoma that does not occur in other neuroblastic tumors with the rare exception of some pineoblastomas and ectopic intracranial retinoblastomas. Flexner-Wintersteiner rosettes are expressions of retinal differentiation. The cells of these rosettes surround a central lumen lined by a refractile structure. The refractile lining corresponds to the external limiting membrane of the retina that represents sites of attachments between photoreceptors and Müller cells. The rosette is characterized by a single row of columnar cells with eosinophilic cytoplasm and peripherally situated nuclei (Fig XI-35, top left). The chromatin of cell nuclei in rosettes is usually looser than that of nuclei from undifferentiated cells in adjacent tumor.

A less commonly encountered rosette without features of retinal differentiation, known as the *Homer Wright rosette,* can be found in other neuroblastic tumors such as neuroblastoma and medulloblastoma of the cerebellum as well as in retinoblastoma. The lumen of a Homer Wright rosette is filled with a tangle of eosinophilic cytoplasmic processes (Fig XI-35, top right).

Evidence of photoreceptor differentiation has been documented as well for another flowerlike structure known as a *fleurette*. Fleurettes are curvilinear clusters of cells composed of rod and cone inner segments that are often attached to abortive outer segments (Fig XI-35, bottom). The fleurette expresses a greater degree of retinal differentiation than does the Flexner-Wintersteiner rosette. In a typical retinoblastoma, the undifferentiated tumor cells greatly outnumber the fleurettes and Flexner-Wintersteiner rosettes, and differentiation is not an important prognostic indicator.

Progression　The most common route for retinoblastoma tumor to escape from the eye is by way of the optic nerve. Although direct infiltration of the optic nerve can lead to extension into the brain, cells that spread into the leptomeninges gain access to the subarachnoid space with the potential for seeding throughout the central nervous system (Fig XI-36). Invasion of the optic nerve is a poor prognostic sign (Fig XI-37). See chapter XIX for discussion of prognosis.

Massive uveal invasion, in contrast, theoretically increases the risk of hematogenous dissemination. Spread to regional lymph nodes may be seen when tumor involving the anterior segment grows into the conjunctival substantia propria, especially when the filtration angle is involved.

Spontaneous regression of retinoblastoma　This process is discussed in chapter XIX; see p 264.

Retinocytoma　Retinocytoma is characterized histologically by numerous fleurettes admixed with individual cells that demonstrate varying degrees of photoreceptor differentiation (Fig XI-38). Retinocytoma should be distinguished from spontaneous regression of retinoblastoma, which is the end result of coagulative necrosis. See discussion in chapter XIX.

Also referred to as *retinoma,* retinocytoma differs from retinoblastoma in the following ways:

□ Retinocytoma cells have more cytoplasm and more evenly dispersed nuclear chromatin than retinoblastoma cells. Mitoses are not observed in retinocytoma.

□ Although calcification may be identified in retinocytoma, necrosis is usually absent.

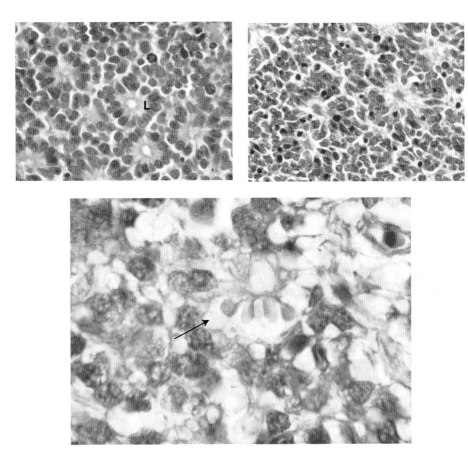

FIG XI-35—Retinoblastoma rosettes. *Upper left,* Flexner-Wintersteiner rosettes: note the central lumen (L). *Upper right,* Homer Wright rosettes: note the central neurofibrillary tangle in the center of these structures. *Bottom:* The fleurette (arrow) demonstrates bulbous cellular extension of retinoblastoma cells that represent differentiation along the lines of photoreceptor outer segments.

Trilateral retinoblastoma This condition is discussed in chapter XIX; see pp 264–265.

Secondary malignancies Patients with the genetic form of retinoblastoma have a 5%–6% risk for the development of secondary malignancies. The most common secondary malignancy is osteosarcoma. External-beam radiation therapy increases the risk of secondary malignancy to 17%–51%. See chapter XIX for more complete discussion of both genetic counseling for and management of retinoblastoma.

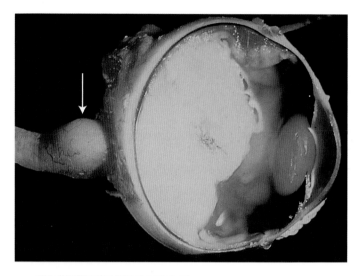

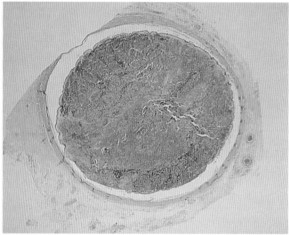

FIG XI-36—Retinoblastoma. *Top,* Massive invasion of the globe posteriorly by retinoblastoma with bulbous enlargement of the optic nerve (arrow) caused by direct extension. *Bottom,* A cross section of the optic nerve taken at the surgical margin of transection. Tumor is present in the nerve at this point, and the prognosis is poor.

Medulloepithelioma

Also known as *diktyoma,* medulloepithelioma is a congenital neuroepithelial tumor arising from primitive medullary epithelium. This tumor usually occurs in the ciliary body but has also been documented in the retina and optic nerve. Although the tumor develops before the medullary epithelium shows substantial signs of differentiation, cells are organized into ribbonlike structures that have a distinct cellular

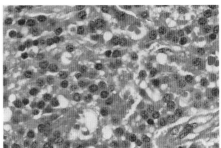

FIG XI-37—Retinoblastoma has invaded the optic nerve and extended to the margin of resection. This is an extremely poor prognostic sign.

FIG XI-38—Retinocytoma. Note the exquisite degree of photoreceptor differentiation.

polarity (Fig XI-39). These ribbonlike structures are composed of undifferentiated round to oval cells possessing little cytoplasm. Cell nuclei are stratified in three to five layers, and the entire structure is lined on one side by a thin basement membrane. One surface secretes a mucinous substance, rich in hyaluronic acid, that resembles primitive vitreous. Stratified sheets of cells are capable of forming mucinous cysts that are clinically characteristic. Flexner-Wintersteiner and Homer Wright rosettes can also be seen.

Medulloepitheliomas that contain solid masses of neuroblastic cells indistinguishable from retinoblastoma are more difficult to classify. Medulloepitheliomas that have substantial amounts of undifferentiated cells with high mitotic rates and that demonstrate tissue invasion are considered malignant, although patients treated with enucleation have high survival rates, and "malignant" medulloepithelioma typically follows a relatively benign course if the tumor remains confined to the eye.

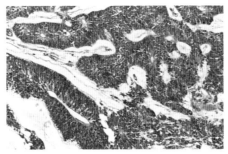

FIG XI-39—Medulloepithelioma. Note the ribbons and cords of tumor cells that seem to recapitulate the morphology of the ciliary epithelium.

Heteroplastic tissue, such as cartilage or smooth muscle, may be found in medulloepitheliomas. Tumors composed of cells from two different embryonic germ layers are referred to as *teratoid medulloepitheliomas*. Malignant teratoid medulloepitheliomas demonstrate either solid areas of undifferentiated neuroblastic cells or sarcomatous transformation of heteroplastic elements.

Fuchs Adenoma

This acquired tumor of the nonpigmented epithelium of the ciliary body may be associated with sectoral cataract and may simulate other iris or ciliary body neoplasms. Fuchs adenomas consist of hyperplastic nonpigmented ciliary epithelium arranged in sheets and tubules with alternating areas of PAS-positive basement membrane material.

Combined Hamartoma of the Retina and RPE

This lesion is characterized clinically by the presence of a slightly elevated, variably pigmented mass involving the RPE, peripapillary retina, optic nerve, and overlying vitreous. Frequently, a preretinal membrane is present that distorts the tumor's inner retinal surface. The lesion is often diagnosed in childhood, supporting a probable hamartomatous origin, but it is possible that the vascular changes are primary with secondary changes in the adjacent RPE.

The tumor is composed of thickening of the optic nerve head and peripapillary retina with an increased number of vessels. The RPE is hyperplastic and has frequently migrated into a perivascular location. Vitreous condensation and fibroglial proliferation may be present on the surface of the tumor.

Other Retinal Tumors

Other tumors of the retina are very rare. Massive gliosis of the retina may occur secondary to chronic retinal detachment or chronic inflammation. Various retinal tumors occur in association with some phakomatoses including astrocytic hamartomas in tuberous sclerosis and hemangioblastomas in von Hippel–Lindau disease. The phakomatoses are discussed in BCSC Section 5, *Neuro-Ophthalmology,* and Section 6, *Pediatric Ophthalmology and Strabismus.*

CHAPTER XII

Uveal Tract

Topography

The *iris, ciliary body,* and *choroid* constitute the uveal tract. The uveal tract is embryologically derived from mesoderm and neural crest. Firm attachments between the uveal tract and the sclera exist at only three sites:

- Scleral spur
- Exit points of the vortex veins
- Optic nerve

Iris

The iris is located in front of the crystalline lens. It separates the anterior segment of the eye into two compartments, the anterior chamber and the posterior chamber, and forms a circular aperture (pupil) that controls the amount of light transmitted into the eye. The iris is composed of five layers:

- Anterior border layer
- Stroma
- Muscular layer
- Anterior pigment epithelium
- Posterior pigment epithelium

The anterior border layer represents a condensation of iris stroma and melanocytes, and it is coarsely ribbed with numerous crypts (Fig XII-1). The stroma contains blood vessels, nerves, melanocytes, fibrocytes, and clump cells. The clump cells are both macrophages containing phagocytosed pigment (Type 1, or clump cells of Koganei) and variants of smooth muscle cells (Type 2 clump cells). The vessels within the stroma appear thick-walled as a result of the presence of a thick collar of collagen fibrils. The dilator and sphincter muscle make up the muscular layer. The posterior portion of the iris is lined by the anterior and posterior pigment epithelium, which is composed of a double layer of pigment epithelium arranged in an apex-to-apex configuration. The cell body of the anterior pigment epithelium gives rise to the dilator muscle. The color of the iris is determined by the number and size of the melanin pigment granules in the stromal melanocytes.

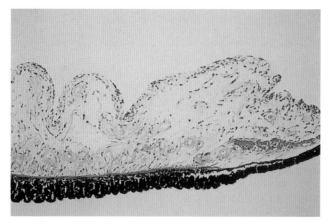

FIG XII-1—Histopathologic appearance of the iris: the anterior border layer is thrown into numerous crypts and folds. The sphincter muscle is present at the pupillary border, while the dilator muscle lies just anterior to the posterior pigment epithelium.

Ciliary Body

The ciliary body, measuring approximately 6.0–6.5 mm wide, extends from the base of the iris and becomes continuous with the choroid at the ora serrata. The ciliary body is composed of two areas:

□ The *pars plicata*, which contains the ciliary processes

□ The *pars plana*

The inner portion is lined by a double layer of epithelial cells, the inner nonpigmented layer and the outer pigmented layer (Fig XII-2). The zonular fibers of the lens attach to the ciliary body processes. The ciliary muscle has three types of fibers:

□ Longitudinal fibers (Brucke's muscle)

□ Radial fibers

□ The innermost circular fibers (Müller's muscle)

These fiber groups function as a group during accommodation.

Choroid

The choroid is the pigmented vascular tissue that forms the middle coat of the posterior part of the eye. It extends from the ora serrata anteriorly to the optic nerve posteriorly and consists of three principle layers:

□ Lamina fusca (suprachoroid layer)

□ Stroma

□ Choriocapillaris

The choriocapillaris provides nutrients for the retinal pigment epithelium (RPE) and the outer retinal layers (Fig XII-3).

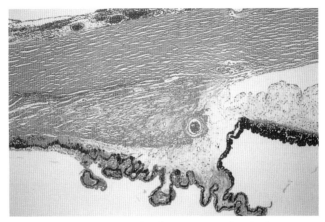

FIG XII-2—Normal ciliary body. The numerous ciliary body processes are covered by a double row of epithelium. The iris root is seen at the right.

Congenital Anomalies

The entities described below are discussed in detail in BCSC Section 2, *Fundamentals and Principles of Ophthalmology,* and Section 6, *Pediatric Ophthalmology and Strabismus.*

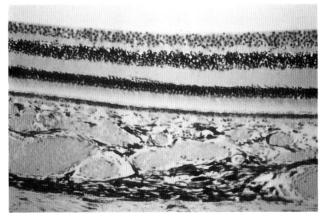

FIG XII-3—The choroid is present in the lower half of the figure. Its relationship to the overlying neurosensory retina and RPE is depicted.

Aniridia

True aniridia, or complete absence of the iris, is rare. Most cases of aniridia are incomplete, and a narrow rim of rudimentary iris tissue is present peripherally. Aniridia is usually bilateral, although it may be asymmetric. Histologically, the rudimentary iris consists of underdeveloped ectodermal-mesodermal neural crest elements. The anterior chamber angle is often incompletely developed, and peripheral anterior synechiae with overgrowth of corneal endothelium is often present. These changes are most likely responsible for the high incidence of glaucoma associated with aniridia. Other ocular findings in aniridia include cataract, corneal pannus, and foveal hypoplasia.

Both autosomal dominant and recessive inheritance patterns for aniridia have been described. An association between sporadic aniridia and an increased incidence of Wilms tumor has been linked to an 11p13 deletion. Microcephaly, mental retardation, and other genitourinary abnormalities have also been described in association with aniridia.

Coloboma

An absence of part or all of a tissue, coloboma may affect the iris, ciliary body, choroid, or all three structures. Colobomas may occur as isolated defects or as portions of more complex malformations. Typical colobomas occur as a result of faulty closure of the fetal fissure (optic groove) anywhere from the optic disc to the pupil in the inferonasal meridian. Atypical colobomas occur in locations outside the region of the embryonic fissure. More than half of typical colobomas are bilateral, although they may be asymmetric.

Inflammations

BCSC Section 9, *Intraocular Inflammation and Uveitis,* discusses the conditions described below and also explains the immunologic processes involved in depth.

Infectious

The uveal tract may be involved in infectious processes that either seem restricted to a single intraocular structure or may be part of a generalized inflammation affecting several or all coats of the eye. If the source of the infectious agent is introduced from outside the body, as with posttraumatic bacterial infection, the infection is termed *exogenous.* If, however, the infection is introduced from elsewhere in the body, such as a ruptured diverticulum, and subsequently spreads hematogenously to involve the uveal tract, the infection is referred to as *endogenous.* A wide variety of organisms have been shown to cause infections of the uveal tract, including bacteria, fungi, viruses, and protozoa. Obtaining a careful clinical history will usually help guide the clinician in the consideration of causative agents.

Histopathology will often show a mixed acute and chronic inflammatory infiltrate within the choroid, ciliary body, or iris stroma. In cases of viral, fungal, or protozoal (e.g., toxoplasmosis) agents, a granulomatous pattern of inflammation may be observed. Special tissue stains for microorganisms (B&B, Gomori's methenamine silver, PAS, Ziehl-Neelsen) are often helpful in identifying organisms admixed within the inflammatory reaction.

Noninfectious

Sympathetic ophthalmia   This rare bilateral granulomatous panuveitis occurs after accidental or surgical injury to one eye (the *exciting,* or *inciting, eye*), followed by a latent period and development of uveitis in the uninjured globe (the *sympathizing eye*). The inflammation in the sympathizing eye may occur as early as 10 days or as late as 50 years following the suspected triggering incident, but 4–8 weeks is the typical period of latency.

Histologically, a diffuse granulomatous inflammatory reaction appears within the uveal tract composed of lymphocytes and epithelioid histiocytes containing phagocytosed melanin pigment (Figs XII-4, XII-5). Typically, the choriocapillaris is

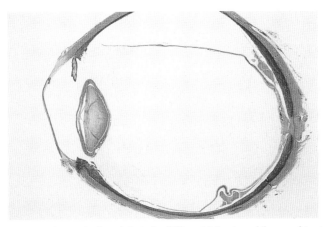

FIG XII-4—Sympathetic ophthalmia. Diffuse thickening of the uveal tract.

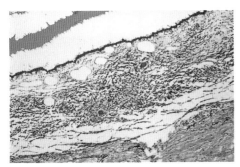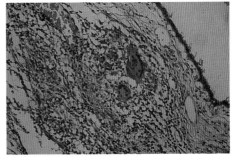

FIG XII-5—Sympathetic ophthalmia. *Left,* Diffuse granulomatous inflammation within the choroid. *Right,* Higher magnification shows the presence of multinucleated giant cells.

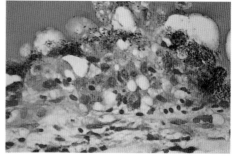

FIG XII-6—Dalen-Fuchs nodules in sympathetic ophthalmia. *Left,* Focal collections of inflammatory cells are located between the RPE and Bruch's membrane. *Right,* Higher magnification demonstrates the presence of epithelioid histiocytes within the nodules.

spared. Varying degrees of inflammation in the anterior chamber may be present, as evidenced by collections of histiocytes deposited on the corneal endothelium (mutton-fat keratic precipitates). Dalen-Fuchs nodules, which are collections of epithelioid histiocytes, lymphocytes, and RPE on the inner surface of Bruch's membrane, may be seen in some cases (Fig XII-6). Dalen-Fuchs nodules may be present in other diseases such as Vogt-Koyanagi-Harada (VKH) syndrome and are, therefore, not pathognomonic of sympathetic ophthalmia.

Although the etiology of sympathetic ophthalmia is not known, the pathogenesis may involve a hypersensitivity to melanin pigment, retinal S antigen, or other retinal or uveal proteins. Experimental animal studies suggest that the penetrating ocular injury allows antigens to gain access to the lymphatic system where they are processed and subsequently incite an immune response.

Vogt-Koyanagi-Harada syndrome VKH is a rare cause of posterior or diffuse uveitis that may have both ocular and systemic manifestations. The syndrome occurs more commonly in patients with Asian or American Indian ancestry and usually affects individuals between 30 and 50 years of age. Ocular symptoms include bilateral decreased visual acuity, pain, redness, and photophobia. Systemic manifestations include alopecia, poliosis (loss of pigmentation of eyebrows and eyelashes), vitiligo, dysacusis, headaches, and seizures.

A chronic, diffuse granulomatous uveitis resembles that seen in sympathetic ophthalmia. Classically, the entire choroid is involved by the inflammatory reaction, however, without sparing of the choriocapillaris. The granulomatous inflammation may extend to involve the retina. Because the disease is one of exacerbation and remission, chorioretinal scarring and RPE hyperplasia may also be observed. Choroidal neovascularization has been described in some cases. The etiology of VKH is unknown. A proposed mechanism involves an immune reaction to uveal melanin-associated protein, melanocytes, or pigment epithelium. There is a strong association between HLA-DR4 and VKH syndrome.

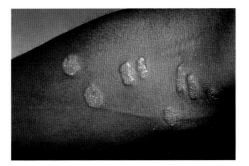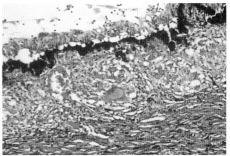

FIG XII-7—Sarcoid. *Left,* Gross appearance of multiple discrete nodules. (Photograph courtesy of Curtis E. Margo, MD.) *Right,* Histopathology of sarcoid nodule showing epithelioid histiocytes and multinucleated giant cells.

Sarcoidosis   The uveal tract is the most common site of ocular involvement by sarcoid. Anteriorly, inflammatory nodules of the iris may be seen, either at the pupillary margin (Koeppe nodules) or elsewhere on the iris (Busacca nodules). These nodules are composed of collections of noncaseating epithelioid histiocytes admixed with lymphocytes (Fig XII-7). In the posterior segment chorioretinitis, periphlebitis, and chorioretinal nodules may be seen. Periphlebitis may appear clinically as inflammatory lesions described as *candle wax drippings.* Histologically, the involved tissues show infiltration by noncaseating granulomatous inflammation. Multinucleated giant cells are often present, and asteroid bodies (star-shaped acidophilic bodies) and Schaumann's bodies (spherical, basophilic, often calcified bodies) may be seen within the giant cells. Neither asteroid nor Schaumann's bodies are pathognomonic for sarcoidosis, however.

Degenerations

Rubeosis Iridis

Rubeosis iridis, or neovascularization of the iris, is a somewhat common finding in surgically enucleated eyes. It may be associated with a wide variety of conditions (Table XII-1). Histopathologically, new vessels grow on the anterior iridic surface and may extend to involve the angle, causing a secondary type of glaucoma, *neovascular glaucoma.* Initially, the vessels lack supporting tissue and do not possess the encircling thick fibrous cuff seen in normal iris vessels. The anterior surface of the iris leaflets often becomes flattened.

Vessels may, less commonly, arise from the posterior surface of the iris. Fibrous tissue develops around the new vessels, creating fibrovascular membranes that line the anterior surface of the iris and cover the chamber angle. Myofibroblasts in the fibrovascular tissue may contract and lead to an anterior displacement of the posterior iris epithelium past the level of the sphincter muscle commonly known as *ectropion uveae.* In the chamber angle these fibrovascular membranes contribute to the formation of peripheral anterior synechiae. In advanced cases atrophy of the dilator muscle, attenuation of the pigment epithelium, and stromal fibrosis occur.

TABLE XII-1

CONDITIONS ASSOCIATED WITH RUBEOSIS IRIDIS

Vascular Disorders
    Central retinal vein occlusion
    Central retinal artery occlusion
    Branch retinal vein occlusion
    Carotid occlusive disease

Ocular Diseases
    Sympathetic ophthalmia
    Vogt-Koyanagi-Harada syndrome
    Retinal detachment
    Coats disease
    Secondary glaucoma

Surgery and Radiation Therapy
    Retinal detachment surgery
    Radiation

Systemic Diseases
    Diabetes mellitus
    Sickle cell disease

Neoplastic Diseases
    Retinoblastoma
    Melanoma of the choroid/iris
    Metastatic carcinoma

Trauma

A nonprogressive form of rubeosis iridis, consisting of small iris neovascular tufts at the pupillary margin, has also been described. The neovascular tissue may be isolated to one sector of the pupillary margin, or it may involve the entire margin. This condition has been described in patients with adult-onset diabetes mellitus and with myotonic dystrophy.

Hyalinization of the Ciliary Body

Over time the ciliary body processes become hyalinized and fibrosed. The thin delicate processes become blunted and attenuated, and the stroma becomes more eosinophilic. This process is a normal aging change of the ciliary body and is not considered pathologic.

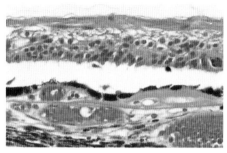

FIG XII-8—Sub-RPE neovascularization. A new blood vessel (arrow) lies between the RPE and Bruch's membrane.

Choroidal Neovascularization

New blood vessels may grow between the RPE and Bruch's membrane, a condition called *choroidal neovascularization*. Any condition that produces a disruption or break in Bruch's membrane may predispose the eye to choroidal neovascularization, including age-related macular degeneration (AMD), angioid streaks, ocular histoplasmosis, and trauma. Complications of choroidal neovascularization include serous or hemorrhagic detachment of the RPE or retina, leading to fibrous tissue proliferation and disciform scarring (Fig XII-8).

Neoplasia

Iris

Nevus   The iris nevus represents a localized proliferation of melanocytic cells that generally appears as a darkly pigmented lesion of the iris stroma with minimal distortion of the iris architecture. In some cases the nevus may cause a distortion of the iris pupil or, less commonly, a sector cataract. There is an increased incidence of iris nevi in patients with neurofibromatosis. The data as to whether or not iris nevi occur more commonly in eyes containing posterior choroidal melanomas is conflicting.

Iris nevi appear histologically as accumulations of branching dendritic cells or collections of banal-appearing spindle cells. A variety of growth patterns and cytologic appearances are possible, but cellular atypia and significant mitotic activity are not present. If the nevus is located near the pupillary margin, it may cause anterior displacement of the associated posterior pigment epithelium (ectropion uveae).

No treatment is indicated for iris nevi. They should be observed carefully over time, either through the use of photographs or with detailed drawings, to ascertain growth. See Figure XVII-1.

Melanoma   Melanomas arising in the iris tend to display a nonaggressive clinical course as compared to posterior melanomas arising in the ciliary body and choroid. The majority of iris melanomas occur in the inferior sectors of the iris. The lesions can be quite vascularized and may occasionally cause spontaneous hyphema. Iris melanomas are uncommon, accounting for between 3.3% and 16.6% of all uveal melanomas. The average age of presentation of patients with iris melanomas is 10–20 years earlier than that for posterior melanomas, ranging between 40 and 50 years old. Iris melanomas may occur in the pediatric age group, however.

The modified Callender classification for posterior melanomas (see below) may not be applicable to iris melanomas in terms of prognostic significance, because even iris melanomas containing epithelioid melanoma cell types have a relatively benign course compared to their posterior melanoma counterparts.

While iris melanomas may grow in a localized aggressive fashion, they rarely metastasize. One exception occurs when melanomas grow to diffusely involve the entire iris stroma (Fig XII-9). In such cases the melanoma may extend posteriorly into the chamber angle and involve the ciliary body, giving rise to the so-called ring melanoma. Cataract and secondary glaucoma may develop as complications of the tumor growth.

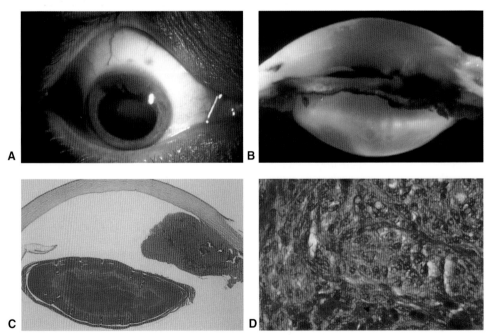

FIG XII-9—*A,* Clinical appearance of iris melanoma. The pigmented tumor is seen occupying the iris superiorly. *B,* Gross appearance of pigmented iris mass. *C,* Low magnification shows the iris melanoma completely replacing the normal iris stroma, extending into the anterior chamber, and touching the posterior cornea. *D,* Histopathology of iris melanoma shows numerous plump epithelioid melanoma cells containing prominent nucleoli.

Choroid and Ciliary Body

Nevus Most nevi of the uveal tract occur in the choroid. One review of 100 nevi showed that fewer than 6% involved the ciliary body, while the remainder were present in the choroid. Four types of nevus cells have been described:

- Plump polyhedral
- Slender spindle
- Plump fusiform dendritic
- Balloon cells

Depending on the size and location of the nevus, it may exert nonspecific effects on adjacent ocular tissues. The associated choriocapillaris may become compressed or obliterated, and drusen may be seen overlying the nevus. Less commonly, localized serous detachments of the overlying RPE or neurosensory retina develop.

The majority of choroidal nevi remain stationary over long periods of observation. However, the presence of nevus cells associated with some melanomas supplies evidence that melanomas may arise from previous choroidal nevi (Fig XII-10).

Melanocytoma The melanocytoma is a specific type of uveal tract nevus that warrants separate consideration. These jet-black lesions may occur anywhere in the uveal tract, but they most commonly appear in the peripapillary region.

Histologically, a melanocytoma is composed of plump polyhedral cells with small nuclei and abundant cytoplasm. Because the nevus cells are so heavily pigmented, it is usually necessary to obtain bleached sections to accurately study the cytologic features. Areas of cystic degeneration or necrosis may be observed.

Melanoma Choroidal melanoma is the most common primary intraocular tumor in adults. The incidence in the United States is approximately six cases per million. The tumor is rare in children and primarily affects patients between 60 and 70 years old. Melanomas occur most commonly in whites or other lightly pigmented individuals.

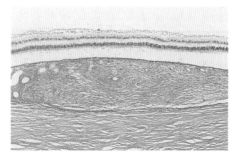

FIG XII-10—Spindle cell nevi are composed of delicate bipolar cells with thin tapering nuclei.

Ocular melanocytic conditions such as melanosis oculi and oculodermal melano-cytosis (nevus of Ota) have been shown to be risk factors for the development of choroidal melanoma.

Ciliary body melanomas may be asymptomatic in their early stages, as they can remain hidden behind the iris. As they enlarge, they may cause displacement of the lens and sector cataracts. Ciliary body tumors may erode through the iris root and present as a peripheral iris mass. Other ciliary body melanomas can extend directly through the sclera, creating an epibulbar mass. Dilated episcleral vessels, *sentinel vessels,* may be visible directly over the tumor. In rare cases the tumor may grow cir-cumferentially to involve the entire ciliary body. This growth pattern is referred to as a *ring melanoma.*

The location and size of posterior choroidal melanomas will determine the patient's presenting symptoms. A peripheral lesion may go undetected for a pro-tracted period, whereas a posterior pole tumor affecting the macula, and therefore vision, may present quite early.

Choroidal melanomas are typically brown, elevated, dome-shaped subretinal masses. The degree of pigmentation is variable, ranging from dark brown to com-pletely amelanotic. Over time the tumor may break through the overlying Bruch's membrane, producing a collar-button or mushroom-shaped configuration. Promi-nent clumps of orange pigment (lipofuscin) at the level of the RPE may be present overlying the melanomas, and localized serous detachment of the sensory retina is frequently present.

Several factors have been significantly correlated with survival in patients with choroidal and ciliary body melanomas. The two most important variables associated with survival are

□ The size of the largest tumor dimension in contact with the sclera

□ The cell type making up the tumor

The modified Callender classification is used for the cytologic classification of uveal melanomas:

□ Spindle cell nevus

□ Spindle cell melanoma

□ Epithelioid melanoma

□ Mixed-cell type (mixture of spindle and epithelioid cells)

On occasion a melanoma may have undergone extensive necrosis, precluding classification.

Spindle cell melanoma has the best prognosis and epithelioid melanoma the worst. Melanomas of mixed-cell type have an intermediate prognosis. Some authors have suggested that survival following enucleation decreases with increasing pro-portions of epithelioid cells in mixed-cell melanomas. Totally necrotic melanomas assume the same prognosis as mixed-cell melanomas.

The modified Callender classification has some disadvantages. First, there is no way to precisely define a melanoma of mixed-cell type, since disagreement persists regarding the minimal number of epithelioid cells needed for a melanoma to be classified as mixed-cell type. Second, the scheme is difficult to reproduce even among experienced ophthalmic pathologists. This difficulty arises because the cyto-logic features of the melanoma cells reflect a continuous spectrum (Figs XII-11 through XII-13).

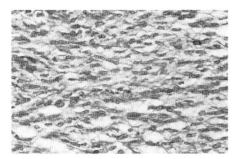

FIG XII-11—Spindle-A cells are characterized by low nuclear-to-cytoplasmic ratios. Neither nucleoli nor mitoses are observed, and a central stripe may be noted down the long axis of the nucleus. Tumors composed exclusively of spindle-A cells are considered to be nevi.

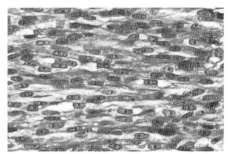

FIG XII-12—Spindle-B cells demonstrate a higher nuclear-to-cytoplasmic ratio; more coarsely granular chromatin; and plumper, large nuclei. Mitotic figures and nucleoli are present, although not in large numbers. Tumors composed of mixtures of spindle-A and spindle-B cells are designated spindle cell melanomas.

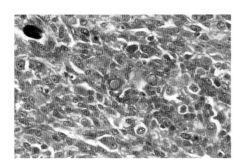

FIG XII-13—Patients with epithelioid melanomas have the poorest prognosis. Cells resemble epithelium because of abundant eosinophilic cytoplasm and enlarged oval to polygonal nuclei. Epithelioid melanoma cells often lack cohesiveness and demonstrate marked pleomorphism, including the formation of multinucleated tumor giant cells. Nuclei have a conspicuous nuclear membrane, very coarse chromatin, and large nucleoli.

Cytomorphometric measurements of melanoma cells have been studied. One such measurement is the *mean of the ten largest melanoma cell nuclei (MLN)*. This parameter has been shown to correlate well with mortality after enucleation. The correlation of morphometry is enhanced further when combined with the largest dimension of scleral contact by tumor.

Intrinsic tumor microvascular patterns have also been studied and shown to have prognostic significance. Tumors containing vascular closed loops or vascular networks (three vascular loops located back-to-back) are associated with an increased incidence of the development of subsequent metastases.

As mentioned, melanomas may break through the overlying Bruch's membrane and assume a mushroom-shaped configuration (Fig XII-14). Tumors may also contribute to serous detachments of the overlying and adjacent retina, with subsequent degenerative changes in the outer segments of the photoreceptors. Melanomas may extend through scleral emissary channels to gain access to the epibulbar surface and the orbit (Fig XII-15). Less commonly, aggressive melanomas may invade directly the underlying sclera or overlying retina (Fig XII-16).

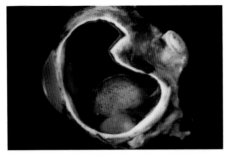
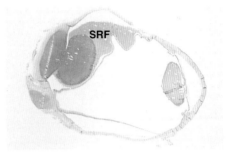

FIG XII-14—Choroidal melanoma with rupture through Bruch's membrane. *Left,* Gross appearance. *Right,* Microscopic appearance. Note the subretinal fluid adjacent to the tumor (SRF).

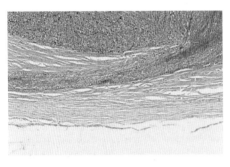
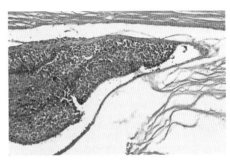

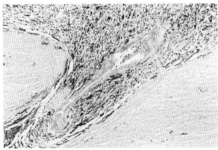

FIG XII-15—*Upper left,* Note the melanoma cells tracking along scleral emissary canals. *Right,* Melanoma is found within the vortex vein. *Lower left,* Some melanomas track along the outer sheaths of vortex veins and nerves.

FIG XII-16—Note the retinal degeneration overlying this choroidal melanoma and the retinal invasion by tumor.

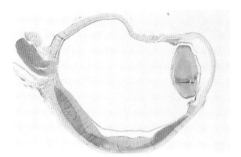

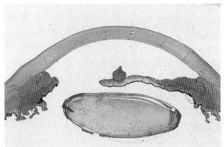

FIG XII-17—Some melanomas form diffuse, plac-oid growths.

FIG XII-18—By definition, a ring melanoma fol-lows the major arterial circle of the iris circum-ferentially around the eye.

Tumor necrosis can incite variable degrees of intraocular inflammation. Direct invasion of the anterior chamber may lead to secondary glaucoma. Additionally, tumor necrosis may lead to the liberation of melanin pigment, which can then gain access to the anterior chamber and angle, causing a type of secondary glaucoma called *melanomalytic glaucoma*.

Lymphatic spread of ciliary body and choroidal melanoma is rare. Metastases almost invariably result from the hematogenous spread of melanoma to the liver. The reason for the propensity of melanoma to spread to the liver is unknown, al-though more than 95% of tumor-related deaths have liver involvement. In as many as one third of tumor-related deaths, the liver is the sole site of metastasis.

Some types of uveal melanomas show biological behavior that cannot be pre-dicted according to the criteria discussed above. Survival rates of patients with dif-fuse ciliary body melanomas (ring melanoma) are particularly poor. These relatively flat tumors are almost always of mixed-cell type, and they may grow circumferen-tially without becoming significantly elevated. Diffuse choroidal melanomas simi-larly have a poor prognosis (Figs XII-17, XII-18).

Metastatic Tumors

Metastatic lesions represent the most common intraocular tumor in the adult. These lesions most often involve the choroid, but any ocular structure can be affected. Unlike primary uveal melanoma, metastatic lesions are often multiple and may be bilateral. Although these lesions typically assume a flattened growth pattern, rare cases of collar-button or mushroom-shaped lesions have been reported. The most common primary tumors metastasizing to the eye are breast carcinoma in women and lung carcinoma in men (Fig XII-19). Other primary tumors with reported metas-tases to the uveal tract include cutaneous melanoma, prostate adenocarcinoma, renal cell carcinoma, and carcinoid tumors. Histologically, metastatic tumors may recapitulate the appearance of the primary lesion, or they may appear less differen-tiated. Special histochemical and immunohistochemical stains can be helpful in diagnosing the metastatic lesion and determining its origin. The importance of a careful clinical history cannot be overemphasized. See also chapter XX.

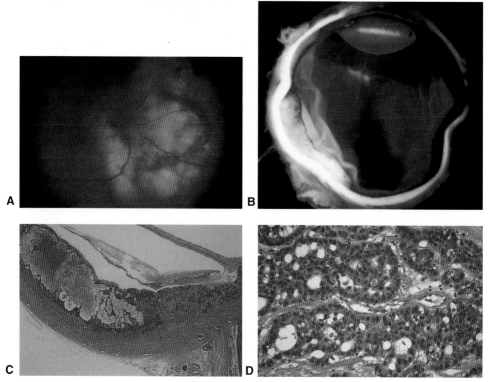

FIG XII-19—*A,* Clinical appearance of metastatic lesion from lung primary. *B,* Gross appearance of lesion. *C,* Choroidal metastasis from lung adenocarcinoma; histopathology shows adenocarcinoma with mucin production. *D,* Higher magnification depicts a well-differentiated adenocarcinoma with distinct glandular appearance.

Other Uveal Tumors

Hemangioma Hemangiomas of the choroid occur in two specific forms. The *localized* choroidal hemangioma typically occurs in patients without other systemic disorders. It generally appears as a red or orange tumor located in the postequatorial zone of the fundus. Such tumors commonly produce a secondary retinal detachment. If the detachment extends into the foveal region, blurred vision, metamorphopsia, and micropsia may occur. These benign vascular tumors characteristically affect the overlying RPE and cause cystoid degeneration of the outer retinal layers.

The *diffuse* choroidal hemangioma is generally seen in patients with Sturge-Weber syndrome (encephalofacial angiomatosis). This choroidal tumor produces diffuse reddish orange thickening of the entire fundus, resulting in an ophthalmoscopic pattern commonly referred to as the *tomato catsup fundus.* Retinal detachment and glaucoma often occur in eyes with this lesion.

Histopathologically, both the diffuse and localized hemangiomas show collections of variably sized vessels within the choroid. The lesions may appear as predominantly capillary hemangiomas, cavernous hemangiomas, or a mixed pattern of both. The adjacent and overlying choroid may show compressed melanocytes, hyperplastic RPE, and fibrous tissue proliferation.

When choroidal hemangiomas are asymptomatic, generally no treatment is indicated. The most common complication is serous detachment of the retina involving the fovea with resultant visual loss. If this occurs, the surface of the tumor can be treated lightly with argon laser or xenon arc photocoagulation. The goal of this type of treatment is not to destroy the tumor but rather to create a chorioretinal adhesion that prevents further accumulation of fluid. If the retinal detachment is extensive, this type of photocoagulation is usually unsuccessful. Recurrent detachments are common, and the long-term visual prognosis in patients with macular detachment or edema is guarded.

Choroidal osteoma   These benign bony tumors typically arise from the juxtapapillary choroid and are seen in adolescent to young adult patients, more commonly women than men. The characteristic lesion appears yellow to orange and has well-defined margins. Histopathologically, the tumor is composed of unremarkable-appearing compact bone located in the peripapillary choroid. The intratrabecular spaces are filled with a loose connective tissue containing large and small blood vessels, vacuolated mesenchymal cells, and scattered mast cells. The bone trabeculae contain osteocytes, cement lines, and occasional osteoclasts.

Choroidal osteomas typically enlarge slowly over many years. If the tumor involves the macula, vision is generally impaired. Subretinal neovascularization is a common complication of macular choroidal osteoma. Both choroidal osteoma and hemangioma may mimic a choroidal melanoma clinically and should, therefore, be included in the differential diagnosis of choroidal melanoma.

Neural sheath tumors   Schwannoma (neurilemoma) and neurofibroma are rare tumors of the uveal tract. Multiple neurofibromas may occur in the ciliary body, iris, and choroid in patients with neurofibromatosis. The histopathologic features of neurofibroma are discussed in chapter XIV, Orbit.

Leiomyoma   Neoplasms arising from the smooth muscle of the ciliary body have been reported rarely. These tumors may exhibit both myogenic and neurogenic features by light and transmission electron microscopy. In such cases the term *mesectodermal leiomyoma* is employed.

Lymphoid proliferation   The choroid may be the site of lymphoid proliferation, either as a primary ocular process or in association with systemic lymphoproliferative disease.

Uveal lymphoid infiltration (formerly reactive lymphoid hyperplasia) of the uveal tract is similar to the spectrum of low-grade lymphoid lesions that occur in the orbit (see chapter XIV, Orbit) and conjunctiva. There may be diffuse involvement of the uveal tract by a mixture of lymphocytes and plasma cells, and lymphoid follicles may be present. Lymphocyte typing reveals a polymorphic population without clonal restriction; this finding distinguishes inflammatory pseudotumor from lymphoma.

Grossniklaus HE, Martin DF, Avery R, et al. Uveal lymphoid infiltration: report of four cases and clinicopathologic review. *Ophthalmology.* 1998;105:1265–1273.

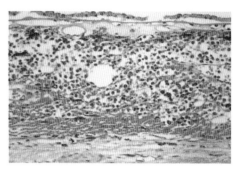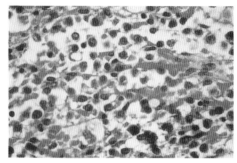

FIG XII-20—*Left,* Diffuse expansion of choroid by lymphoma. *Right,* Higher magnification depicts atypical lymphocytes.

Lymphoma of the uveal tract occurs almost exclusively in association with systemic lymphoma. The classification of lymphomas is discussed in chapter XIV (Fig XII-20).

Trauma

The uveal tract is frequently involved in cases of ocular trauma. *Prolapse* of uveal tissue through a perforating ocular injury is a common association. *Rupture* of the choroid may occur as the result of a blunt or penetrating injury. The pattern of the rupture most frequently appears as semicircular lines circumscribing the peripapillary region. If the macula is involved, the prognosis for vision recovery is guarded. Subretinal neovascularization can occur as a late complication. More severe injury may cause rupture of both the choroid and retina, a condition termed *chorioretinitis sclopetaria.*

Choroidal detachment, either localized or diffuse, may occur after accidental or surgical trauma. Serous or hemorrhagic fluid accumulates in the suprachoroidal space between the choroid and the sclera. Depending on the etiology, the fluid may spontaneously resorb, allowing for reattachment of the choroid. In other cases surgical drainage of the fluid may be required.

CHAPTER XIII

Eyelids

Topography

The eyelids extend from the eyebrow superiorly to the cheek inferiorly, and they can be subdivided into orbital and tarsal components. At the level of the tarsus the eyelid consists of four main histologic layers, from anterior to posterior:

☐ Skin

☐ Orbicularis oculi muscle

☐ Tarsus

☐ Palpebral conjunctiva

A surgical plane of dissection through an incision along the gray line of the eyelid margin is possible between the orbicularis and tarsus, functionally dividing the eyelid into anterior and posterior lamellae (Fig XIII-1). BCSC Section 7, *Orbit, Eyelids, and Lacrimal System,* covers the anatomy of the eyelids as well as the conditions discussed later in this chapter in detail.

The *skin* of the eyelid is thinner than that of most other body sites. It consists of an epidermis of keratinizing stratified squamous epithelium, which also contains

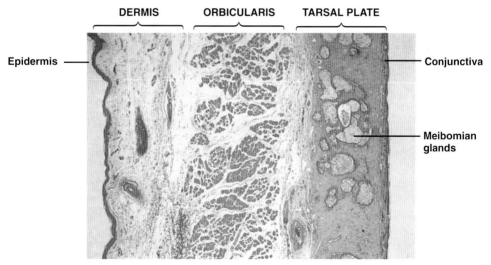

FIG XIII-1—This is a cross section of normal eyelid. Proceeding from left to right, note the epidermis, the dermis resting upon the orbicularis, the tarsus surrounding the meibomian glands, and the palpebral (tarsal) conjunctiva.

melanocytes and antigen-presenting Langerhans cells; and a dermis of loose collagenous connective tissue that contains the following:

- Cilia and associated sebaceous glands (of Zeis)
- Apocrine sweat glands (of Moll)
- Eccrine sweat glands
- Pilosebaceous units

The *orbicularis oculi* is composed of striated muscle. The *tarsal plate,* a thick plaque of dense fibrous connective tissue, contains the sebaceous meibomian glands. Inserting into the superior border of the tarsus of the upper eyelid is the levator palpebrae superioris, which exists only as a collagenous aponeurosis in the eyelid; the true muscular portion of the levator lies within the orbit. The sympathetically innervated smooth muscle of Müller lies posterior to the levator. Also present near the upper border of the superior tarsal plate (and less so in the lower border of the inferior tarsal plate) are the accessory lacrimal glands of Wolfring; the accessory lacrimal glands of Krause are present in the conjunctival fornices. The *palpebral conjunctiva* is tightly adherent to the posterior surface of the tarsus and is composed of nonkeratinizing stratified columnar epithelium containing mucin-producing goblet cells, with minimal subepithelial fibrovascular stroma. The conjunctival epithelium becomes more squamous in appearance near its termination at the eyelid margin and the corneoscleral limbus. Table XIII-1 lists the normal functions of the eyelid glands and some of the pathologic conditions related to them.

TABLE XIII-1

GLANDS OF THE EYELID: FUNCTION AND PATHOLOGY

SECRETORY ELEMENT	NORMAL FUNCTION	PATHOLOGY
Conjunctival goblet cells	Mucin secretion to enhance corneal wetting	Numbers diminished in some dry eye states
		Present in mucoepidermoid carcinoma
Accessory lacrimal glands of Krause and Wolfring	Basal tear secretion of the aqueous layer	Sjögren syndrome
		Graft vs host disease
		Rare tumors (benign mixed tumor)
Meibomian glands	Secretion of lipid layer of tears to retard evaporation	Chalazion
		Sebaceous carcinoma
Sebaceous glands of Zeis	Lubrication of the cilia	External hordeolum
		Sebaceous carcinoma
Glands of Moll	Lubrication of the cilia	Ductal cyst (sudoriferous cyst, apocrine hidrocystoma)
		Apocrine carcinoma
Eccrine glands	Secretions for temperature control, electrolyte balance	Ductal cyst (sudoriferous cyst, eccrine hidrocystoma)
		Syringoma
		Sweat gland carcinoma

Congenital Anomalies

BCSC Section 8, *External Disease and Cornea*, discusses many of the conditions mentioned below and later in this chapter.

Distichiasis

Distichiasis is the aberrant formation within the tarsus of cilia that exit the eyelid margin through the orifices of meibomian glands. Although these lashes may rub against the eye, they are relatively well tolerated initially and may not cause symptoms of irritation until early childhood. Distichiasis is inherited in an autosomal dominant fashion and is usually the only congenital anomaly present. It may, however, be associated with other anomalies such as mandibulofacial dysostosis and trisomy 18. The pathogenesis of distichiasis is thought to be anomalous formation within the tarsus of a complete pilosebaceous unit rather than the normal sebaceous (meibomian) gland.

Phakomatous Choristoma

A rare congenital tumor, phakomatous choristoma (Zimmerman tumor) is formed from the aberrant location of lens epithelium within the inferonasal portion of the lower eyelid. These cells may undergo cytoplasmic enlargement, identical to the "bladder" cell in a cataractous lens. PAS-positive basement membrane material is produced, recapitulating lens capsule. The nodule formed is usually present at birth and enlarges slowly. Complete excision is the usual treatment.

Dermoid Cyst

Dermoid cysts may occur in the eyelid, but they are more common in the orbit and will discussed in the next chapter.

Inflammations

Infectious

Depending on the causative agent, infections of the eyelids may produce disease that is localized (e.g., hordeolum), multicentric (e.g., papillomas), or diffuse (cellulitis). Routes of infection may be primary inoculation through a bite or wound, direct spread from a contiguous site such as a paranasal sinus infection, or by hematogenous dissemination from a remote site. Infectious agents may be

- Bacterial such as *Staphylococcus aureus* in hordeolum and infectious blepharitis
- Viral as in papillomas caused by human papilloma virus (HPV)
- Fungal such as blastomycosis, coccidioidomycosis, or aspergillosis

Hordeolum   Also known as a *stye*, hordeolum is a primary acute self-limited inflammatory process typically involving the glands of Zeis and, less often, the meibomian glands of the upper eyelid. A small abscess, or focal collection of polymorphonuclear leukocytes and necrotic debris, forms at the site of infection. Healing occurs without visible scarring in most cases.

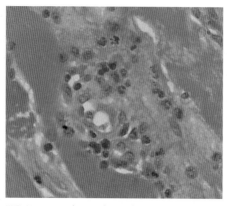

FIG XIII-2—Polymorphonuclear leukocytes dissect between the skeletal muscle fibers of the orbicularis in this biopsy of a preseptal cellulitis of the eyelid.

Cellulitis   The diffuse spread of acute inflammatory cells through tissue planes is known as *cellulitis*. The pathologic change is often accompanied by vascular congestion and edema (Fig XIII-2). *Preseptal cellulitis* involves the tissues of the eyelid anterior to the orbital septum, the fibrous membrane connecting the borders of the tarsal plates to the bony orbital rim. The condition most commonly affects the pediatric population and is most often secondary to upper respiratory tract infections caused by bacteria such as *Streptococcus pneumoniae.*

Viral infections   Examples of two types of viral infections involving the eyelids are viral papillomas and molluscum contagiosum. Virally induced *papillomas* of the eyelid are seen in young patients and are caused by HPV subtypes 6 and 11, those also associated with verruca. The papillomas are pedunculated growths along the eyelid margin composed of acanthotic and hperkeratotic epidermis lining papillary fibrovascular cores. Koilocytotic cytoplasmic clearing of infected epithelial cells may be present. The growths may spontaneously regress over months to years if not surgically excised or ablated by cryotherapy. Lesions with a papillomatous appearance seen in middle-aged or elderly persons include seborrheic keratosis, actinic keratosis, intradermal nevus, and acrochordon (fibroepithelial polyp).

Molluscum contagiosum is caused by a member of the poxvirus family and also typically affects young or immunocompromised persons. Dome-shaped, waxy epidermal nodules with central umbilication form and, if present on the eyelid margin, may cause a secondary follicular conjunctivitis (Fig XIII-3). Histopathologically, the lesions are distinctive, with a nodular proliferation of infected epithelium producing a central focus of necrotic cells that is extruded to the skin surface (Fig XIII-4). As the replicating virus fills the cytoplasm, the nucleus is displaced peripherally and finally disappears as the cells are shed. Incision and curettage are usually curative.

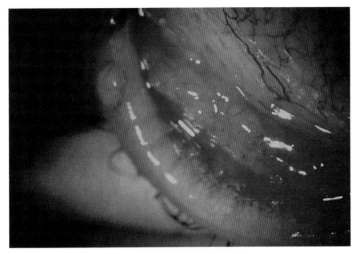

FIG XIII-3—Molluscum contagiosum. Note the follicular conjunctivitis.

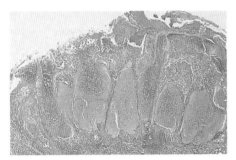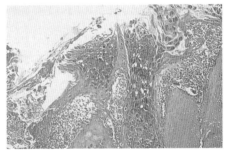

FIG XIII-4—Molluscum contagiosum. *Left,* Note the thickened epidermis with a central crater. *Right,* Note the eosinophilic and basophilic inclusion bodies.

Noninfectious

Chalazion This chronic, often painless nodule of the eyelid occurs when the lipid secretions of the meibomian glands or, less often, the glands of Zeis are discharged into the surrounding tissues, inciting a lipogranulomatous reaction (Fig XIII-5). The lipid is dissolved by solvents during routine tissue processing, so that histologic sections show histiocytes and multinucleated giant cells enveloping optically clear spaces. Lymphocytes, plasma cells, and neutrophils may also be present.

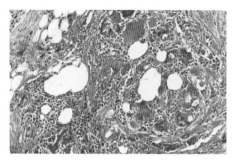

FIG XIII-5—Chalazion. Granulomatous inflammation surrounds clear spaces, formerly occupied by lipid (lipogranuloma).

Degenerations

Xanthelasma

Xanthelasma are single or multiple yellow soft plaques occurring in the nasal aspect of the upper and lower eyelids in middle-aged to elderly individuals, predominantly females. Associated hyperlipoproteinemic states, particularly hyperlipoproteinemia types II and III, are present in 30%–40% of patients with xanthelasma. These eyelid xanthomas consist of collections of histiocytes with microvesicular foamy cytoplasm clustered around vessels and adnexal structures within the dermis (Fig XIII-6). Associated inflammation is minimal to nonexistent. Treatment is either by surgical or carbon dioxide laser ablation.

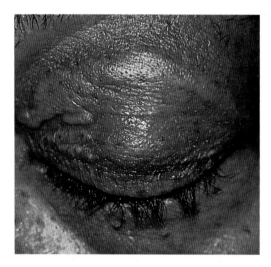

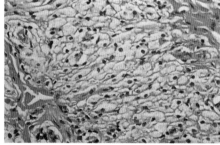

FIG XIII-6—Xanthelasma. Note the foam cells (filled with lipid) surrounding a venule at the left margin of the right photograph.

Amyloid

The term *amyloid* refers to a heterogeneous group of extracellular proteins that exhibit birefringence and dichroism under polarized light when stained with Congo red (see Figure X-8). These features result from the three-dimensional configuration of the proteins into a β pleated sheet. Examples of proteins that may form amyloid deposits include

☐ Immunoglobulin light chain fragments (AL amyloid) in plasma cell dyscrasias

☐ Transthyretin mutations in familial amyloid polyneuropathy (FAP) types I and II (see chapter X, Vitreous)

☐ Gelsolin mutations in FAP type IV (Meretoja syndrome; lattice corneal dystrophy type II)

Amyloid within the skin of the eyelid is highly indicative of a systemic disease process, either primary or secondary, while deposits elsewhere in the ocular adnexa but not in the eyelid are more likely a localized disease process. Other systemic diseases with eyelid manifestations are listed in Table XIII-2.

Amyloid deposits in the skin are usually multiple, bilateral, and symmetric waxy yellow-white nodules. The deposition of amyloid within blood vessel walls in the skin causes increased vascular fragility and often results in intradermal hemorrhages, accounting for the purpura seen clinically (Fig XIII-7). On routine histologic sections amyloid appears as an amorphous to fibrillogranular eosinophilic extracellular deposit, usually within vessel walls but also in the connective tissue and around peripheral nerves and sweat glands. Other stains useful in demonstrating

TABLE XIII-2

EYELID MANIFESTATIONS OF SYSTEMIC DISEASES

SYSTEMIC CONDITION	EYELID MANIFESTATION
Erdheim-Chester disease	Xanthelasma, xanthogranuloma
Hyperlipoproteinemia	Xanthelasma
Amyloidosis	Waxy papules, ptosis, purpura
Sarcoidosis	Papules
Wegener granulomatosis	Edema, ptosis, lower eyelid retraction
Scleroderma	Reduced mobility, taut skin
Polyarteritis nodosa	Focal infarct
Systemic lupus erythematosus	Telangiectasias, edema
Dermatomyositis	Edema, erythema
Relapsing polychondritis	Papules
Carney complex	Myxoma
Fraser syndrome	Cryptophthalmos
Treacher Collins syndrome	Lower eyelid coloboma

Modified from Wiggs JL, Jakobiec FA. Eyelid manifestations of systemic disease. In: Albert DM, Jakobiec FA, eds. *Principles and Practice of Ophthalmology.* 2nd ed. Philadelphia: Saunders; 1994:1859.

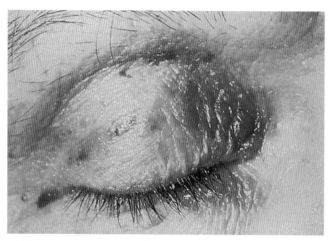

FIG XIII-7—Cutaneous amyloid in a patient with multiple myeloma. Note the waxy elevation and the purpura.

amyloid deposits include crystal violet and thioflavin t. Electron microscopy reveals the deposits to be composed of randomly oriented extracellular fibrils measuring 7.5–10.0 nm in diameter.

Albert DM, Jakobiec FA, eds. *Principles and Practice of Ophthalmology.* 2nd ed. Philadelphia: Saunders; 1994:2956–2974.

Garner A, Klintworth GK, eds. *Pathobiology of Ocular Disease: A Dynamic Approach.* 2nd ed. New York: Dekker; 1994:993–1007.

Neoplasia

Epidermal Neoplasms

Seborrheic keratosis This common benign epithelial proliferation occurs in middle age. Clinically, one or more well-circumscribed, oval, dome-shaped to verrucoid "stuck-on" papules appears, principally on the trunk and face, varying from millimeters to centimeters in greatest dimension and from pinkish to brown in color. Histopathologically, several architectural patterns are possible, although all demonstrate hyperkeratosis, acanthosis, and some degree of papillomatosis. The acanthosis is a result of proliferation of either polygonal or basaloid squamous cells without dysplasia.

A characteristic finding in most types of seborrheic keratosis is the formation of pseudohorn cysts, concentrically laminated collections of surface keratin within the acanthotic epithelium (Fig XIII-8). Irritated seborrheic keratosis, also termed *inverted follicular keratosis* by some authors, shows nonkeratinizing squamous epithelial whorling, or squamous "eddies," instead of pseudohorn cysts (Fig XIII-9). Heavy melanin phagocytosis by keratinocytes may impart a dark brown color to an otherwise typical seborrheic keratosis that may then be confused clinically with malignant melanoma.

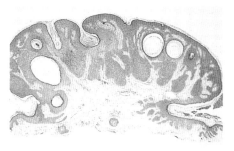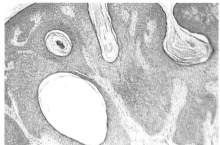

FIG XIII-8—Seborrheic keratosis. *Left,* The epidermis is acanthotic, and an excessive amount of keratin appears on the surface (hyperkeratosis). *Right,* Pseudohorn cysts appear to be present within the epidermis but actually represent crevices or infoldings of epidermis.

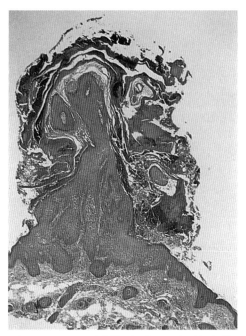

FIG XIII-9—Inverted follicular keratosis. Clinically, this lesion appeared to be a cutaneous horn.

Sudden onset of multiple seborrheic keratoses is known as the *Leser-Trélat sign* and is associated with a malignancy, usually a gastrointestinal adenocarcinoma; these keratoses may in fact represent evolving acanthosis nigricans. Table XIII-3 lists other systemic malignancies with cutaneous manifestations.

TABLE XIII-3

EYELID NEOPLASMS IN ASSOCIATION WITH SYSTEMIC MALIGNANCIES

SYNDROME	EYELID MANIFESTATION
Muir-Torre syndrome (visceral carcinoma, usually colon)	Keratoacanthoma, sebaceous neoplasm (adenoma, carcinoma)
Cowden disease (breast carcinoma, fibrous hamartomas of breast, thyroid, GI tract)	Multiple trichilemmomas
Basal cell nevus syndrome (medulloblastoma, fibrosarcoma)	Multiple basal cell carcinomas

Modified from Wiggs JL, Jakobiec FA. Eyelid manifestations of systemic disease. In: Albert DM, Jakobiec FA, eds. *Principles and Practice of Ophthalmology.* 2nd ed. Philadelphia: Saunders; 1994:1859.

Keratoacanthoma   This rapidly growing epithelial proliferation with a potential for spontaneous involution may be difficult to distinguish from squamous cell carcinoma both clinically and histopathologically. Dome-shaped nodules with a keratin-filled central crater may attain a considerable size, up to 2.5 cm diameter, within a matter of 1–2 months (Fig XIII-10). The natural history is typically spontaneous involution over several months, resulting in a slightly depressed scar. Histopathologically, keratoacanthomas show a cup-shaped invagination of well-differentiated squamous cells forming irregularly configured nests and strands and inciting a lymphoplasmacytic host response. The proliferating epithelial cells undermine the adjacent normal epidermis so that the edges of the lesion are likened to the flying but-

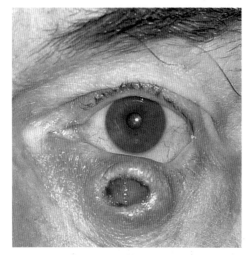

FIG XIII-10—Keratoacanthoma. Note the cuplike configuration. In this case the central crater was originally filled with keratin.

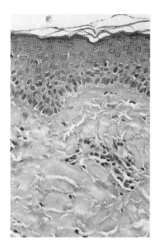

FIG XIII-11—Solar elastosis. The collagen of the dermis appears blue in this H&E stain, instead of pink. This is a marker of ultraviolet light–induced damage.

tresses of a Gothic cathedral. At the deep aspect of proliferating nodules mitotic activity and nuclear atypia may occur, making the distinction between keratoacanthoma and invasive squamous cell carcinoma problematic. If unequivocal invasion is present, the lesion should be considered a well-differentiated squamous cell carcinoma. When keratoacanthoma versus squamous cell carcinoma is the clinical differential diagnosis, the lesion should be completely excised in order to permit optimal histopathologic examination of the lateral and deep margins of the tumor–host interface.

Actinic keratoses More specifically known as *solar keratoses,* these are erythematous, scaly macules or papules developing in middle age on sun-exposed skin, particularly the face and the dorsal surfaces of the hands (Fig XIII-11). They range from millimeters up to 1 cm in greatest dimension. Hyperkeratotic types may form a cutaneous horn, and hyperpigmented forms may clinically simulate lentigo maligna. Squamous cell carcinoma may develop from preexisting actinic keratosis, and thus biopsy of suspicious lesions and long-term follow-up are necessary in patients with this condition. However, when squamous cell carcinoma arises in actinic keratosis, the risk of subsequent metastatic dissemination is very low (0.5%–3.0%).

Histopathologically, five subtypes range from hypertrophic to atrophic; the sine qua non for diagnosis in all types is the presence of

☐ Nuclear dysplasia

☐ Nuclear enlargement

☐ Nuclear hyperchromasia

☐ Nuclear membrane irregularity

☐ Increased nuclear-to-cytoplasmic ratio

Nuclear changes in actinic keratosis range from mild, involving only the basal epithelial layers, to frank carcinoma in situ, or full-thickness involvement of the epidermis.

Dyskeratosis (premature individual cell keratinization) and mitotic figures above the basal epithelial layer are often present (Fig XIII-12). The underlying dermis shows

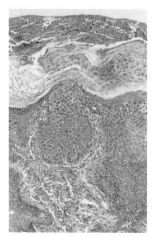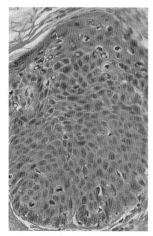

FIG XIII-12—Actinic keratosis. *Left,* Note the epidermal thickening (acanthosis), disorganization within the epidermis (dysplasia), parakeratosis, and inflammation within the dermis. Solar elastosis is also noted. *Right,* Note the epidermal disorganization and mitotic figures.

solar elastosis (fragmentation, clumping, and loss of eosinophilia) of dermal collagen and a lichenoid chronic inflammatory infiltrate of varying intensity. The base of the lesion must be examined histopathologically in order to determine whether invasive squamous cell carcinoma has supervened; as with keratoacanthoma, superficial shave biopsies not including the base of the lesion are contraindicated.

Carcinomas Although *squamous cell carcinoma* may occur in the eyelids, it is at least 10 and perhaps up to 40 times less common than basal cell carcinoma. Since the majority of squamous cell carcinomas arise in solar-damaged skin (actinic keratoses), the lower eyelid is more frequently involved than the upper. The clinical appearance is diverse, ranging from ulcers to plaques to fungating or nodular growths. Correspondingly, the clinical differential diagnosis is long, and pathologic examination of excised tissue is necessary for accurate diagnosis. Histopathologic examination shows atypical squamous cells forming nests and strands, extending beyond the epidermal basement membrane, infiltrating the dermis, and inciting a desmoplastic fibrous tissue reaction (Fig XIII-13). Tumor cells may be

□ Well differentiated, forming keratin and easily recognizable as squamous

□ Moderately differentiated

□ Poorly differentiated, requiring ancillary studies to confirm the nature of the neoplasm

The presence of intercellular bridges between tumor cells should be sought when the diagnosis is in question. Perineural and lymphatic space invasion may be present and should be reported when identified microscopically. Regional lymph node metastasis is reported to occur in from 1% to 21% of patients with eyelid squamous cell carcinoma.

FIG XIII-13—*Top right,* Squamous cell carcinoma. *Below,* Note the tumor cells invading into the dermis. *Bottom right,* Keratin is produced in this well-differentiated squamous cell carcinoma.

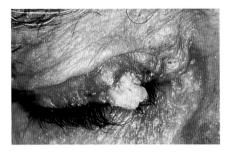

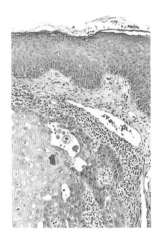

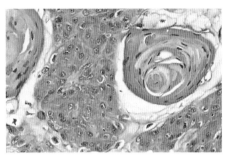

Basal cell carcinoma is by far the most common malignant neoplasm of the eyelids, accounting for more than 90% of all eyelid malignancies. As with squamous cell carcinoma, exposure to sunlight is a risk factor. Lesions typically occur on the face, and the lower eyelid is more commonly involved than the upper. Tumors in the medial canthal area are more likely to be deeply invasive and involve the orbit. The classic description is that of a "rodent" ulcer, that is a slowly enlarging ulcer with pearly, raised, rolled edges. The morpheaform, or fibrosing, basal cell carcinoma, however, is a flat or slightly depressed pale yellow indurated plaque; this type is often infiltrative, and its extent is difficult to determine clinically (Fig XIII-14). Other growth patterns include nodular and multicentric.

As the name implies, basal cell carcinomas originate from the stratum basale, or stratum germinativum, of the epidermis. Tumor cells are characterized by relatively bland, monomorphous nuclei and a high nuclear-to-cytoplasmic ratio; anaplastic features and abnormal mitotic figures are uncommon. Basal cell carcinoma forms cohesive nests with nuclear palisading of the peripheral cell layer (Fig XIII-15). A helpful diagnostic feature, albeit a presumed artifact of tissue processing, is the characteristic cleftlike separation of the tumor from its surrounding stroma. Basal cell carcinomas may exhibit a variety of cytologic and architectural patterns, including squamous (metatypical), sebaceous, adenoid, and cystic differentiation. Fibrosing basal cell carcinomas are almost always undifferentiated.

Complete excision is the treatment of choice. Multicentric and fibrosing basal cell carcinomas require frozen-section examination of surgical margins or Mohs' micrographic surgical technique for adequate excision. Morbidity in basal cell carcinomas is almost always the result of local spread; metastatic spread is extremely unusual.

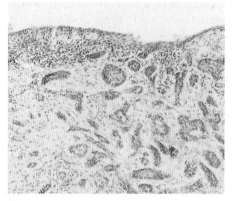

FIG XIII-14—Basal cell carcinoma, morpheaform (sclerosing) type. There are thin strands and cords of tumor cells in a fibrotic (desmoplastic) dermis.

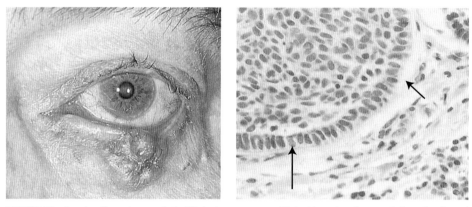

FIG XIII-15—Basal cell carcinoma. *Left,* Clinical appearance. *Right,* Note the characteristic palisading of the cells around the outer edge of the tumor (long arrow) and the artifactitious separation between the nest of tumor cells and the dermis (cracking artifact, short arrow).

Dermal Neoplasms

Capillary hemangiomas are common in the eyelids of children. They usually present at or shortly after birth as a red-purple nodule that may exhibit slow but worrisome growth over weeks to months. Spontaneous involution, however, is the rule, and lesions usually disappear by school age. Intervention is reserved for those lesions that diminish vision through proptosis or astigmatism, promoting amblyopia. The histopathologic appearance is dependent on the stage of evolution of the hemangioma. Early lesions may be very cellular with solid nests of plump endothelial cells and correspondingly little vascular luminal formation. Established lesions typically show well-developed flattened endothelium-lined capillary channels in a lobular configuration. Involuting lesions demonstrate increased fibrosis and hyalinization of capillary walls with luminal occlusion.

Appendage Neoplasms

Sebaceous carcinoma most commonly involves the upper eyelid of elderly persons. It may originate in the meibomian glands of the tarsus, the glands of Zeis in the skin of the eyelid, or the sebaceous glands of the caruncle. Clinical diagnosis is often missed or delayed because of its propensity to mimic a chalazion or chronic blepharoconjunctivitis (Fig XIII-16). Histopathologically, well-differentiated sebaceous carcinomas are readily identified through the microvesicular foamy nature of the tumor cell cytoplasm (Fig XIII-17). Moderately differentiated tumors may exhibit

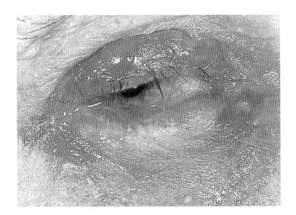

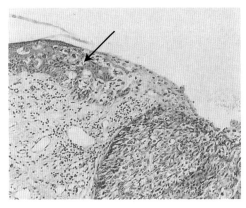

FIG XIII-16—Sebaceous carcinoma. *Top,* Note the eyelid erythema suggesting blepharitis. Note also the loss of eyelashes and the irregular eyelid thickening. *Left,* Pagetoid invasion of the epithelium by tumor cells (arrow).

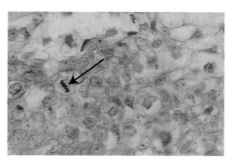

FIG XIII-17—Sebaceous carcinoma. Note the mitotic figures (arrow) and foamy cytoplasm.

some degree of sebaceous differentiation. Poorly differentiated tumors, however, may be difficult to distinguish from the other more common epithelial malignancies. The demonstration of lipid within the cytoplasm of tumor cells by special stains, such as oil red O or Sudan black, is diagnostic, but it must be performed on tissue prior to processing and paraffin embedding. Alternatively, osmium staining of tissue processed for electron microscopy will highlight intracytoplasmic lipid.

When sebaceous carcinoma is suspected clinically, the pathologist should be alerted so that frozen-section slides can be generated for lipid stains. Another feature, characteristic but not pathognomonic for sebaceous cell carcinoma, is the dissemination of individual and clusters of tumor cells within the epidermis or conjunctival epithelium known as *pagetoid spread* (see Figure XIII-16). Another pattern in the conjunctiva is that of complete replacement of conjunctival epithelium by tumor cells. A rare variant of sebaceous carcinoma involves only the epidermis and conjunctiva without demonstrable invasive tumor.

Treatment recommendations include wide local excision of nodular lesions. Large or deeply invasive tumors may require exenteration. Suboptimal cytologic preservation and difficulty in distinguishing goblet cells from pagetoid spread of tumor cells may reduce the accuracy of intraoperative frozen-section diagnosis of margins. Preoperative mapping by routine processing of multiple biopsies may afford a more accurate assessment of the extent of spread of the carcinoma. Survival rates for sebaceous carcinoma are worse than those for squamous cell carcinoma but have improved in recent years as a result of increased awareness, earlier detection, more accurate diagnosis, and appropriate treatment. Metastases first involve regional lymph nodes.

Albert DM, Jakobiec FA, eds. *Principles and Practice of Ophthalmology.* 2nd ed. Philadelphia: Saunders; 1994:1713–1823.

Melanocytic Neoplasms

Nevocellular nevi occur commonly on the eyelids, and they may be visible at birth (congenital nevi) or become apparent in adolescence or adulthood. Congenital nevi are often larger than those appearing in later years, sometimes reaching substantial size. Nevi greater than 20 cm in dimension are referred to as *giant congenital melanocytic nevi.* The risk for development of melanoma in congenital nevi is pro-

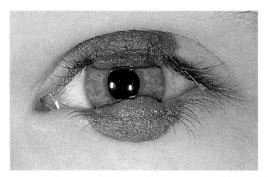

FIG XIII-18—Congenital split, or "kissing," nevus of the eyelid.

portional to the size of the nevus; close follow-up and/or excision of congenital nevi is warranted. Congenital melanocytic nevi in the eyelid may develop in utero prior to the separation of the upper and lower eyelids and result in the clinical appearance of "kissing" nevi (Fig XIII-18). Features associated with congenital nevi include the presence of nevus cells within and around adnexal structures, vessel walls, and perineurium; extension into the deep reticular dermis or subcutaneous tissue; and single- or double-file arrangement of nevus cells.

Melanocytic nevi appearing after childhood typically begin as small (less than 0.5 cm) round brown macules, gradually attaining increased thickness to become papules that may or may not be pigmented. This growth pattern corresponds to the histopathologic classification of melanocytic nevi. Macular (flat) nevi histopathologically show nests of melanocytes along the dermal–epidermal junction and are consequently termed *junctional nevi* (Fig XIII-19). A junctional nevus is clinically

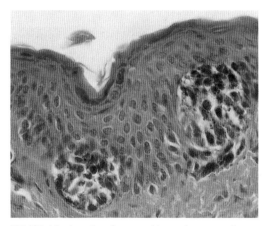

FIG XIII-19—Junctional nevus. Nests of nevus cells are seen at the junction between epidermis and dermis.

indistinguishable from an ephelis, or freckle. Histopathologically, however, an ephelis is a result of increased melanization of basal keratinocytes, without proliferation or aggregation of melanocytes. As the junctional nests, or theques, of the nevus begin to migrate into the superficial dermis, the nevus becomes a dome-shaped, or papillomatous, papule. When both a junctional and an intradermal component are present, the histopathologic classification becomes a *compound nevus* (Fig XIII-20). Finally, the junctional component disappears, leaving only nevus cells within the dermis, and the classification accordingly becomes *intradermal nevus* (Fig XIII-21).

An evolution in cytomorphology of the nevus cells also takes place: those in the superficial portion of the nevus are polygonal, or epithelioid, in shape (type A nevus cells). Within the midportion of the nevus the cells become smaller with less cytoplasm and resemble lymphocytes (type B nevus cells). At the deepest levels the nevus cells become spindled and appear similar to Schwann cells of peripheral nerves (type C nevus cells). Recognition of this "maturation" is useful in classifying melanocytic neoplasms as benign. Other histopathologic criteria favoring a benign melanocytic process include the following:

- Absence of intraepidermal migration of nevus cells
- Absence of mitotic activity in the dermal component of the mass
- Absence of nuclear enlargement or prominent nucleoli
- Cytoplasmic melanin pigment content greatest in the superficial layers and absent in deeper layers

Multinucleated giant melanocytes and interspersed adipose tissue are common in older nevi.

Nevi that show some clinical or pathologic atypicality include *Spitz nevus* and *dysplastic nevus*. Spitz nevus develop in late childhood or in adolescence and are uncommon after the second decade. In contrast to the clinical picture of the usual nevus, they may be larger (up to 1.0 cm) and have a pink-red color. Histopathologically, they are usually compound and exhibit nuclear and cytoplasmic enlargement and pleomorphism. Other features suggesting malignancy, however, such as atypical mitotic figures, intraepidermal migration, and lack of maturation, are generally lacking.

Clinical features suggesting that a nevus may be dysplastic include size greater than 0.5 cm, irregular margins, and irregular pigmentation. Nevi are considered dysplastic when they demonstrate certain architectural and/or cytomorphologic characteristics on histopathologic examination. Architectural features include lentiginous (single cell) melanocytic hyperplasia, bridging of melanocytes across the bases of adjacent rete pegs, and lamellar fibrosis of the papillary dermis. Cytologic atypia is characterized by nuclear enlargement, hyperchromasia, and prominent nucleoli. Clinically suspicious lesions should be completely excised. Persons with multiple dysplastic nevi are at increased risk for development of melanoma and may represent a genetic susceptibility, suggesting that family members should also be examined and followed closely.

Cutaneous malignant melanoma is a rare occurrence on the eyelids. It may be associated with a preexisting nevus or may develop de novo. Clinical features suggesting malignancy are the same as mentioned above for dysplastic nevi; in addition, invasive melanoma is heralded by a vertical (perpendicular to the skin surface)

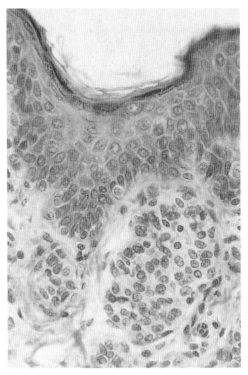

FIG XIII-20—Compound nevus. Nests of nevus cells are present in the dermis as well as at the junction of epidermis and dermis.

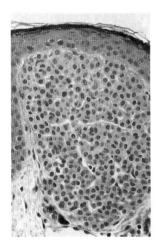

FIG XIII-21 — Intradermal nevus. The nests of nevus cells are confined to the dermis.

growth phase that results in an elevated or indurated mass. There are four main histopathologic subtypes of malignant melanoma:

- Superficial spreading
- Lentigo maligna
- Nodular
- Acral-lentiginous

Superficial spreading is the most common type of cutaneous melanoma and demonstrates a radial (intraepidermal) growth pattern extending beyond the invasive component, distinguishing it from nodular melanoma. Lentigo maligna melanoma occurs on the face of elderly individuals, with a long preinvasive phase (lentigo maligna) prior to the development of invasion. Acral-lentiginous melanoma, as the name implies, involves the extremities and is not seen in the eyelid.

Histopathologic features characteristic of melanoma include pagetoid intraepidermal spread of atypical melanocytic nests and single cells, nuclear abnormalities as listed above, lack of maturation in the deeper portions of the mass, and atypical mitotic figures. A bandlike lymphocytic host response along the base of the mass is more common in melanoma than in benign proliferations, with the exception of halo nevus. Prognosis is correlated with depth of invasion in stage I (localized) disease. Metastases, when they occur, typically involve regional lymph nodes first.

McLean IW, Burnier MN, Zimmerman LE, et al. *Tumors of the Eye and Ocular Adnexa.* Washington: Armed Forces Institute of Pathology; 1994.

Spencer WH, ed. *Ophthalmic Pathology: An Atlas and Textbook.* 4th ed. Philadelphia: Saunders; 1996:2263–2277.

CHAPTER XIV

Orbit

Topography

Bony Orbit, Soft Tissues

Seven bones form the boundaries of the orbit, all of them thick except those forming the medial and inferior walls, which are easily eroded and fractured. These seven bones are

- Frontal
- Zygomatic
- Palatine
- Lacrimal
- Sphenoid
- Ethmoid
- Maxillary

The orbital cavity is pear shaped with a volume of 30 cc. Other elements occupying the cavity are the following:

- Globe
- Lacrimal gland
- Muscles
- Tendons
- Fat
- Fascia
- Vessels
- Nerves
- Sympathetic ganglia
- Cartilaginous trochlea

Inflammatory and neoplastic processes that increase the volume of the orbital contents lead to *proptosis* (protrusion) of the globe and/or *displacement* (deviation) from the horizontal or vertical position. The degree and direction of ocular displacement help to localize the position of the mass. The term *exophthalmos* denotes endocrine dysfunction.

The *lacrimal gland* is situated anteriorly in the superotemporal quadrant of the orbit. The gland is divided into orbital and palpebral lobes by the aponeurosis of the levator palpebrae superioris muscle. The acini of the glands are composed of low cuboidal epithelium. The ducts, which lie within the fibrovascular stroma, are lined by low cuboidal epithelium with a second outer layer of low flat myoepithelial cells.

BCSC Section 2, *Fundamentals and Principles of Ophthalmology*, covers orbital anatomy in Part 1, Anatomy. BCSC Section 7, *Orbit, Eyelids, and Lacrimal System*, also discusses orbital anatomy, as well as the conditions covered in the following pages, in detail.

Congenital Anomalies

Dermoid and Other Epithelial Cysts

Dermoid cysts are believed to arise as embryonic epithelial nests that became entrapped during embryogenesis. They may protrude through the frontozygomatic suture to take a dumbbell shape. Most manifest in childhood as a mass in the superotemporal quadrants of the orbit. Rupture of cyst contents may produce a marked granulomatous reaction. Histologically, dermoid cysts are encapsulated, lined by keratinized stratified squamous epithelium. The cysts contain keratin and hair, and the walls of the cysts are lined with adnexal structures including sebaceous glands, hair roots, sweat glands, and even lacrimal glands (Fig XIV-1). If the wall does not bear adnexal structures, the term *epidermal cyst* is applied. Intraorbital cysts may also be lined by respiratory epithelium or conjunctival epithelium.

Inflammations

Infectious

Bacterial infections   The causes of bacterial infections of the orbit include bacteremia, trauma, retained surgical hardware, and adjacent sinus infection. Infection may involve a variety of genera including *Haemophilus influenzae, Streptococcus, Staphylococcus (S aureus), Clostridium,* Bacterioides, *Klebsiella,* and *Proteus.* Histologically, acute inflammation, necrosis, and abscess formation may be present. Tuberculosis rarely involves the orbit; it produces a granulomatous reaction.

Fungal and parasitic infections   A common fungal infection of the orbit is caused by sinus infection from mucormycosis (zygomycosis). Poorly controlled diabetes

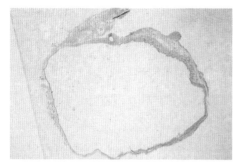 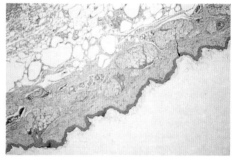

FIG XIV-1—Photomicrographs show a dermoid cyst surrounded by stratified squamous epithelium. The wall of the cyst contains sebaceous glands and adnexal structures.

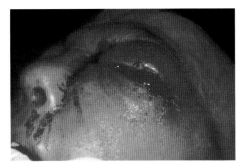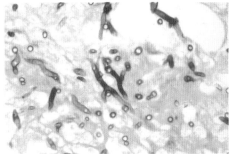

FIG XIV-2—*Aspergillus* infections of the orbit generally produce severe insidious orbital inflammation. Microscopic sections demonstrate the branching hyphal structure on silver stains.

can make patients particularly prone to mucormycosis, although any immunocompromised condition may increase susceptibility. Histologically, acute and chronic inflammation appear in a background of necrosis, often with histiocytes. Broad, nonseptated hyphae may be identified in PAS or GMS stains.

Aspergillus infection of the orbit may occur in immunocompromised or otherwise healthy individuals. Often the symptoms are slowly progressive and insidious, producing a sclerosing granulomatous disease. *Aspergillus* has often been difficult to culture but may be observed in tissue as septated hyphae with 45°-angle branching (Fig XIV-2). Despite aggressive surgical therapy and adjunctive therapy with amphotericin B, extension into the brain may be fatal with orbital infections of both *Aspergillus* and mucormycosis. Allergic fungal sinusitis has also been noted to extend into the orbit in some instances.

Parasitic infections of the orbit are rare and may be produced by *Echinoccocus*, *Taenia solium* (cysticercosis), *Onchocerca volvulus* (onchocerciasis), and *Loa loa* (loiasis). These infections are mostly seen in patients who come from or have traveled to endemic areas.

Noninfectious

Thyroid orbitopathy   Also known as *Graves disease* and *thyroid ophthalmopathy*, this condition is related to thyroid dysfunction and is the most common cause of unilateral or bilateral proptosis (exophthalmos) in the adult. A cellular infiltrate of mononuclear cells, lymphocytes, plasma cells, mast cells, and fibroblasts involves the interstitial tissues of the extraocular muscles, most commonly the inferior and medial rectus muscles (Fig XIV-3). The muscles appear firm and white, and the tendons are usually not involved. The fibroblasts produce mucopolysaccharide, which leads to an increased water content of the tissues. As a result of the increased bulk, the optic nerve is compromised at the orbital apex and papilledema may result. Progressive fibrosis results in restriction of ocular movement, and exposure keratitis is

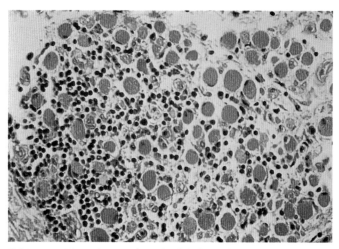

FIG XIV-3—Graves disease (thyroid ophthalmopathy or orbitopathy). The muscle bundles of the extraocular muscle are separated by fluid, accompanied by an infiltrate of mononuclear inflammatory cells. The inflammatory process expands the volume of the muscles, potentially causing proptosis and, in extreme cases, corneal exposure.

also a complication. BCSC Section 1, *Update on General Medicine,* discusses thyroid disease in greater detail.

Albert DM, Jakobiec FA, eds. *Principles and Practice of Ophthalmology.* 2nd ed. Philadelphia: Saunders; 1994:2937-2951.

Idiopathic orbital inflammation, orbital inflammatory syndrome (sclerosing orbitis)

This clinicopathologic entity refers to a space-occupying inflammatory disorder that simulates a neoplasm (i.e., a pseudotumor) but has no recognizable cause of infection or inflammation such as Graves disease or ruptured epidermal inclusion cyst. This disorder accounts for about 5% of orbital lesions. Clinically, patients have an abrupt course and usually complain of pain. The condition may affect children as well as adults. The inflammatory response may be diffuse or compartmentalized: when localized to an extraocular muscle, the condition is called *orbital myositis* (Fig XIV-4); when localized to the lacrimal gland, it is frequently called *sclerosing dacryoadenitis.*

In the early stages inflammation predominates with a polymorphous inflammatory response (eosinophils, neutrophils, plasma cells, lymphocytes, and macrophages) that is often perivascular and frequently infiltrates muscle and produces fat necrosis. In later stages fibrosis is the predominant feature, often with interspersed lymphoid follicles bearing germinal centers. The fibrosis may inexorably replace orbital fat and encase extraocular muscles and the optic nerve (Fig XIV-5). The majority of patients with early idiopathic orbital inflammation respond promptly to corticosteroids, while patients with the advanced stages of fibrosis may be unresponsive.

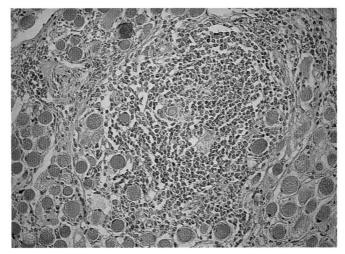

FIG XIV-4—Orbital pseudotumor (idiopathic orbital inflammation). In this case an inflammatory infiltrate involves extraocular muscle. In contrast to Graves disease, where the tendons of the muscles are spared, orbital pseudotumor can inflame any orbital structure, including the muscle tendons.

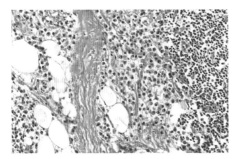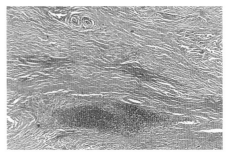

FIG XIV-5—Idiopathic orbital inflammation. *Left,* Note the mixture of inflammatory cells in the bundle of collagen running through the orbital fat. *Right,* Diffuse fibrosis dominates the histologic picture of this sclerosing pseudotumor, considered by some authorities to represent a later stage of the condition illustrated on the left.

Degenerations

Amyloid

Amyloid deposition of the orbit occurs in primary systemic amyloidosis, involving extraocular muscles and nerves to produce ophthalmoplegia and ptosis. Amyloidosis may also be localized within the orbit with no systemic manifestations. Histologic sections stained with Congo red dye show deposits of a hyalinized amorphous

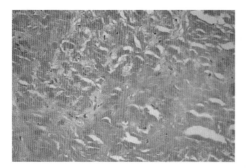 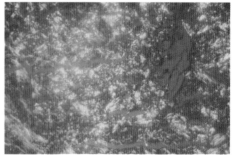

FIG XIV-6—Photomicrographs show the tissue infiltration by pink amorphous material in a case of orbital amyloidosis *(left). Right,* Polarized light of Congo red–stained section demonstrates red-green dichroism.

material that exhibits green-red dichroism with polarized light (Fig XIV-6). Electron microscopy demonstrates characteristic fibrils. BCSC Section 8, *External Disease and Cornea,* discusses both systemic and localized amyloidosis in greater detail.

Neoplasia

Neoplasms of the orbit may be primary, secondary from adjacent structures, or metastatic. The incidence of primary neoplasms is low, hemangioma and lymphoma being the most common of this type. Secondary tumors from adjacent sinuses are slightly more common than primary tumors.

In children approximately 90% of orbital tumors are benign and 10% are malignant. Most benign lesions are cystic (dermoid or epidermoid cysts), and most malignant tumors are rhabdomyosarcomas. The orbit may be involved secondarily by retinoblastoma, neuroblastoma, or leukemia/lymphoma.

Lacrimal Gland Neoplasia

Benign mixed tumor (pleomorphic adenoma)   This term describes the most common epithelial tumor of the lacrimal gland. Initially, the tumor is encapsulated, and it grows slowly by expansion. This progressive expansile growth may indent the bone of the lacrimal fossa, producing excavation of this area. Tumor growth stimulates the periosteum to deposit a thin layer of new bone (cortication). The adjacent orbital bone is not eroded. Typically, the patient experiences no pain. This tumor is more common in men than women, and the median age is 34 years.

The histologic appearance of benign mixed tumor, as the name implies, is a mixture of epithelial and stromal elements. The epithelial component may form nests or tubules lined by two layers of cells, the outermost layer blending imperceptibly with the stroma (Fig XIV-7). The stroma may appear myxoid and contain heterologous elements, including cartilage and bone. Although the tumor may appear to be encapsulated, microscopic lobules can prolapse through the capsule, which is formed by the compression of adjacent normal orbital tissue and is not an anatomic barrier cleanly separating the tumor from the adjacent orbit.

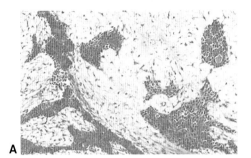

FIG XIV-7—*A*, Benign mixed tumor (pleomorphic adenoma) of the lacrimal gland. Note both the epithelial and the mesenchymal elements in this tumor. *B*, Low power shows the circumscribed nature of this benign mixed tumor. *C*, Well-differentiated glandular structures (epithelial component).

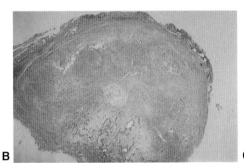

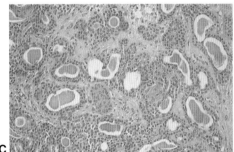

Although benign mixed tumor is a benign neoplasm, tumor left behind in the orbit after incomplete surgical removal may produce clinically significant recurrences that are difficult to extirpate surgically. The possibility of orbital recurrence leads to two important surgical principles:

☐ Try to excise the tumor with a rim of normal orbital tissue and don't merely shell it out

☐ Avoid incisional biopsies into this tumor to prevent seeding of the orbit

Adenocarcinoma, including adenoid cystic carcinoma, may arise in long-standing and recurrent benign mixed tumors.

Spencer WH, ed. *Ophthalmic Pathology: An Atlas and Textbook*. 4th ed. Philadelphia: Saunders; 1996:2484-2494.

Adenoid cystic carcinoma As mentioned above, this adenocarcinoma can arise in benign mixed tumor or de novo in the lacrimal gland. Unlike benign mixed tumor, adenoid cystic carcinoma is not encapsulated; tends to erode the adjacent bone; and invades nerves, accounting for the pain that is a frequent presenting complaint. Grossly, the appearance is grayish white, firm, and nodular. Histologically, a variety of patterns may appear, including the swiss cheese (cribriform) pattern (Fig XIV-8). Other histologic patterns include basaloid (solid), comedo, sclerosing, and tubular. Presence of the basaloid pattern has been associated with a worse prognosis (5-year survival of 21%) than those tumors without a basaloid component (5-year survival of 71%). Because of the diffuse infiltration of this tumor, exenteration may be recommended, often with removal of adjacent bone. Despite aggressive surgical intervention, the long-term prognosis is poor.

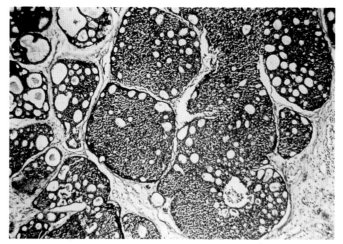

FIG XIV-8—Adenoid cystic carcinoma of the lacrimal gland. Note the characteristic swiss cheese arrangement of tumor cells.

Font RL, Smith SL, Bryan RG. Malignant epithelial tumors of the lacrimal gland: a clinicopathologic study of 21 cases. *Arch Ophthalmol.* 1998; 116:613–616.

Lymphoproliferative Lesions

Most classifications of lymphoid lesions have been based on lymph node architecture, and such nodal classifications have been difficult to apply to so-called extranodal lymphoid lesions. There are no lymph nodes in the orbit, and therefore it is problematic to classify these lesions by the same criteria used for lymph nodes. In general, lymphoid lesions of the orbit may be considered a spectrum from reactive to malignant in which absolute distinctions frequently become blurred.

Reactive lymphoid hyperplasia   Mature lymphocytes, admixed with plasma cells and histiocytes, appear together with capillary hyperplasia and plump endothelial cells. Irregularly shaped follicles contain a center of macrophages and large lymphocytes with mitotic figures. Surrounding these collections is a zone of small lymphocytes (Fig XIV-9).

Malignant lymphoma   Malignant lymphomas of the orbit may be a presenting manifestation of systemic lymphomas, or they may arise primarily from the orbit. Incidence of orbital involvement in systemic lymphomas is 1.3%. Hodgkin disease is exceedingly rare in the orbit, and the majority of primary malignant orbital lymphomas are non-Hodgkin lymphomas of diffuse architecture that mark immunophenotypically as B cells (Fig XIV-10). Only 15% of primary orbital lymphomas show a follicular growth pattern.

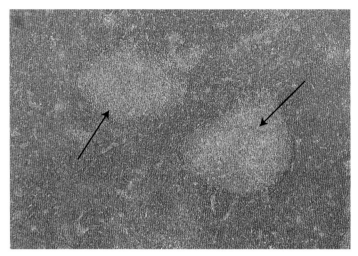

FIG XIV-9—Note the well-demarcated germinal centers (arrows) in this case of benign reactive lymphoid hyperplasia.

The classifications for non-Hodgkin lymphomas are controversial and continue to evolve. The current Revised European-American Lymphoma (REAL) classification reflects attempts to include extranodal lymphomas. However, the categories in this scheme have not been extensively tested for reproducibility or prognosis in orbital lesions. Much of the data predicting prognosis for specific types of orbital lymphomas were collected prior to the REAL classification and its concepts.

Harris NL, Jaffe ES, Stein H, et al. A revised European-American classification of lymphoid neoplasms: a proposal from the International Lymphoma Study Group. *Blood.* 1994;84:1361–1392.

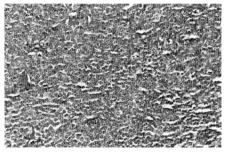

FIG XIV-10—B-cell lymphoma of the orbit. Orbital soft tissues are diffusely replaced by sheets of cytologically malignant lymphocytes.

The most commonly encountered low-grade orbital lymphomas in the REAL classification include B-cell chronic lymphocytic leukemia (CLL) type, and marginal zone or mucosa-associated lymphoid tissue (MALT) lymphoma. The lymphomas of the CLL type are composed of homogeneous sheets of small, mature-appearing lymphocytes. The MALT lymphomas often show poorly formed follicles with heterogeneous cellular composition including small atypical cells with cleaved nuclei, monocytoid cells, small lymphocytes, and plasma cells. The neoplastic monocytoid B-cell population may expand the marginal zone and infiltrate follicles. MALT lymphomas are characterized by a B cell immunophenotype that is CD5 and CD10 negative. See also BCSC Section 9, *Intraocular Inflammation and Uveitis,* Part 1, Immunology.

High-grade lymphomas of the orbit in the REAL classification include large cell lymphoma, lymphoblastic lymphoma, and Burkitt lymphoma. With the exception of Burkitt lymphoma, orbital lymphoma is not likely to occur in children, although leukemic infiltrates and so-called granulocytic sarcoma are encountered in children.

In many cases of lymphoid orbital tumors, up to 50% in some series, the pathologic studies are indeterminant. A similar incidence of systemic lymphoma (35%) has been reported for lymphoid hyperplasia and B-cell lymphoma, so differentiation may not be clinically critical (Fig XIV-11).

Neither immunophenotypic nor gene rearrangement studies to identify clonal lymphocyte populations have thus far been shown to be helpful in predicting the development of systemic disease. Location is one factor that may have a bearing on prognosis; conjunctival lesions have a better prognosis than orbital lesions. Eyelid lesions may have the highest association with systemic lymphoma (67%).

It is important for the ophthalmologist to distinguish orbital lymphoproliferative lesions from orbital inflammatory syndrome. Unlike patients with orbital inflammatory syndrome, patients with orbital lymphoproliferative lesions present with a gradual painless progression of proptosis. Every patient with an orbital lymphoprolifera-

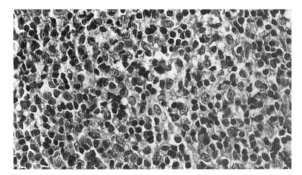

FIG XIV-11—Cytologically, this lesion falls between reactive lymphoid hyperplasia and lymphoma. Cells resembling plasma cells (plasmacytoid cells) are identified. In this type of tumor immunohistochemistry and molecular pathology studies may be helpful in determining whether the tumor is polyclonal or monoclonal.

tive lesion must be investigated for evidence of systemic lymphoma, including a complete blood count (CBC) and differential, examination for lymphadenopathy and imaging of thoracic and abdominal viscera. A bone marrow biopsy is preferred to an aspirate because it includes bone spicules; the presence of a paratrabecular lymphoid infiltrate may indicate systemic lymphoma. In contrast to most cases of idiopathic orbital inflammation, which are treated with corticosteroids, lymphoid lesions confined to the orbit are treated with radiation. Typically, patients with lymphoid hyperplasia receive 1500–2000 centigrays (cGy), and those who have B-cell lymphoma receive 2000–3000 cGy.

The ophthalmologist taking a biopsy of an orbital or conjunctival lymphoproliferative lesion should consult with the pathologist to determine the optimal method for handling the tissue. Fresh (unfixed) tissue is preferred for touch preparations, immunohistochemistry, flow cytometry, and gene rearrangement studies. The type of fixative used for permanent sections varies from one laboratory to another. Exposure of the biopsy specimen to air for long periods of time should be avoided. It is very important that the tissue be handled gently; crush artifact can prevent the pathologist from rendering a diagnosis.

Albert DM, Jakobiec FA, eds. *Principles and Practice of Ophthalmology.* 2nd ed. Philadelphia: Saunders; 1994:2005–2016.

Vascular Tumors

Lymphangiomas occur in children and are characterized by fluctuation in proptosis. Lymphangiomas of the orbit are unencapsulated, diffusely infiltrating tumors that feature lymphatic vascular spaces and well-formed lymphoid aggregates in a fibrotic interstitium (Fig XIV-12).

Hemangioma in the adult is encapsulated and consists of cavernous spaces *(cavernous hemangioma)* with thick, fibrosed walls (Fig XIV-13). Vessels may show thrombosis and calcification. Hemangioma in the child is unencapsulated, more cellular, and composed of capillary-sized vessels *(capillary hemangioma)* (Fig XIV-14).

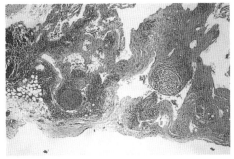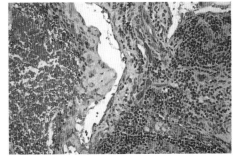

FIG XIV-12—Photomicrograph shows numerous vascular channels with a fibrotic interstitium. Higher magnification demonstrates the lymphocytes and plasma cells within the fibrous walls.

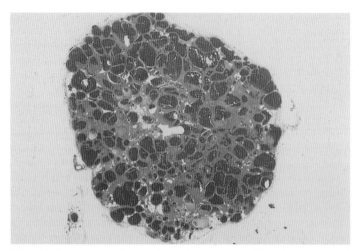

FIG XIV-13—Cavernous hemangioma. Large spaces of blood are separated by thick septa.

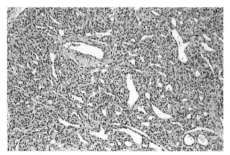

FIG XIV-14—Capillary hemangioma. Note the small capillary-sized vessels and the proliferation of benign endothelial cells.

Hemangiopericytoma occurs mainly in adults (median age 42 years) and manifests with proptosis, pain, diplopia, and decreased visual acuity. Histologically, a staghorn vascular pattern is displayed with densely packed oval to spindle-shaped cells. The reticulin stain is useful to demonstrate tumor cells that are individually wrapped in a network of collagenous material (Fig XIV-15). Hemangiopericytomas include a spectrum of benign, intermediate, and malignant lesions. Features of malignancy include an infiltrating border, anaplasia, mitotic figures, and necrosis. However, these features may be absent in tumors that eventually metastasize.

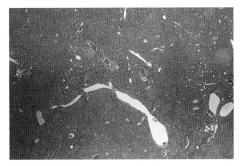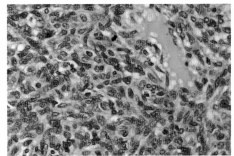

FIG XIV-15—Photomicrographs demonstrate a dense spindle cell tumor with a branching vascular pattern characteristic of hemangiopericytoma. Higher magnification demonstrates closely packed round to oval cells with vesicular nuclei.

Tumors with Muscle Differentiation

Rhabdomyosarcoma This is the most common primary malignant orbital tumor of childhood (average age of onset 7–8 years). Proptosis is often sudden and rapidly progressive, and it requires emergency treatment. Reddish discoloration of the eyelids is *not* accompanied by local heat or systemic fever as it is in cellulitis. Orbital rhabdomyosarcomas are classified slightly differently and have a better prognosis (5-year survival overall of 92%) than their extraorbital counterparts.

Three histologic types of orbital rhabdomyosarcoma are recognized (Fig XIV-16):

☐ Embryonal (the most common)

☐ Alveolar

☐ Differentiated

Embryonal rhabdomyosarcoma may develop in the conjunctiva and present as grapelike submucosal clusters *(botryoid variant)*. Histologically, spindle cells are arranged in a loose syncytium with occasional cells bearing cross-striations, which are found in about 60% of embryonal rhabdomyosarcomas. Well-differentiated rhabdomyosarcomas feature numerous cells with striking cross-striations. Immunohistochemical reactivity for desmin and muscle-specific actin may be identified. Electron microscopy is often helpful, especially in the less well differentiated cases of embryonal rhabdomyosarcoma, to demonstrate the typical sarcomeric banding pattern. See also BCSC Section 6, *Pediatric Ophthalmology and Strabismus.*

Leiomyomas and leiomyosarcomas Tumors with smooth muscle differentiation are rare. *Leiomyomas* are benign tumors that typically manifest with slowly progressive proptosis in patients in the fourth and fifth decades. Histologically, these spindle cell tumors show blunt-ended cigar-shaped nuclei and trichrome-positive filamentous cytoplasm. *Leiomyosarcomas* are malignant lesions, typically occurring in patients in the seventh decade. Histologically, more cellularity, necrosis, pleomorphism, and mitotic figures appear than in the leiomyoma.

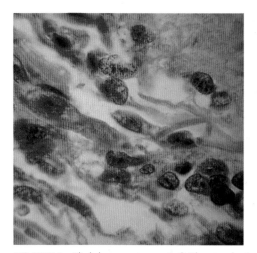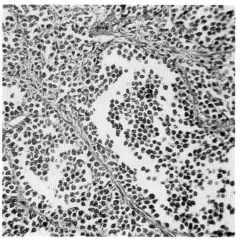

FIG XIV-16—Rhabdomyosarcoma. *Left,* The neoplastic cells tend to differentiate toward muscle cells. In this moderately differentiated embryonal example, cross-striations representing Z-bands of actin-myosin complexes within the cytoplasm can be easily identified. It is more common for these cells to be more primitive with a featureless abundant cytoplasm. In the less differentiated cases, electron microscopy and immunohistochemistry may be necessary to correctly identify this neoplasm. *Right,* Poorly cohesive rhabdomyoblasts separated by fibrous septa into "alveoli" are low-magnification histologic features of the alveolar variant of rhabdomyosarcoma. This variant may have a less favorable natural history than the more common embryonal type.

Tumors with Fibrous Differentiation

Fibrous histiocytoma (fibroxanthoma) is one of the most common mesenchymal tumors of the orbit in adults. The median age at presentation is 43 years with a range of 6 months to 85 years, and the upper nasal orbit is the most common site. Most fibrous histiocytomas are benign. The tumor is composed of an admixture of histiocytes and fibroblasts, some of which form a cartwheel (storiform) pattern (Fig XIV-17). Although most are benign, intermediate and malignant varieties do exist.

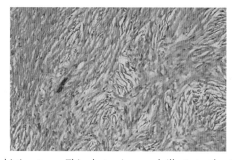

FIG XIV-17—Fibrous histiocytoma. This photomicrograph illustrates the storiform (cartwheel or matlike) pattern.

Malignant tumors are identified by a high rate of mitotic activity (more than one mitotic figure per high-power field), pleomorphism, and necrosis. Other primary tumors of fibrous connective tissue include nodular fasciitis, fibroma, solitary fibrous tumor, and fibrosarcoma.

Fibrous dysplasia of bone may be monostotic or polyostotic. When the orbit is affected, the condition is usually monostotic and the patient often presents during the first three decades of life. The tumor may cross suture lines to involve multiple orbital bones. Narrowing of the optic canal and lacrimal drainage system can occur. Plain radiographic studies show a ground-glass appearance with lytic foci. Cysts containing fluid also appear. As a result of arrest in the maturation of bone, trabeculae are composed of woven bone with a fibrous stroma that is highly vascularized rather than lamellar bone. The bony trabeculae often have a C-shaped appearance.

Katz BJ, Nerad JA. Ophthalmic manifestations of fibrous dysplasia: a disease of children and adults. *Ophthalmology.* 1998;105:2207–2215.

Juvenile ossifying fibroma, a variant of fibrous dysplasia, is characterized histologically by spicules of bone rimmed by osteoblasts. At low magnification ossifying fibroma may be confused with a psammomatous meningioma. The inexperienced histologist can find the correct identification difficult.

Osseous and cartilaginous tumors are rare; of these, *osteoma* is the most common. It is slow growing, well circumscribed, and composed of mature bone. Most commonly, osteoma arises from the frontal sinus. Other primary tumors in this group include

☐ Osteoblastoma

☐ Giant cell tumor

☐ Chondroma

☐ Ewing sarcoma

☐ Osteogenic sarcoma

☐ Chondrosarcoma

Nerve Sheath Tumors

The *neurofibroma* is the most common of the nerve sheath tumors. This is a slow-growing tumor that includes an admixture of endoneural fibroblasts, Schwann cells, and axons. Neurofibromas may be circumscribed but are not encapsulated. The consistency is firm and rubbery. Microscopically, the spindle-shaped cells are arranged in ribbons and cords in a matrix of myxoid tissue and collagen that contains axons.

Isolated neurofibromas do not necessarily indicate systemic involvement, but the plexiform type of neurofibroma is associated with neurofibromatosis, or von Recklinghausen disease type 1 (Fig XIV-18).

Neurilemoma (Schwannoma) arises from Schwann cells. Slow growing and encapsulated, it may be solitary or associated with neurofibromatosis. The yellowish tumor may show cysts and areas of hemorrhagic necrosis. Two histologic patterns appear microscopically: Antoni-A spindle cells are arranged in interlacing cords, whorls, or palisades; and Verocay bodies, or collections of cells, resemble sensory corpuscles (Fig XIV-19). Antoni-B tissue is made up of stellate cells with a mucoid stroma. Vessels are usually prominent and thick walled, and no axons are present.

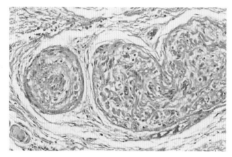

FIG XIV-18—Plexiform neurofibroma. The trunk of the nerve is enlarged by proliferation of endoneural fibroblasts and Schwann cells. Axons may be demonstrated within the lesion.

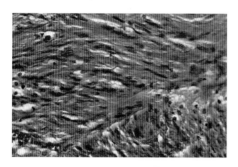

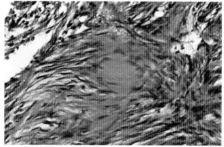

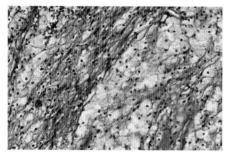

FIG XIV-19—Neurilemoma (Schwannoma). *Upper left,* This is the Antoni-A pattern. Spindle cells are packed together, and palisading of nuclei may be seen. *Right,* The palisading of nuclei may form a Verocay body. *Lower left,* The Antoni-B pattern represents degeneration within the tumor. The histologic structures are loosely teased apart.

Adipose Tumors

Lipomas are rare in the orbit. Pathologic characteristics include encapsulation and a distinctive lobular appearance. Because lipomas are histologically difficult to distinguish from normal or prolapsed fat, the incidence may have been previously overestimated.

Liposarcomas are malignant tumors that are extremely rare in the orbit. Histologic criteria depend on the type of liposarcoma, but the unifying diagnostic feature is the presence of lipoblasts. These tumors tend to recur before they metastasize.

Metastatic Tumors

Secondary tumors are those that invade the orbit by direct extension from adjacent structures such as sinus, bone, or eye. Metastatic tumors are those that spread from a primary site such as breast in women and prostate in men. In the child a neuroblastoma is the most common primary site.

McLean IW, Burnier MN, Zimmerman LE, et al. *Tumors of the Eye and Ocular Adnexa.* Washington: Armed Forces Institute of Pathology; 1994:215–298.

CHAPTER XV

Optic Nerve

Topography

The optic nerve, embryologically derived from the optic stalk, is a continuation of the optic tract; thus, the pathology of the optic nerve reflects that of the central nervous system (CNS). Running 35–55 mm in length, the optic nerve extends from the eye to the optic chiasm (Fig XV-1). Its axons originate from the retinal ganglion cell layer and have a myelin coat posterior to the lamina cribrosa. The intraocular portion is 0.7–1.0 mm in length, the intraorbital portion 25–30 mm, and the intracanalicular portion 4–10 mm. The diameter is 3.0–3.5 mm, tapering to 1.5 mm in the scleral canal.

Oligodendrocytes, astrocytes, and microglial cells are glial cells (*glia* = glue). Oligodendrocytes produce and maintain the myelin that sheaths the optic nerve. Myelinization stops at the lamina cribrosa (Fig XV-2). Occasionally, aberrant patches of myelin are seen in the nerve fiber layer of the retina as discrete, flat, feathery white patches. Astrocytes are involved with support and nutrition. Microglial cells (CNS histiocytes) have a phagocytic function.

The coat of meninges includes the dura mater, which merges with the sclera; the cellular arachnoid layer; and the vascular pia. Arachnoid cells may lie in nests that can contain corpora aranacia; these nests are most obvious in young patients. The pial vessels extend into the optic nerve and subdivide the nerve fibers into fascicles. The subarachnoid space, which contains cerebrospinal fluid (CSF), ends blindly at the termination of the meninges (Fig XV-3).

FIG XV-1—Low-power photomicrograph shows the relationship of the optic nerve to the eye and extraocular muscle.

FIG XV-2—Photomicrograph shows the termination of myelinated axons at the lamina cribrosa.

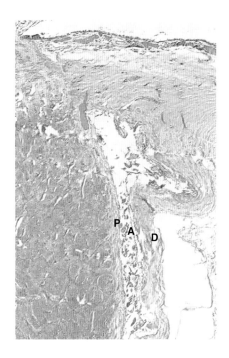

FIG XV-3—Normal optic nerve. The dura mater (D) is continuous with the sclera anteriorly. Note the arachnoid (A) and the pia (P).

Blood supply to different portions of the optic nerve comes from a variety of sources. The ophthalmic artery comes through the pia and supplies the intraorbital and intraocular portion. In general, the periaxial fibers are supplied by the pial vessels and the axial fibers by the central retinal artery, which passes directly through the subarachnoid space to the nerve. The vein, however, is oblique and has a variable course.

BCSC Section 2, *Fundamentals and Principles of Ophthalmology,* discusses and illustrates the anatomy of the optic nerve. Section 5, *Neuro-Ophthalmology,* also covers the physiology and pathology of the optic disc and optic nerve.

Congenital Anomalies

Pits

Optic nerve head pits presumably arise as defects in closure of the fetal fissure. Pits usually appear temporally and are associated with field defects, serous retinal detachments, and occasionally colobomas in the fellow eye. Loss of retinal ganglion cells and nerve fibers occurs in the region of the pit, and meningeal cysts have been described in association with closed pits.

Colobomas

Colobomas of the optic nerve head result from failure of closure of the fetal fissure. Optic nerve head colobomas are located inferior to the nerve head and are associated with colobomas of the retina, choroid, ciliary body, and iris. Cystic outpouchings in the sclera may produce a cyst lined by degenerated choroid and gliotic retina (microphthalmos with cyst).

Inflammations

Infectious

Infections of the optic nerve may be secondary to bacterial and mycotic infections of adjacent anatomic structures such as the eye, brain, or sinus, or they may occur as part of a systemic infection, particularly in the immunosuppressed patient. Fungal infections include mucormycosis, cryptococcosis, and coccidioidomycosis. Mucormycosis generally results from contiguous sinus infection. Cryptococcosis results from direct extension along the CNS and often produces multiple foci of necrosis with little inflammatory reaction. Coccidioidomycosis produces necrotizing granulomas.

Viral infections of the optic nerve are usually associated with other CNS lesions. Multiple sclerosis and acute disseminated myelitis produce loss of myelin early, but initially the axons are undamaged so that visual function may return. The damaged myelin is removed by macrophages (Fig XV-4). Astrocytic proliferation then occurs to produce a glial scar, which is known as a *plaque.*

Noninfectious

Noninfectious inflammatory disorders of the optic nerve include giant cell arteritis and sarcoidosis. *Giant cell arteritis* may produce granulomatous mural inflammation and occlusion of posterior ciliary vessels with liquefactive necrosis of the optic nerve.

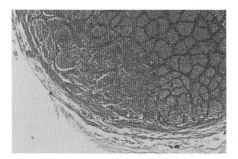 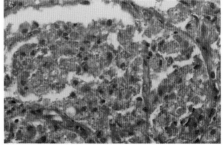

FIG XV-4—Multiple sclerosis, optic nerve. *Left,* Luxol-fast blue stain, counterstained with H&E. The blue-staining area indicates normal myelin. Note the absence of myelin in the lower left corner of the optic nerve, corresponding to a focal lesion. *Right,* Higher magnification. The blue material (myelin) is engulfed by macrophages.

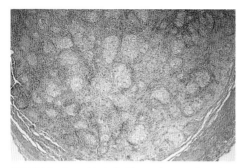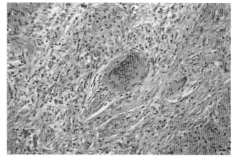

FIG XV-5—Sarcoid. *Left,* Photomicrograph at low power of the optic nerve with discrete noncaseating granuloma. *Right,* Higher magnification. Multinucleated giant cells are featured in the granulomas.

Sarcoidosis of the optic nerve is often associated with retinal, vitreal, and uveitic lesions (Fig XV-5; see also Figure XII-7). Unlike the characteristic noncaseating granulomas in the eye, the optic nerve lesions may feature necrosis.

Degenerations

Optic Atrophy

Loss of retinal ganglion cells because of glaucoma or infarction results in degeneration of their axons and is known as *ascending atrophy. Descending atrophy* results from pathology within the cranial cavity or orbit. Axonal degeneration is accompanied by loss of myelin and oligodendrocytes. The optic nerve shrinks despite the proliferation of astrocytes, and thickened pial strands result from proliferation of connective tissue (Fig XV-6).

The portion of the optic nerve nearer the lateral geniculate body is described as *central,* and the portion nearer the retina is described as *peripheral.* Injury to the retina or to any peripheral portion of the optic nerve results in rapid ascending atrophy of the central portion. Initially, the axons at the peripheral portion swell. Retrograde degeneration of the axons then occurs with loss of retinal ganglion cells.

Cavernous optic atrophy of Schnabel is characterized microscopically by large cystic spaces containing mucopolysaccharide material, which stains with alcian blue, posterior to the lamina cribrosa (Fig XV-7). The intracystic material is thought to be vitreous that penetrates into the parenchyma through the internal limiting membrane of the optic nerve head. These changes occur most commonly in patients with glaucoma after acute rises in IOP, but they have also been seen in nonglaucomatous elderly patients with generalized arteriosclerotic disease.

Albert DM, Jakobiec FA, eds. *Principles and Practice of Ophthalmology.* 2nd ed. Philadelphia: Saunders; 1994:2529-2534.

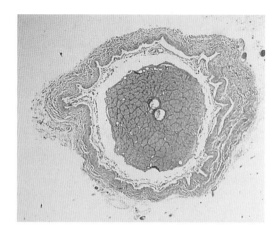

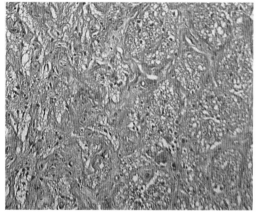

FIG XV-6—Atrophic optic nerve. *Top,* Low magnification. Note the widened subdural space. *Bottom,* High magnification shows changes in the dura mater, arachnoid, and pia.

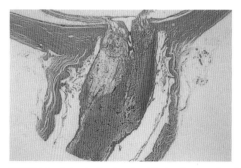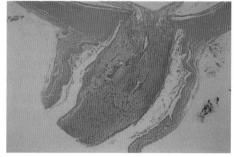

FIG XV-7—Schnabel's atrophy. Photomicrographs show cystic atrophy within the optic nerve. The cystic space is filled with alcian blue staining material.

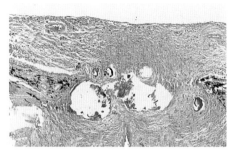

FIG XV-8—Drusen of the optic nerve head. Note the local zones of calcification just anterior to the lamina.

Drusen

Drusen of the optic disc consist of hyaline-like calcified material within the nerve substance (Fig XV-8). They are usually bilateral and may be complicated by neovascularization and hemorrhage. They are thought to result from intracellular mitochondrial calcification within the axons. Optic disc drusen may produce field defects, and their presence can cause enlargement of the papilla that may be mistaken for papilledema.

Giant drusen are associated with the phakomatoses such as tuberous sclerosis and neurofibromatosis, which are considered to be hamartomatous proliferations of astrocytes with secondary calcification. (See BCSC Section 6, *Pediatric Ophthalmology and Strabismus,* for further discussion of the phakomatoses.) Giant drusen lie anterior to the lamina cribrosa.

Optic disc drusen may be associated with acquired disease such as angioid streaks, papillitis, optic atrophy, chronic glaucoma, and vascular occlusions. They may occur in otherwise normal eyes and are occasionally dominantly inherited.

Spencer WH, ed. *Ophthalmic Pathology: An Atlas and Textbook.* 4th ed. Philadelphia: Saunders; 1996:537–541.

Neoplasia

Tumors may affect the optic nerve head (e.g., melanocytoma, peripapillary choroidal melanoma, pigment epithelium proliferation, hemangioma) or the retrobulbar portion of the optic nerve (e.g., glioma, meningioma).

Melanocytoma

This benign, deeply pigmented melanocytic tumor is situated eccentrically on the disc, projecting for less than 2 mm into the vitreous and extending into the lower temporal retina and posteriorly beyond the lamina (Fig XV-9). Slow growth may occur. A bleached section shows closely apposed, plump cells of uniform character with abundant cytoplasm and small nuclei with little chromatin. Nucleoli are small and regular.

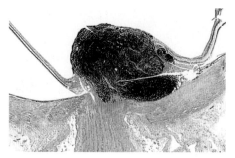

FIG XV-9—Melanocytoma of the optic nerve. The choroid adjacent to the optic nerve is also involved by this tumor. The cells of the tumor are so densely packed with melanin that the cytologic detail is not visible without higher magnification and melanin bleaching.

Gliomas

These tumors may arise in any part of the visual pathway, including the optic disc and nerve. The most common cell of origin is the spindle-shaped or hairlike (pilocytic) astrocyte (juvenile pilocytic astrocytoma) (Fig XV-10, upper left and right). Optic nerve gliomas are frequently associated with neurofibromatosis (NF-1), an autosomal dominant disorder with the gene, a tumor suppressor, located on the long arm of chromosome 17q11. The tumors most commonly present in the first decade and are of low grade.

Enlarged, deeply eosinophilic cell processes known as *Rosenthal fibers* may be found in these low-grade tumors (Fig XV-10, lower left). Foci of microcystic degeneration and calcification may occur, and the pial septa are thickened. The meninges show a reactive hyperplasia with proliferation of spindle-shaped meningeal cells and infiltration with astrocytes. The dura mater remains intact so the nerve appears tubular or sausage shaped. Some evidence indicates that these tumors may show slow, progressive growth.

High-grade tumors (glioblastoma multiforme) rarely involve the optic nerve. When this does occur, the optic nerve is usually involved secondarily from a brain tumor.

Meningioma

The majority of orbital meningiomas, which arise from arachnoid cells, are extensions of intracranial meningioma (secondary type). Those that arise primarily within the orbit are less common; of these, most arise within the arachnoid of the optic nerve (Fig XV-11, upper left and right). Extradural tumors that arise from ectopic meningothelial cells, within the muscle cone or at the roof or orbital floor, are rare.

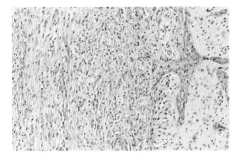

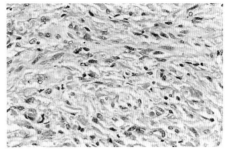

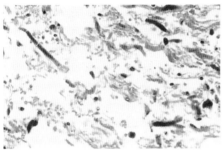

FIG XV-10—Astrocytoma of the optic nerve. *Upper left,* The right side of this photograph demonstrates normal optic nerve, and the left side shows a pilocytic astrocytoma. *Right,* The neoplastic glial cells are elongated to resemble hairs (hence the *pilocytic* in the name). *Lower left,* Degenerating eosinophilic filaments known as *Rosenthal fibers* are not unique to astrocytoma of the optic nerve.

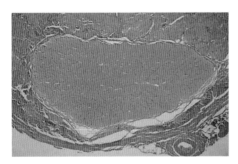

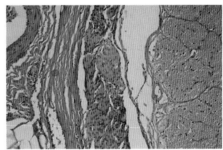

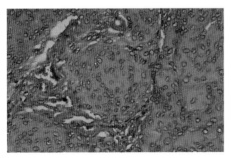

FIG XV-11—Meningioma of the optic nerve. *Upper left,* This meningioma has grown circumferentially around the optic nerve and has compressed the nerve. *Right,* Meningioma of the optic nerve originates from the arachnoid. *Lower left,* Note the whorls of tumor cells, characteristic of the meningothelial type of meningioma, the most common histologic variant arising from the optic nerve.

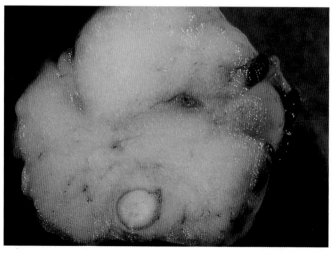

FIG XV-12—Optic nerve meningioma. The shaggy border of this gross specimen emphasizes the tendency of the perioptic meningioma to invade surrounding orbital tissues.

The mean age at presentation of primary meningioma is lower than that of the secondary type (20% are less than 10 years of age). Tumor growth is slow. Primary optic nerve meningiomas may invade the nerve and the eye and may extend through the dura mater to invade muscle (Fig XV-12).

Microscopically, the tumor (primary or secondary) is usually of the meningotheliomatous type with plump cells arranged in whorls (Fig XV-11, lower left). Psammoma bodies tend to be sparse. Patient survival is longer (up to 19 years) with primary orbital meningiomas than with those of secondary type (up to 15 years). Although the meningioma may rarely be associated with neurofibromatosis in the younger age group, it is a less frequent hallmark of NF-1 than is optic nerve glioma.

Albert DM, Jakobiec FA, eds. *Principles and Practice of Ophthalmology.* 2nd ed. Philadelphia: Saunders; 1994:2359–2370.

PART 2

INTRAOCULAR TUMORS: CLINICAL ASPECTS

CHAPTER XVI

Introduction to Part 2

Intraocular tumors comprise a broad spectrum of benign and malignant lesions that can lead to loss of vision and loss of life. Effective management of these lesions depends on accurate diagnosis. In most cases experienced ophthalmologists diagnose intraocular neoplasms by clinical examination and ancillary diagnostic tests. For example, investigators in the Collaborative Ocular Melanoma Study (COMS) have reported a misdiagnosis rate of less than 0.2%. The incidence of clinically missed intraocular tumors reported by ophthalmic pathology laboratories also appears to be decreasing. Although intraocular tumors may be evaluated with fine-needle aspiration biopsy (FNAB), the indications for this technique are limited; moreover, FNAB of intraocular tumors such as retinoblastoma may result in orbital seeding of tumor. FNAB is discussed in greater detail in chapter IV; see pp 42–44.

Important new information is available concerning the most common primary intraocular malignancies: choroidal melanoma in adults and retinoblastoma in children. The major clinical trial mentioned above, the COMS, was funded in 1985 and has completed patient accrual into both the medium and large tumor trials and the small tumor observational study. Survival data from the large tumor trial and small tumor observational study have been reported. A multicenter randomized clinical trial to evaluate management of presumed small choroidal melanoma is anticipated.

The predisposing gene for retinoblastoma has been isolated, cloned, and sequenced. The first multicenter randomized trial in retinoblastoma has been funded by the National Cancer Institute to evaluate the application of combined systemic chemotherapy and local treatments on intraocular retinoblastoma.

Chang M, Zimmerman LE, McLean IW. The persisting pseudomelanoma problem. *Arch Ophthalmol.* 1984;102:726–727.

The Collaborative Ocular Melanoma Study Group. Accuracy of diagnosis of choroidal melanomas in the Collaborative Ocular Melanoma Study: COMS report no. 1. *Arch Ophthalmol.* 1990;108:1268–1273.

Shields JA, Shields CL. *Intraocular Tumors: A Text and Atlas.* Philadelphia: Saunders; 1992.

ACKNOWLEDGMENTS

The authors acknowledge the contributions of Drs. Andrew Schachat, David Abramson, and Robert Folberg, who were responsible for the previous editions of the following chapters. Their work established a framework for the significant revisions included within this updated volume. Ingrid U. Scott, MD, MPH, Assistant Professor of Ophthalmology, Bascom Palmer Eye Institute, was instrumental in the final revision and review of the present text.

CHAPTER XVII

Melanocytic Tumors

Iris Nevus

Iris nevus generally appears as a darkly pigmented lesion of the iris stroma with minimal distortion of the iris architecture (Fig XVII-1). The true incidence of iris nevi remains uncertain, as many of these lesions produce no symptoms and are incidentally recognized during routine ophthalmic examination. Iris nevi may present in two forms:

☐ Circumscribed iris nevus: typically nodular, involving a discrete portion of the iris

☐ Diffuse iris nevus: may involve an entire sector or, rarely, the entire iris

In some cases the lesion causes slight ectropion iridis and sector cataract. The incidence of iris nevi may be higher in the eyes of patients with neurofibromatosis, although no convincing evidence suggests an increased incidence of iris nevi in eyes containing a posterior uveal malignant melanoma.

Iris nevi are best evaluated by slit-lamp biomicroscopy coupled with gonioscopic evaluation of the angle structures. Specific attention should be given to lesions involving the angle structures to assure that a previously unrecognized ciliary body lesion is not present. The most important possibility in the differential diagnosis is iris melanoma. When iris melanoma is included within the differential, close observation with scheduled serial reevaluation is indicated. Iris nevi usually require no treatment once the diagnosis is made, but they should be followed closely and photographed to evaluate for growth.

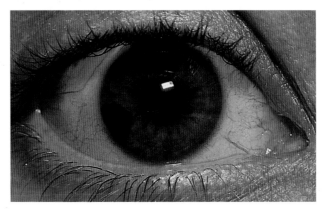

FIG XVII-1—Iris nevus, clinical appearance. The lesion is only slightly raised from the iris surface, and lesion color is homogeneous brown.

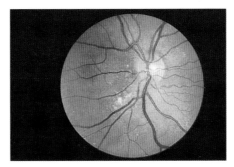

FIG XVII-2—Choroidal nevus, clinical appearance. Note the rather indistinct margins and surface drusen.

Nevus of the Ciliary Body or Choroid

Nevi of the ciliary body are occasionally incidental findings in globes that are enucleated for other reasons. Choroidal nevi may occur in up to 7% of the population. Often they are not associated with clinical symptoms and become recognized on routine ophthalmic examination. The typical choroidal nevus appears ophthalmoscopically as a flat or minimally elevated brown choroidal lesion with indistinct margins (Fig XVII-2). Some nevi are amelanotic and may be less apparent. Choroidal nevi can have overlying RPE disturbance, serous detachment, drusen, choroidal neovascular membranes, and orange pigment; they may produce visual field defects. On fluorescein angiography choroidal nevi may either hypofluoresce or hyperfluoresce, depending on the associated findings. Ocular and oculodermal melanocytosis may predispose to uveal malignancy, with 4.6% of reported cases of nevus of Ota showing ocular melanoma development.

Choroidal nevi are distinguished from choroidal melanomas by clinical evaluation and ancillary testing. No single clinical factor is pathognomonic for benign versus malignant choroidal melanocytic lesions. The differential diagnosis for melanocytic lesions most commonly includes the following:

☐ Malignant melanoma

☐ Atypical disciform scar associated with age-related macular degeneration (AMD)

☐ Suprachoroidal hemorrhage

☐ Congenital hypertrophy of the retinal pigment epithelium (CHRPE)

☐ Choroidal hemangioma

☐ Melanocytoma

☐ Metastatic carcinoma

☐ Choroidal osteoma

Virtually all choroidal melanocytic tumors thicker than 3 mm are melanomas, and virtually all choroidal melanocytic lesions thinner than 1 mm are nevi. Many lesions 1–3 mm in thickness (apical height) may be benign, although the risk of malignancy increases with height. It is rarely possible to classify tumors 1–3 mm in thickness with certainty. Flat lesions with a maximum basal diameter of 10 mm or less are almost always benign. The risk of malignancy increases for lesions that are larger than 10 mm in basal diameter.

Clinical risk factors for enlargement have been well characterized and include the following:

- Presence of orange pigmentation
- Associated subretinal fluid
- Increased size at presentation
- Juxtapapillary location
- Absence of drusen or RPE changes
- Subjective clinical symptoms

If definite enlargement is documented, malignant change should be suspected.

The recommended management of choroidal nevi is photographic documentation and/or clinical drawings for lesions <1 mm in thickness and photographic and ultrasonographic documentation of lesions >1 mm in thickness coupled with regular, periodic reassessment for signs of growth. The small tumor observational study within the COMS is aimed at determining the appropriateness of immediate versus delayed treatment for suspected small choroidal melanomas.

Melanocytoma of the Ciliary Body or Choroid

Melanocytomas of the ciliary body or choroid are rare, but they may appear as elevated pigmented tumors simulating a nevus or melanoma. Melanocytomas have been reported to undergo malignant change in some instances. When a melanocytoma is suspected, photographic and echographic studies are appropriate. If growth is documented, the lesion should be treated as a malignancy. Pathologically, melanocytoma cells are distinct with a characteristic large, polyhedral shape, small nuclei, and cytoplasm filled with melanin granules (see Figure XV-9).

Iris Melanoma

Iris melanomas account for fewer than 10% of all intraocular melanomas. Small malignant melanomas of the iris may be impossible to differentiate clinically from benign iris nevi and other simulating lesions. The following conditions may be included in a differential diagnosis of iris melanoma:

- Iris nevus
- Primary iris cyst (pigment epithelial and stromal)
- Essential iris atrophy
- Iris foreign body
- Peripheral anterior synechiae
- Metastatic carcinoma to iris
- Aphakic iris cyst
- Iris atrophy, miscellaneous
- Pigment epithelial hyperplasia or migration
- Juvenile xanthogranuloma
- Medulloepithelioma
- Retained lens material simulating iris nodule

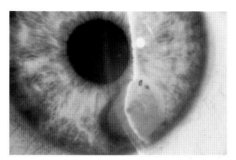

FIG XVII-3—Melanoma of the iris exhibits prominent vascularity.

Signs suggestive of malignancy include extensive ectropion iridis, prominent vascularity, sector cataract, secondary glaucoma, seeding of the peripheral angle structures, extrascleral extension, lesion size, and documented progressive growth. Iris melanomas range in appearance from amelanotic to dark brown lesions, and three quarters of them will be found to involve the inferior iris (Fig XVII-3). In rare instances they assume a diffuse growth pattern, producing a syndrome of unilateral acquired hyperchromic heterochromia and secondary glaucoma. Clinical evaluation is identical to that for iris nevi. Table XVII-1 and Figures XVII-4a–4h describe and illustrate the various iris nodules. See also Figure XII-9, p 162.

Recent advances in high-resolution ultrasonography allow for excellent characterization of tumor size and anatomic relationship to normal ocular structures. Fluorescein angiography may document intrinisic vascularity, although this is of limited value in the determination of a differential diagnosis. Rarely, when the management of the lesion is in question, FNAB may be considered. In most cases, when growth or severe glaucoma occurs, diagnostic and therapeutic excisional treatment is indicated. Brachytherapy using custom-designed plaques may be employed in select instances. The prognosis for most patients with iris melanomas is excellent with a lower mortality than ciliary body and choroidal melanoma, possibly because the biological behavior of most of these iris tumors appears distinctly different from ciliary or choroidal melanoma.

Augsburger JJ, Schroeder RP, Territo C, et al. Clinical parameters predictive of enlargement of melanocytic choroidal lesions. *Br J Ophthalmol.* 1989;73:911–917.

Butler P, Char DH, Zarbin M, et al. Natural history of indeterminate pigmented choroidal tumors. *Ophthalmology.* 1994;101:710–716.

The Collaborative Ocular Melanoma Study Group. Factors predictive of growth and treatment of small choroidal melanoma: COMS report no. 5. *Arch Ophthalmol.* 1997; 115:1537–1544.

Gass JD. Observation of suspected choroidal and ciliary body melanoma for evidence of growth prior to enucleation. *Ophthalmology.* 1980;87:523–528.

Shields CL, Shields JA, Kiratli H, et al. Risk factors for growth and metastasis of small choroidal melanocytic lesions. *Ophthalmology.* 1995;102:1351–1361.

TABLE XVII-1

DIFFERENTIAL DIAGNOSTIC FEATURES OF IRIS NODULES
(alphabetical list)

LESION	FEATURES
Down syndrome (Brushfield spots) (Fig XVII-4a)	Wolfflin (1902)—elevated white to light yellow spots in periphery of iris, 10–20 per eye. Brushfield (1924) noted association with Down syndrome. Incidence in Down syndrome is 85%; otherwise, 24% (Donaldson 1961). Histopathologically, the spots are areas of relatively normal iris stroma surrounded by a ring of mild iris hypoplasia. Anterior border layer slightly increased in density.
Epithelial invasion, serous cyst, solid or pearl cyst, implantation membrane	Each follows surgery or injury. Appears as serous or solid cysts in continuity with the wound or as implantation cysts or membranes on the anterior iris surface.
Foreign body retained	Usually becomes secondarily pigmented and may be associated with chronic iridocyclitis and peripheral anterior synechiae.
Fungal endophthalmitis	Irregular yellow-white mass on iris. May be accompanied by hypopyon or only mild inflammatory signs.
Iridocyclitis	The iris nodules of classic granulomatous anterior uveitis occur either superficially or deeply within the iris. Koeppe's nodules occur at the pupillary border, and Busacca's nodules lie upon the anterior iris surface. Microscopically, they are composed of large and small mononuclear cells.
Iris freckle (Fig XVII-4b)	Stationary, lightly to darkly pigmented flat areas on the anterior iris surface composed of anterior border layer melanocytes containing increased pigmentation without increase in number of melanocytes.
Iris nevus (Fig XVII-1)	Discrete mass(es) or nodule(s) on anterior iris surface. Variable pigmentation. Composed of benign nevus cells. Increased incidence of iris nevi in patients with neurofibromatosis.
Iris nevus syndrome (Cogan-Reese)	Acquired diffuse nevus of iris associated with unilateral glaucoma, heterochromia, peripheral anterior synechiae, and extension of endothelium and Descemet's membrane over trabecular meshwork. Obliteration of normal iris architecture. (See ICE syndrome, p 81.)
Iris pigment epithelial cysts (Figs XVII-4c, 4d)	Cysts encompassing both layers of neuroepithelium. Produce a localized elevation of stroma and may be pigmented. May transilluminate. May be better seen after dilation. B-scan ultrasonography of value in diagnosis.
Iris pigment epithelial proliferation	Congenital or acquired (trauma or surgery) plaques of pigment epithelium displaying a black, velvety appearance.
Juvenile xanthogranuloma	Yellowish to gray, poorly demarcated iris lesions associated with raised orange skin lesion(s) (single or multiple) appearing in the first year of life. May be associated with spontaneous hyphema and secondary glaucoma. Histopathologically, there is a diffuse granulomatous infiltrate with lipid-containing histiocytes and Touton giant cells. The lesions regress spontaneously. May also be found in ciliary body, anterior choroid, episclera, cornea, eyelids, and orbit.
Leiomyoma	May be well localized and even pedunculated, often diffuse and flat, and usually lightly pigmented. Electron microscopy required for clear differentiation between leiomyoma and amelanotic spindle cell melanoma.

TABLE XVII-1

DIFFERENTIAL DIAGNOSTIC FEATURES OF IRIS NODULES (continued)
(alphabetical list)

LESION	FEATURES
Leukemia (Figs XVII-4e, 4f)	Very rare nodular or diffuse milky lesions with intense hyperemia. Iris usually loses its architecture, becomes quite thickened along with the development of heterochromia. Pseudohypopyon common.
Malignant melanoma (Fig XVII-3)	Occurring as nodular or flat growths usually in the periphery, especially inferiorly or inferotemporally. Variably pigmented, often with satellite pigmentation and pigmentation in the anterior chamber angle and nutrient vessels. Pupil may dilate irregularly, and elevated intraocular tension may be present.
Tapioca melanoma	Tapioca-like nodules lying over a portion or all of the iris. May be translucent to lightly pigmented in color. Often associated with unilateral glaucoma.
Melanocytosis, congenital ocular and oculodermal	Generally unilateral with diffuse uveal nevus causing heterochromia iridis associated with blue or slate gray patches of sclera and episclera. In oculodermal melanocytosis, there is also eyelid and brow involvement. Malignant potential exists.
Metastatic carcinoma	Gelatinous to white vascularized nodules on the anterior iris surface and in the anterior chamber angle. Associated with anterior uveitis, hyphema, rubeosis, and glaucoma.
Neurofibromatosis (von Recklinghausen disease) (Fig XVII-4g)	Multiple lesions varying from tan to dark brown and about the size of a pinhead. May be flat or project from the surface. Histopathologically, they are composed of collections of nevus cells.
Retinoblastoma (Fig XVII-4h)	White foci upon the anterior iris surface, in the anterior chamber angle, or a pseudohypopyon.

FIG XVII-4a-h—Iris nodules.

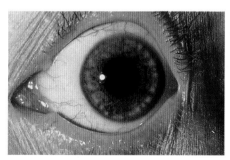

FIG XVII-4a: Brushfield spots. (Photograph courtesy of WR Green, MD.)

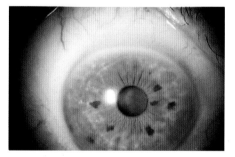

FIG XVII-4b: Iris freckles.

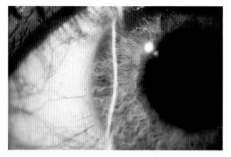

FIG XVII-4c: Pigment epithelial cyst. Prior to dilation the iris stroma is bowed forward in the area of the cyst, which is invisible posteriorly.

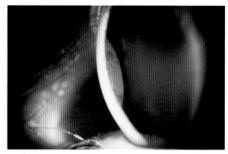

FIG XVII-4d: Pigment epithelial cyst. After dilation the cyst of the posterior iris epithelium can be seen.

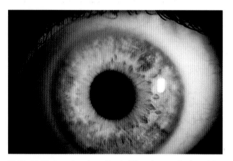

FIG XVII-4e: Leukemic infiltration of the iris. Note heterochromia, prominent vascularity, and stromal thickening.

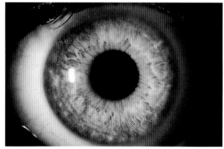

FIG XVII-4f: Normal fellow eye in leukemia.

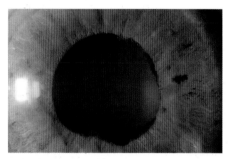

FIG XVII-4g: Neurofibromatosis. Note presence of multiple small iris nodules.

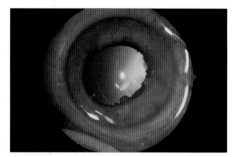

FIG XVII-4h: Retinoblastoma. Diffuse iris involvement with white tumor. (Photograph courtesy of JA Shields, MD, and JJ Augsburger, MD.)

Shields JA, Sanborn GE, Augsburger JJ. The differential diagnosis of malignant melanoma of the iris: a clinical study of 200 patients. *Ophthalmology.* 1983;90:716–720.

Spencer WH, ed. *Ophthalmic Pathology: An Atlas and Textbook.* 4th ed. Philadelphia: Saunders; 1996:1607–1621.

Sumich P, Mitchell P, Wang JJ. Choroial nevi in a white population: The Blue Mountains Eye Study. *Arch Ophthalmol.* 1998;116:645–650.

Melanoma of the Ciliary Body or Choroid

Choroidal/ciliary body melanoma is the most common primary intraocular tumor in adults. The incidence in the United States is approximately 6–7 cases per million. The tumor, extremely rare in children, primarily affects patients in their early 60s, although a bimodal distribution with involvement in the third decade is also noted. The tumor has a predilection for lightly pigmented individuals. Risk factors have not been conclusively identified but may include

☐ Genetic predisposition (dysplastic nevus syndrome)

☐ Ocular melanocytic conditions such as melanosis oculi and oculodermal melanocytosis

☐ Light-colored irides

☐ Cigarette smoking

Ciliary body melanomas can be asymptomatic in their early stages because of their hidden location behind the iris; by the time of detection they may have become rather large. When patients do present with symptoms, they most commonly note visual loss, photopsias, or visual field alterations. Ciliary body melanomas are not usually visible unless the pupil is widely dilated (Fig XVII-5, upper left). Some erode through the iris root into the anterior chamber and eventually become visible on external examination or with gonioscopy. Other tumors extend directly through the sclera in the ciliary region, producing a dark epibulbar mass. The initial sign of a ciliary body melanoma may be dilated episcleral sentinel vessels in the quadrant of the tumor (Fig XVII-5, right). The tumor may eventually become quite large, producing a sectoral or diffuse cataract, subluxated lens (Fig XVII-5, lower left), secondary glaucoma, retinal detachment, and even iris neovascularization. Rarely, a ciliary body melanoma assumes a diffuse growth pattern and extends 180°–360° around the ciliary body. This type of melanoma is referred to as a *ring melanoma* (see Figure XII-18, p 167).

The typical *choroidal melanoma* is a brown, elevated, dome-shaped subretinal mass (Fig XVII-6, left). The degree of pigmentation ranges from dark brown to totally amelanotic. With time many tumors erupt through Bruch's membrane to assume a mushroomlike cross-sectional shape (Fig XVII-6, right). Prominent clumps of orange pigment at the RPE level may appear over the surface of the tumor, as well as serous detachment of the sensory retina. If extensive retinal detachment develops, anterior displacement of the lens–iris diaphragm and secondary angle-closure glaucoma occasionally occur. Neovascularization of the iris may also appear in such eyes, and spontaneous hemorrhage into the subretinal space may occur. Vitreous hemorrhage is usually seen only in cases when the melanoma has erupted through Bruch's membrane.

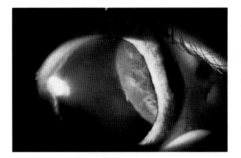

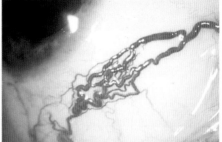

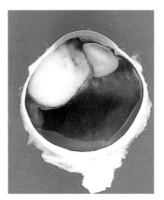

FIG XVII-5—*Upper left,* Ciliary body melanoma, clinical appearance. Such tumors may not be evident unless the pupil is widely dilated. *Right,* Sentinel vessels. *Lower left,* Ciliary body melanoma, gross pathology. Note mostly amelanotic appearance of this tumor, which is subluxing the lens and causing secondary angle closure.

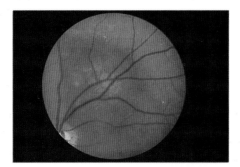

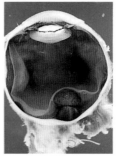

FIG XVII-6—*Left,* Small choroidal melanoma, clinical appearance. Note clumps of orange pigment on the tumor surface. *Right,* Choroidal melanoma, gross pathology. Note the mushroom-shaped cross-sectional contour of this darkly pigmented tumor and the associated retinal detachment.

Cutler SJ, Young JL, eds. Third national cancer survey: incidence data. *National Cancer Institute Monograph 14.* Washington, DC: National Institutes of Health; 1975.

Gallagher RP, Elwood JM, Rootman J, et al. Risk factors for ocular melanoma: Western Canada Melanoma Study. *J Natl Cancer Inst.* 1985;74:775–778.

Mahoney MC, Burnett WS, Majerovics A, et al. The epidemiology of ophthalmic malignancies in New York State. *Ophthalmology.* 1990;97:1143–1147.

Scotto J, Fraumeni JF Jr, Lee JA. Melanomas of the eye and other noncutaneous sites: epidemiologic aspects. *J Natl Cancer Inst.* 1976;56:489–491.

Seddon JM, Gragoudas ES, Glynn RJ, et al. Host factors, UV radiation, and risk of uveal melanoma: a case-control study. *Arch Ophthalmol.* 1990;108:1274–1280.

Wilkes SR, Robertson DM, Kurland LT, et al. Incidence of uveal malignant melanoma in the resident population of Rochester and Olmsted County, Minnesota. *Am J Ophthalmol.* 1979;87:639–641.

Diagnostic Testing

Clinical evaluation of all suspected posterior uveal melanomas, of the ciliary body and the choroid, should include an extensive history, ophthalmoscopic evaluation, and ancillary testing to definitively establish the diagnosis. The tests described below, when applied appropriately, will allow for accurate diagnosis of melanocytic tumors in more than 95% of cases. Atypical lesions may be characterized by several other testing modalities such as FNAB, or, when appropriate, lesions may be observed for characteristic changes in clinical behavior that will establish a correct diagnosis.

Indirect ophthalmoscopic viewing of the tumor remains the gold standard for testing. It is the single most important diagnostic technique for evaluating patients with intraocular tumors, as it provides stereopsis and a wide field of view and facilitates visualization of the peripheral fundus, particularly when used with scleral depression. Indirect ophthalmoscopy allows for an accurate clinical assessment of tumor basal dimension and apical height. It is not useful in eyes with opaque media, however, which require other diagnostic methods such as transillumination, ultrasonography, computed tomography (CT), and/or magnetic resonance imaging (MRI).

Slit-lamp biomicroscopy used in combination with *gonioscopy* offers the best method for establishing the presence and extent of anterior involvement in ciliary body tumors. In addition, the presence of sectoral cataract, secondary angle involvement, or sentinel vessel formation may be clues for the diagnosis of ciliary body tumor. Hruby, Goldmann, and other wide-field fundus lenses can be used with the slit lamp to evaluate lesions of the posterior fundus under high magnification. High-magnification fundus evaluation can delineate neurosensory retinal detachment, orange pigmentation, rupture of Bruch's membrane, intraretinal tumor invasion, and vitreous involvement. Fundus biomicroscopy with the three-mirror contact lens is useful in the assessment of lesions of the peripheral fundus.

Transillumination is often helpful in evaluating suspected ciliary body or choroidal melanomas. It is valuable in assessing the degree of pigmentation within a lesion and in determining basal diameters of anterior tumors. The shadow of a tumor is visible with a transilluminating light source, preferably a high-intensity fiberoptic device, placed either on the surface of the topically anesthetized eye in a quadrant opposite the lesion or directly on the cornea with a smooth, dark, specially designed corneal cap (Fig XVII-7).

Transillumination can also be performed with indirect ophthalmoscopy, letting the transilluminating light serve as the only source for visualization of the fundus through the dilated pupil. When this technique is used, the degree of light blocked

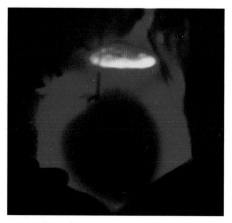

FIG XVII-7—Choroidal melanoma, transillumination shadow.

by a lesion can be measured with calipers. The approximate basal size of a pigmented ciliary body tumor can often be determined by transillumination because the intrinsic pigment of the lesion blocks light transmission. Serous ciliochoroidal detachments and amelanotic ciliary body tumors usually glow brightly in transilluminated light, and, therefore, transillumination of amelanotic melanomas is not particularly effective.

Although photographic and fluorescein angiographic studies are excellent in documenting the baseline clinical appearance of the tumor, because of the difficulty of photographing most peripheral fundus lesions, photographic studies may not be helpful in evaluating melanomas of the ciliary body. *Fundus photography* is valuable in documenting the ophthalmoscopic appearance of an intraocular tumor and in identifying interval changes in the basal size of a lesion in follow-up examinations. Wide-angle fundus photographs (60°–180°) taken during serial examinations of intraocular tumors can reveal the full extent of most lesions and document the relationship between lesions and other intraocular structures. The relative positions of retinal blood vessels can be helpful markers of changes in the size of a lesion. However, an examiner comparing serial photographs must allow for variations in film processing, the effect of serous fluid, and photographic techniques.

Fluorescein angiography is of some help in the diagnostic evaluation of intraocular tumors and simulating lesions. This technique reveals information about the vascular supply to a tumor that can be particularly helpful in determining whether the lesion is choroidal or retinal in origin. Fluorescein angiography is of greatest use in ruling out lesions that simulate choroidal melanoma. For example, in cases of choroidal or subretinal hemorrhage, diffuse hypofluorescence of the lesion may be noted along with an absence of an intrinsic vasculature. Fluorescein angiography of choroidal melanoma may show fluorescence of deep intralesional vessels during the arterial and arteriovenous phases as well as late staining of the mass. Early punctate fluorescence at the level of the RPE can have a "starry sky" appearance that may be associated with late hyperfluorescence (Fig XVII-8). Fluorescein angiography will typically not differentiate a melanoma from a large nevus, a metastatic carcinoma,

FIG XVII-8a–e—Fluorescein angiography in choroidal melanoma.

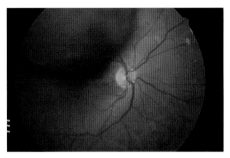

FIG XVII-8a: Large melanoma along the supero-temporal arcade.

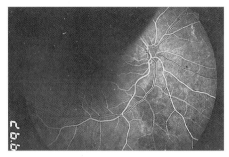

FIG XVII-8b: Usually, the degree of early hypo-fluorescence parallels the degree of pigment seen clinically. In this case early hypofluores-cence of the tumor is marked.

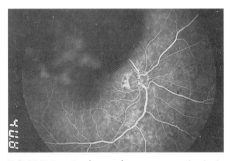

FIG XVII-8c: As the study progresses, intrinsic tumor vessels begin to leak and some hyperfluo-rescence is seen.

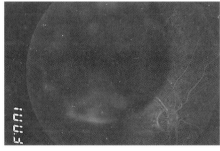

FIG XVII-8d: Hyperfluorescence in the late phases of the study is patchy.

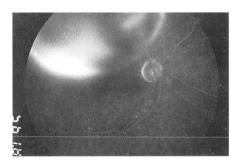

FIG XVII-8e: Approximately 5 minutes after the injection, hyperfluorescence of the tumor is dif-fuse. Melanomas almost always show some degree of late hyperfluorescence; if it is not pres-ent, the diagnosis is suspect.

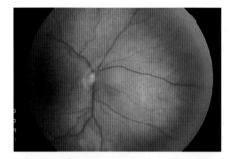

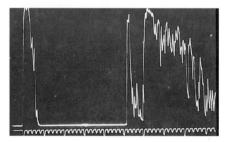

FIG XVII-9—*Upper left,* Peripapillary choroidal melanoma. *Lower left,* The peripapillary tumor is seen nasal to the optic nerve. B-scan ultrasonography is used primarily to show the tumor location and its topography. *Right,* The A-scan ultrasonogram shows characteristic low internal reflectivity. The pattern of the A-scan is used to differentiate tumor types more reliably than the B-scan pattern.

or a choroidal hemangioma. Unfortunately, no patterns of fluorescein angiography are pathognomonic of any single intraocular tumor.

Ultrasonography is the most important ancillary study in evaluating choroidal and ciliary body melanomas (Fig XVII-9). Standardized A-scan ultrasonography provides an accurate assessment of a lesion's internal reflectivity, vascularity, and measurement. Serial examination with A-scan ultrasonography can be used to document growth or regression of an intraocular tumor.

A-scan ultrasonography usually demonstrates a solid tumor pattern with high-amplitude initial echoes and low-amplitude internal reflections (low internal reflectivity). Spontaneous vascular pulsations can also be demonstrated in most cases. B-scan examination provides information about the relative size (height and basal diameters), general shape, and position of intraocular tumors. Occasionally, cross-sectional tumor shape and associated retinal detachment can be detected more easily by ultrasonography than by ophthalmoscopy. B-scan ultrasonography usually shows a dome- or mushroom-shaped choroidal mass with a highly reflective anterior border, acoustic hollowness, choroidal excavation, and occasional orbital shadowing. B-scan ultrasonography can be used to detect intraocular tumors in eyes with either clear or opaque media.

Ultrasonography is generally less satisfactory for ciliary body melanomas because the peripheral location of these tumors makes the test more difficult to perform. Although ultrasonography is generally considered highly reliable in the differential diagnosis of posterior uveal malignant melanoma, it may be difficult or impossible to differentiate a necrotic melanoma from a small subretinal hematoma or a metastatic carcinoma. Recent advances in three-dimensional ultrasound imaging may allow for better evaluation of tumor volume, and advances in high resolution imaging may be able to establish tumor microvasculature patterns predictive of tumor biology.

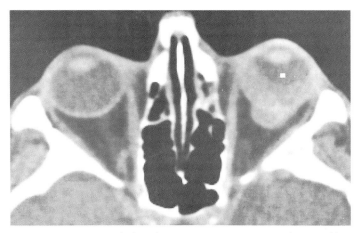

FIG XVII-10—CT scan of orbits demonstrates massive intraocular retinoblastoma with extraocular extension posteriorly in the left eye.

Perimetric evaluation, although nondiagnostic and rarely performed, may show response differences. Flat choroidal nevi rarely have overlying visual field defects, whereas elevated choroidal nevi may have relative and/or absolute defects. Testable choroidal melanomas demonstrate an absolute scotoma over the tumor and an associated relative scotoma from the serous detachment.

CT and *MRI* are two ancillary testing modalities that are not widely used in the assessment of uncomplicated intraocular melanocytic tumors. CT or MRI scans are useful for identification of tumors in eyes with opaque media and are also helpful in determining extrascleral extension and involvement of other organs (Fig XVII-10). MRI may be useful in differentiating atypical vascular lesions from melanocytic tumors.

Albert DM, Jakobiec FA, eds. *Principles and Practice of Ophthalmology.* 2nd ed. Philadelphia: Saunders; 1994:3209–3217.

Shields JA, Shields CL. *Intraocular Tumors: A Text and Atlas.* Philadelphia: Saunders; 1992.

Categorization of Posterior Uveal Melanomas

Melanomas of the choroid and ciliary body have been categorized arbitrarily by size in a number of different ways. Although a size categorization based on tumor volume is logical, no simple and reliable method for assessing tumor volume is currently available. The common practice of estimating tumor volume by multiplying maximal basal diameter, minimal basal diameter, and thickness yields only a crude assessment of actual tumor size. The most commonly employed convention for classification of posterior uveal melanomas by size is based on the simultaneous categorization of maximal basal diameter and thickness (Table XVII-2). Using this categorization, tumors can be classified as small, medium, or large. The two major

TABLE XVII-2

CATEGORIZATION OF POSTERIOR UVEAL MELANOMA BY TUMOR DIMENSION

SIZE CATEGORY	BASAL DIAMETER (mm)	THICKNESS (mm)
Small	4.0–8.0	1.0–2.4
Medium	6.0–<16.0	2.5–<10.0
Large	≥16.0	≥10.0

Modified from Shields JA. *Diagnosis and Management of Intraocular Tumors*. St. Louis: CV Mosby Co; 1983:211.

categories of the diagnostic problems for choroidal melanomas are unsuspected melanomas and pseudomelanomas.

Unsuspected melanomas are present but unrecognized clinically in a blind eye enucleated for reasons such as severe pain associated with intractable glaucoma. Several studies have indicated that an unsuspected melanoma has been found in approximately 10% of cases of this type, although these studies are outdated, and modern imaging techniques have reduced this incidence. Often in these instances opaque ocular media from advanced unilateral cataract or glaucoma have obstructed ophthalmoscopic detection of the tumor. Any patient with unexplained unilateral opaque media should be suspected of having a malignant melanoma until proven otherwise. Melanoma can be ruled out in patients with opaque media through the application of diagnostic ultrasound (in the office) or use of MRI or CT.

Pseudomelanomas are fundus lesions mistakenly diagnosed as malignant melanomas. Many eyes containing such a lesion have, historically, been enucleated when another method of management would have been preferable. Fortunately, recent reports indicate a decreasing incidence of pseudomelanomas in eyes enucleated for presumed melanoma, possibly as a result of the use of ancillary diagnostic tests, primarily ultrasonography. Improved techniques of examination—especially the use of indirect ophthalmoscopy—and greater clinical suspicion by ophthalmologists are probably even more important reasons for improved diagnosis.

Differential Diagnosis

The most common lesions that should be considered in the differential diagnosis of posterior uveal malignant melanoma include suspicious choroidal nevus, disciform macular and extramacular lesions, congenital hypertrophy of the RPE, choroidal hemangioma (see chapter XVIII), melanocytoma, hemorrhagic detachment of the choroid or RPE, metastatic carcinoma (see chapter XX and p 242 in this chapter), and choroidal osteoma. Table XVII-3 offers a more complete list.

Choroidal nevus has been discussed previously, but it should be reemphasized that no single clinical characteristic is diagnostic of choroidal melanoma. Diagnostic accuracy is associated with clinical experience and outstanding ancillary testing facilities. Evaluation and management of these complex cases within regional ocular oncology referral centers appears to enhance patient outcome.

TABLE XVII-3

Amelanotic melanoma

Choroidal metastasis

Choroidal hemangioma

Choroidal osteoma

Age-related macular or extramacular degeneration

Choroidal detachment

Uveal effusion syndrome

Posterior scleritis

Chorioretinal granuloma

Toxoplasmic retinochoroiditis

Rhegmatogenous retinal detachment

Degenerative retinoschisis

Presumed acquired retinal hemangioma

Neurilemmoma

Leiomyoma

Retinal cavernous hemangioma

Combined hamartoma of the retinal pigment epithelium

Modified from Shields JA, Shields CL. Differential diagnosis of posterior uveal melanoma. In: Shields JA, Shields CL. *Intraocular Tumors: A Text and Atlas.* Philadelphia: Saunders; 1992:137–153.

Age-related macular degeneration (AMD) may present with extramacular or macular subretinal neovascularization and fibrosis accompanied by varying degrees and patterns of pigmentation. Significantly, hemorrhage (a common finding associated with disciform lesions) is only rarely seen with melanomas, and then typically with tumors extending through Bruch's membrane. Clinical evaluation of the fellow eye is important to document the presence of age-related macular degenerative changes. Fluorescein angiography results are virtually pathognomonic, revealing early hypofluorescence secondary to blockage from the hemorrhage, often followed by late hyperfluorescence in the distribution of the choroidal neovascular membrane. Ultrasound testing may reveal increased heterogeneity and a lack of intrinsic vascularity on standardized A scan. Serial observation will document involutional alterations of the evolving disciform lesion.

Melanomas less than 5 mm in height rarely produce hemorrhage, and a choroidal mass that is less than 4 mm in thickness and is associated with choroidal, subretinal, or vitreous hemorrhage generally implies a benign process.

Congenital hypertrophy of the RPE (CHRPE) is a well-defined, flat, darkly pigmented lesion ranging in size from less than 1 DD to 10 mm or more. Patients are asymptomatic and the lesion is noted during ophthalmic examination, typically in

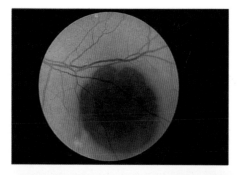

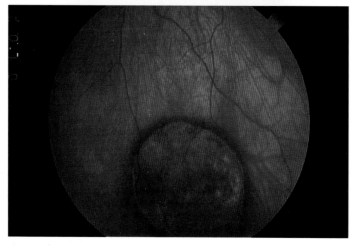

FIG XVII-11—Congenital hypertrophy of the RPE, clinical appearance. *Top*, Note the homogeneous black color and well-defined margins of this nummular fundus lesion. *Bottom*, This lesion has lost much of its pigment, resulting in the formation of depigmented lacunae within the lesion.

patients in their teens or twenties. In younger patients CHRPE often appears homogeneously black, but in older individuals foci of depigmentation (lacunae) often develop (Fig XVII-11). This lesion may grow but has no potential for malignancy.

Histologically, CHRPE consists of tall, melanin-containing pigment epithelial cells that contain large spherical pigment granules. The histology is identical to a condition known as *grouped pigmentation of the retina*, or *bear tracks* (Fig XVII-12). The presence of multiple patches of congenital hypertrophy in family members of patients with Gardner syndrome appears to be a marker for associated colon carcinoma, although the histopathologic features of these patches of congenital hypertrophy may not be identical to those seen in non-Gardner patients. Patients with Gardner syndrome, one of the familial polyposes, carry an extremely high lifetime

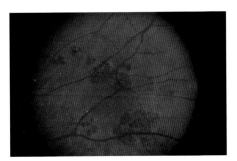

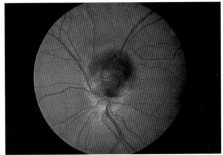

FIG XVII-12—Bear tracks represent small scattered foci of congenital hypertrophy of the RPE.

FIG XVII-13—Melanocytoma of the optic disc. Clinical appearance of darkly pigmented mass involving upper half of disc.

risk of developing colon carcinoma. Fundus findings enable the ophthalmologist to help the gastroenterologist determine the recommended frequency of colon carcinoma screening in family members.

Melanocytoma (magnocellular nevus) of the optic disc typically appears as a dark brown to black epipapillary lesion, often with fibrillar margins as a result of extension into the nerve fiber layer (Fig XVII-13). It is usually located eccentrically over the optic disc and may be elevated. Although these lesions apparently occur with equal frequency in whites and blacks, they seem to be much more common than uveal melanomas among black patients. It is important to differentiate this lesion from melanoma, since the melanocytoma has minimal malignant potential.

Recent studies have shown that about one third of optic disc melanocytomas have a peripapillary nevus component and that 10% of cases will show minimal but definite growth over a 5-year period. In addition, these lesions can produce an afferent pupillary defect and a variety of visual field abnormalities ranging from an enlarged blind spot to extensive nerve fiber layer defects.

Suprachoroidal detachments present in two forms: *hemorrhagic* or *serous.* These lesions are often associated with hypotony and may present in the immediate postoperative period after ophthalmic surgery. Clinically, hemorrhagic detachments are often dome shaped, involve multiple quadrants, and are associated with breakthrough vitreous bleeding. A- and B-scan ultrasonography readings may closely resemble melanoma but show an absence of intrinsic vascularity and an evolution of the hemorrhage over time. Observational management is indicated in the majority of cases. MRI with gadolinium enhancement may be of benefit in select cases to document characteristic alterations.

Choroidal osteomas are benign bony tumors that typically arise from the juxtapapillary choroid in adolescent to young adult patients, more commonly in women than men, and are bilateral in 20%–25% of cases. The characteristic lesion appears

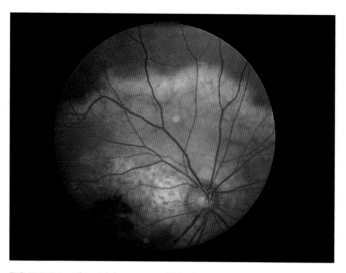

FIG XVII-14—Choroidal osteoma, clinical appearance. Note the yellow-orange color, well-defined pseudopod-like margins, and characteristic spotted pigmentation on the surface of this circumpapillary tumor.

yellow to orange, and it has well-defined pseudopod margins (Fig XVII-14). Ultrasonography reveals a high-amplitude echo corresponding to the plate of bone and loss of the normal orbital echoes behind the lesion. CT scans can also depict these tumors. Choroidal osteomas typically enlarge slowly over many years. If these lesions involve the macula, vision is generally impaired. Subretinal neovascularization is a common complication of macular choroidal osteomas. The etiology of these lesions is unknown, but chronic low-grade choroidal inflammation has been suspected in some cases.

Gass JD, Guerry RK, Jack RL, et al. Choroidal osteoma. *Arch Ophthalmol.* 1978;96: 428–435.

Grand MG, Burgess DB, Singerman LJ, et al. Choroidal osteoma: treatment of associated subretinal neovascular membranes. *Retina.* 1984;4:84–89.

Margo CE. The accuracy of diagnosis of posterior uveal melanoma. *Arch Ophthalmol.* 1997;115:432–434.

Mukai S, Gragoudas ES. Diagnosis of choroidal melanoma. In: Albert DM, Jakobiec FA, eds. *Principles and Practice of Ophthalmology.* 2nd ed. Philadelphia: Saunders; 1994:3209–3217.

Shields CL, Shields JA, Augsburger JJ. Choroial osteoma. *Surv Ophthalmol.* 1988; 33:17–27.

Management and Treatment of Posterior Uveal Melanomas

Management of posterior uveal melanomas has long been the subject of considerable controversy. Two factors lie at the heart of this controversy:

- The limited amount of data on the natural history of untreated patients with posterior uveal malignant melanoma
- The lack of groups of patients matched both for known and unknown risk factors and managed by different therapeutic techniques for assessment of the comparative effectiveness of those treatments

In 1882 Fuchs wrote that all intraocular melanomas were treated by enucleation and the only untreated cases were in the "older literature." Recent advances have utilized both surgical and radiotherapeutic management for intraocular melanoma. The Collaborative Ocular Melanoma Study mentioned in chapter XVI is comparing primary enucleation with radiation therapy in patients with medium or large melanoma. The methods of patient management currently in use depend upon several factors (Table XVII-4):

- Size, location, and extent of the tumor
- Visual status of the affected eye and of the fellow eye
- Age and general health of the patient

TABLE XVII-4

TREATMENT OPTIONS FOR UVEAL MELANOMA

Standard

Observation

Globe-conserving

Brachytherapy (e.g., iodine 125, ruthenium 106, palladium 103)

Charge-particle therapy

Enucleation

Investigational

Combined modality therapy (e.g., brachytherapy and laser hyperthermia)

Transpupillary thermotherapy

Uveoscleral resection

Transvitreal resection

Photodynamic therapy

Observation In certain instances serial observation without treatment of an intraocular tumor is indicated. Most types of benign retinal and choroidal tumors, such as choroidal nevi, choroidal osteoma, or hyperplasia of the RPE, can be managed with observation. Growth of small melanocytic lesions of the posterior uvea that are less than 1.0 mm in thickness can be documented periodically with use of fundus photography and ultrasonography. Significant controversy persists regarding the management of small choroidal melanomas. Lesions greater than 1.0 mm in thickness with documented growth should be evaluated for indications for definitive treatment. Observation of active larger tumors may be appropriate in very elderly and systemically ill patients who are not candidates for any sort of therapeutic intervention.

Enucleation Historically, enucleation has been the gold standard in treatment of malignant intraocular tumors. Zimmerman and McLean hypothesized that surgical manipulation of eyes containing malignant melanoma led to tumor dissemination and increased mortality. This hypothesis is no longer accepted, and enucleation remains appropriate for many medium choroidal melanomas and virtually all large choroidal melanomas. The COMS has compared the application of preenucleation external-beam radiation therapy followed by enucleation to enucleation alone for patients with large choroidal melanoma. No statistically significant survival difference was noted in 5-year mortality rates. Enucleation remains one of the most common primary treatments for choroidal melanoma.

External-beam radiation Conventional external-beam radiation therapy is ineffective as a single modality treatment for malignant melanoma. Combined preenucleation external-beam radiotherapy appears to limit orbital recurrence in large melanoma and showed a non–statistically significant reduction in 5-year mortality within the recently reported COMS large tumor trial.

Radioactive plaque (brachytherapy) The application of a radioactive plaque to the sclera overlying an intraocular tumor allows the delivery of a high dose of radiation to the tumor and a relatively low dose to the surrounding normal structures of the eye. This technique has been available for 50 years. Although various isotopes have been used, the most common are cobalt 60, iodine 125, ruthenium 106, and iridium 192. Within the United States iodine 125 is the most frequently employed isotope for the treatment of ciliary body and choroidal melanomas. Recent advances in intraoperative localization, especially use of ultrasound, have increased the local tumor control rates to as high as 96%. Late radiation complications, especially optic neuropathy and retinopathy, are visually limiting in as many as 50% of patients undergoing treatment. Radiation complications appear dose dependent, and they increase for tumors involving, or adjacent to, the macula or optic nerve.

Charged-particle radiation High-linear-energy transfer radiation with charged particles (protons and helium ions) has been used effectively in managing choroidal and ciliary body melanomas. The technique requires surgical placement of tantalum clips to the sclera to mark the basal margins of the tumor prior to the first radiation fraction. The charged-particle beams deliver a more homogeneous dose of radiation energy to a tumor than does a radioactive plaque, and the lateral spread of radiation energy from such beams is less extensive (Bragg peak effect). Local tumor control rates of up to 98% have been reported.

Unfortunately, charged-particle radiation often delivers a higher dose to anterior segment structures. Radiation complications, more commonly anterior, lead to uncontrolled neovascular glaucoma in 10% of treated eyes and vision loss in approximately 50%. Surgical removal of radiation-induced cataract is indicated if the intraocular tumor is nonviable and the patient appears to have visual limitations attributable to the cataract. No increase in mortality after cataract extraction has been documented.

Alternative treatments *Photoablation/hyperthermia.* Photocoagulation has played a limited role in the treatment of melanocytic tumors. Reports of focal/grid treatment to eradicate active subretinal fluid in choroidal melanoma have documented a propensity for accelerated tumor growth with rupture of Bruch's membrane. Recently, advances in the delivery of hyperthermia (heat) using transpupillary thermotherapy have been reported. Direct diode laser treatment using long duration, large spot size, and relatively low energy laser have been associated with a reduction in tumor volume. No long-term outcome data are available. Currently, photocoagulation coupled with laser ablation/hyperthermia and brachytherapy is being evaluated.

Cryotherapy. Cryotherapy using a triple–freeze/thaw technique has been employed in the treatment of small choroidal melanoma. This therapy is not standard and is not currently undergoing further evaluation for efficacy.

Transscleral diathermy. Diathermy is contraindicated in the treatment of malignant intraocular tumors because the induced scleral damage may provide a route for extrascleral extension of tumor cells.

Chemotherapy. Chemotherapy is currently ineffective in the treatment of primary or metastatic uveal melanoma. Various regimens have been used, however, for palliative treatment of patients with metastatic disease.

Immunotherapy. Presently, immunotherapy is under investigation in the treatment of gross and microscopic metastatic disease. Immunotherapy employs the delivery of systemic cytokines, immunomodulatory agents, or local vaccine therapy aimed toward the activation of a tumor-directed T-cell immune response.

Surgical excision of tumor Surgical excision has been performed successfully in many eyes with malignant and benign intraocular tumors. Concerns regarding surgical excision are the inability to evaluate tumor margins for residual disease and the high incidence of pathologically recognized scleral, retinal, and vitreous involvement in medium and large choroidal melanomas. When this treatment is employed, the surgical techniques are generally quite difficult, requiring an experienced surgeon. In rare instances local excision of the extraocular tumor has been coupled with globe-conserving radiotherapy.

Exenteration Exenteration has traditionally been advocated for patients who have extrascleral extension of a posterior uveal melanoma. Recently the trend has moved toward more conservative treatment for these patients. Local radiotherapy coupled with enucleation appears to obtain survival outcomes similar to exenteration.

Albert DM, Jakobiec FA, eds. *Principles and Practice of Ophthalmology.* 2nd ed. Philadelphia: Saunders; 1994;4:3217–3243.

Bornfeld N, Gragoudas ES, Hopping W, et al, eds. *Tumors of the Eye.* New York: Kugler; 1991:367–587.

The Collaborative Ocular Melanoma Study Group. The Collaborative Ocular Melanoma Study (COMS). Randomized trial of pre-enucleation radiation of large choroidal melanoma. II: Initial mortality findings: COMS report no. 10. *Am J Ophthalmol.* 1998;125:779–796.

Harbour JW, Murray TG, Byrne SF, et al. Intraoperative echographic localization of iodine 125 episcleral radioactive plaques for posterior uveal melanoma. *Retina.* 1996;16:129–134.

Schachat AP. Tumors. In: Ryan SJ, ed. *Retina.* 2nd ed. St Louis: Mosby; 1994.

Shields JA, Shields CL. *Intraocular Tumors: A Text and Atlas.* Philadelphia: Saunders; 1992.

Zimmerman LE, McLean IW, Foster WD. Does enucleation of the eye containing malignant melanoma prevent or accelerate the dissemination of tumour cells? *Br J Ophthalmol.* 1978;62:420–425.

Metastatic Evaluation

All patients require metastatic evaluation prior to definitive treatment of the intraocular melanoma (Table XVII-5). Once the diagnosis of melanoma has been made, but before the patient and physician finalize a treatment plan, the patient should have a medical evaluation. The purpose of this evaluation is two-fold:

□ To determine if any other medical illnesses would contraindicate surgical treatment or need to be ameliorated before surgery. For example, in one small series 15% of the patients had a second malignancy at the time of presentation or during the course of a 10-year follow-up; the COMS found preexisting second independent primary cancers in about 10% of patients. If any question remains that the lesion in the eye is a metastatic tumor, this possibility must be ruled out with a thorough medical evaluation directed at determining the site of primary malignancy.

□ To rule out the possibility of detectable metastatic melanoma from the eye. Few patients have detectable metastatic disease from uveal melanoma noted at the time of initial presentation and before surgical treatment. If metastatic disease is clinically present during the pretreatment evaluation of the eye tumor, enucleation is inappropriate unless the eye is painful. Predominant sites of metastatic disease include liver, lung, and skin or subcutaneous tissue.

Appropriate metastatic evaluation is generally performed on all patients on a yearly follow-up basis and includes comprehensive physical examination, determination of serum levels of liver enzymes, and performance of a chest x-ray. Radionuclide liver scanning, abdominal ultrasonography, and abdominal CT or MRI are generally not appropriate for routine metastatic screening. However, these tests are indicated when abnormalities in liver function profiles are noted. A liver or other organ site biopsy is confirmatory of metastatic disease and is appropriate prior to institution of any treatment for metastatic disease.

The interval between treatment and the onset of metastatic disease is often as early as 2–4 years in patients who develop clinical metastatic disease from a primary

Physical examination, including emphasis on bone and soft tissue

   Chest x-ray: posteroanterior and lateral

   Complete liver function profile

If any of the above are abnormal, a targeted imaging study is warranted. In order of preference, the recommended imaging study is

   MRI of the abdomen and/or chest

   CT of the abdomen and/or chest

   In specific instances high-resolution ultrasonography of the liver may suffice

posterior uveal malignant melanoma, although the median duration to onset of metastasis following treatment is 7 years. Patients who develop clinical metastatic uveal melanoma generally survive less than 6 months, since chemotherapy and other currently available forms of management have limited effectiveness against the disseminated form of this malignancy. The liver appears to be the predominant clinical site of involvement by metastatic melanoma (Table XVII-6). Several treatments have focused on the eradication of isolated liver metastases through surgical resection or chemoembolization.

Currently, it is hypothesized that many patients have nondetectable micrometastatic disease present at the time of their primary therapy. Experimental strategies are aimed at detection and eradication of micrometastatic disease combined with treatment of the primary intraocular malignancy. Several advances have been made in the evaluation and correlation of tumor predictors for metastases. Histopathologic evaluation of choroidal melanoma has documented nine tumor patterns. Rummelt, Folberg, and colleagues have correlated the presence of two of these patterns (networks and parallel with cross-linking) with shortened survival. Mueller and colleagues have reported the noninvasive imaging of tumor vasculature using confocal indocyanine green scanning laser ophthalmoscopy, while Coleman and colleagues have applied ultrasound tissue characterization techniques to image tumor microvasculature. These noninvasive imaging techniques may allow the clinician to assess the malignant/metastatic potential of choroidal melanoma. These modalities may also enhance the diagnostic accuracy in patients with small choroidal tumors.

Coleman DJ, Rondeau MJ, Silverman RH, et al. Correlation of microcirculation architecture with ultrasound backscatter parameters of uveal melanoma. *Europ J Ophthalmol.* 1995;5:96–106.

Mueller AJ, Bartsch D-U, Grossniklaus HE, et al. Identification of microvascularization patterns with confocal indocyanine green angiography. *Ger J Ophthalmol.* 1996; 5:568.

TABLE XVII-6

SITES OF METASTASES IN PATIENTS WITH POSTERIOR UVEAL MELANOMA

| | CLINICAL INCIDENCE (35 CASES) | | | | | | AUTOPSY INCIDENCE (33 CASES) | |
| | INITIAL ORGAN INVOLVEMENT | | SUBSEQUENT INVOLVEMENT | | TOTAL | | | |
ORGAN	NO.	%	NO.	%	NO.	%	NO.	%
Liver	16	45.7	9	25.7	25	71.4	24	72.7
Lung	6	17.1	8	22.9	14	40.0	17	51.5
Subcutaneous tissue, skin	3	8.6	9	25.7	12	34.3	4	12.1
Bone	1	2.9	5	14.3	6	17.1	8	24.2
Lymph nodes	3	8.6	2	5.7	5	14.3	12	36.4
GI tract	1	2.9	4	11.6	5	14.3	9	27.3
Brain	1	2.9	1	2.9	2	5.7	8	24.2
Other	3	8.6	4	11.6	7	19.2	12	36.4

From Rajpal S, Moore R, Karakousis CP. Survival in metastatic ocular melanoma. *Cancer.* 1983;52:334–336.

Rummelt V, Folberg R, Woolson RF, et al. Relation between the microcirculation architecture and the aggressive behavior of ciliary body melanomas. *Ophthalmology.* 1995;102:844–851.

Prognosis

A meta-analysis from the published literature of tumor mortality after treatment documented a 5-year mortality rate of 50% for large choroidal melanoma and 30% for medium choroidal melanoma; 5-year melanoma-related mortality in treated patients with small choroidal melanoma has been reported as high as 12%. Retrospective analysis among patients with melanoma suggests that clinical risk factors for mortality are

☐ Larger tumor size at time of treatment

☐ Tumor growth

☐ Anterior tumor location

☐ Extraocular extension

Local tumor failure (e.g., tumor regrowth) after globe-conserving therapy is a poor prognostic sign for mortality.

Recent reports from the COMS large tumor trial evaluating 1,003 patients have compared enucleation alone to enucleation preceded by preenucleation external-beam radiotherapy and reported 5-year survival rates of 57% and 62%, respectively. Orbital tumor recurrence was noted in six patients treated with enucleation alone and in only one patient treated with preenucleation radiation therapy followed by enucleation.

The COMS small tumor observational study reported on 204 patients and documented a 5-year all-cause mortality rate of 6% and a melanoma-specific mortality rate of 1%. This study also confirmed clinical factors predictive of growth and documented 2- and 5-year Kaplan-Meier estimates of tumor growth of 21% and 31%, respectively.

The medium tumor trial has completed patient accrual at 1350 patients and is awaiting outcomes data for survival comparing enucleation with iodine 125 brachytherapy. Current nonrandomized, non-COMS data suggest a 5-year mortality with iodine 125 brachytherapy or charged-particle radiotherapy of approximately 15%, although there appears to be a selection bias in the group of patients treated.

Adenoma and Adenocarcinoma

Benign adenomas of the nonpigmented and pigmented ciliary epithelium may appear indistinguishable clinically from melanomas arising in the ciliary body. Benign adenomas of the RPE are very rare. These lesions occur as oval, deeply melanotic tumors arising abruptly from the RPE. Adenomas rarely enlarge and seldom undergo malignant change. Adenocarcinoma of the RPE is very rare; only a few cases have ever been reported in the literature. Although these lesions have malignant features histologically, their metastatic potential appears to be minimal.

Rare benign asymptomatic cysts of the ciliary epithelium may occur. Opacified ciliary epithelial cysts are formed in myeloma and macroglobulinemia.

Fuchs adenoma (pseudoadenomatous hyperplasia) is usually an incidental finding at autopsy and rarely becomes apparent clinically. It appears as a glistening white irregular tumor arising from a ciliary crest. Histologically, it consists of benign proliferation of the nonpigmented ciliary epithelium with accumulation of basement membrane–like material.

Spencer WH, ed. *Ophthalmic Pathology: An Atlas and Textbook*. 4th ed. Philadelphia: Saunders; 1996:1291–1313.

Acquired Hyperplasia

Hyperplasia of the pigmented ciliary epithelium usually occurs in response to trauma, inflammation, or other ocular insults. Because of their location, such lesions generally do not become evident clinically. Occasionally, however, they may reach a large size and simulate a ciliary body melanoma. Adenomatous hyperplasia has also been reported to rarely occur and clinically mimic a choroidal melanoma.

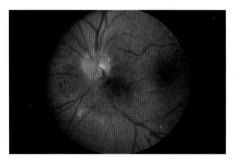

FIG XVII-15—Peripapillary combined hamartoma of the retina and RPE. Note the radiating traction lines through the fovea.

Combined Hamartoma

Combined hamartoma of the RPE and retina is a rare disorder occurring most commonly at the disc margin. Typically, it appears as a darkly pigmented, minimally elevated lesion with retinal traction and tortuous retinal vessels (Fig XVII-15). Histologically, it consists of a proliferation of RPE cells, glial cells, and retinal blood vessels. The glial cells may contract, producing the traction lines seen clinically in the retina. This lesion has been mistaken for malignant melanoma because of its dark pigmentation and slight elevation. In rare cases a combined hamartoma may be situated in the peripheral fundus.

CHAPTER XVIII

Angiomatous Tumors

Hemangiomas

Choroidal Hemangioma

Hemangiomas of the choroid occur in two specific forms: diffuse or circumscribed. The *circumscribed choroidal hemangioma* typically occurs in patients with no other systemic disorder. It generally appears as a red or orange tumor located in the post-equatorial zone of the fundus, often in the macular area (Fig XVIII-1). Such tumors commonly produce a secondary retinal detachment that extends into the foveal region, resulting in visual blurring, metamorphopsia, and micropsia. These benign vascular tumors characteristically affect the overlying RPE and cause cystoid degeneration of the outer retinal layers.

The *diffuse choroidal hemangioma* is generally seen in patients with Sturge-Weber syndrome (encephalofacial angiomatosis). This choroidal tumor produces diffuse reddish orange thickening of the entire fundus, resulting in an ophthalmo-

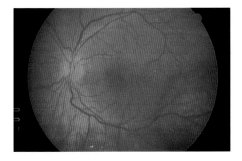

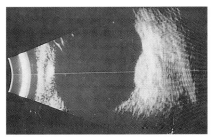

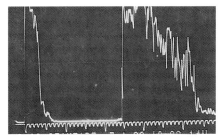

FIG XVIII-1—*Upper left,* Circumscribed choroidal hemangioma. *Lower left,* B-scan ultrasound study shows a highly reflective tumor. *Right,* A-scan ultrasound study shows characteristic high internal reflectivity.

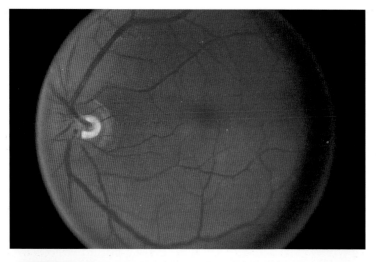

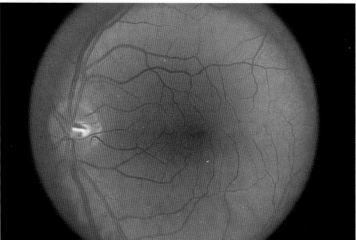

FIG XVIII-2—Choroidal hemangioma, diffuse type, clinical appearance. The saturated red color of the affected fundus *(top)* contrasts markedly with the color of the unaffected fundus *(bottom)* of the same patient.

scopic pattern commonly referred to as *tomato catsup fundus* (Fig XVIII-2). Retinal detachment and glaucoma often occur in eyes with this lesion. See BCSC Section 12, *Retina and Vitreous,* for discussion of choroidal hemangioma, and BCSC Section 6, *Pediatric Ophthalmology and Strabismus,* for discussion of intraocular vascular tumors and Sturge-Weber syndrome.

The principal entities in the differential diagnosis of circumscribed choroidal hemangioma include

□ Amelanotic choroidal melanoma

□ Choroidal osteoma

□ Metastatic carcinoma to the choroid

□ Granuloma of the choroid

Ancillary diagnostic studies may be of considerable help in the evaluation of choroidal hemangiomas. Fluorescein angiography depicts the large choroidal vessels in the prearterial or arterial phases with late staining of the tumor and the overlying cystoid retina. This pattern is not pathognomonic of choroidal hemangiomas, because other choroidal tumors occasionally show a similar pattern. Ultrasonography has been helpful in differentiating choroidal hemangiomas from amelanotic melanomas and from other simulating lesions. A-scan ultrasonography generally shows a high-amplitude initial echo and high-amplitude broad internal echoes ("high internal reflectivity," see Figure XVIII-1, right). B-scan ultrasonography demonstrates localized or diffuse choroidal thickening with prominent internal reflections (acoustic heterogeneity) without choroidal excavation or orbital shadowing (see Figure XVIII-1, lower left). Radiographic studies, particularly CT scanning, can be helpful in differentiating a choroidal hemangioma from a choroidal osteoma.

When choroidal hemangiomas are asymptomatic, generally no treatment is indicated. The most common complication is serous detachment of the retina involving the fovea with resultant visual loss. If this occurs, the surface of the tumor can be treated lightly with laser or xenon arc photocoagulation. The goal of this type of treatment is not to destroy the tumor but rather to create a chorioretinal adhesion that prevents further accumulation of fluid. If the retinal detachment is extensive, this type of photocoagulation is usually unsuccessful. Recurrent detachments are common and the long-term visual prognosis in patients with macular detachment or edema is guarded. Recently, evaluation of brachytherapy and charged-particle radiation in the treatment of choroidal hemangioma has been reported. Involution of the hemangioma is noted, but radiation complications are frequently visually limiting in patients with these tumors, which are often located beneath the macula. External-beam radiotherapy (low dose, fractionated) has also been reported to decrease tumor volume and extent of subretinal fluid and to improve visual function in patients with diffuse choroidal hemangioma.

Albert DM, Jakobiec FA, eds. *Principles and Practice of Ophthalmology.* 2nd ed. Philadelphia: Saunders; 1994:3543–3553.

Garner A, Klintworth GK, eds. *Pathobiology of Ocular Disease: A Dynamic Approach.* 2nd ed. New York: Marcel Dekker, 1994:1449–1451.

Capillary Hemangioma (Hemangioblastoma)

Retinal capillary hemangioma (angiomatosis retinae) is a rare autosomal dominant condition with a reported incidence of 1 in 40,000. Typically, patients are diagnosed in the second to third decades of life, although retinal lesions may be present at birth. The retinal capillary hemangioma (hemangioblastoma) appears as a red to orange tumor arising within the retina with large-caliber, tortuous afferent and efferent retinal blood vessels (Fig XVIII-3). Associated yellow-white retinal and subretinal

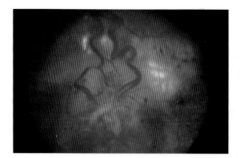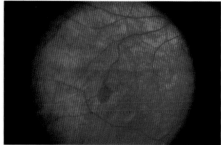

FIG XVIII-3—Retinal capillary hemangioma (hemangioblastoma). *Left,* Note dilated, tortuous retinal blood vessels supplying this vascular tumor. (Photograph courtesy of JA Shields, MD, and JJ Augsburger, MD.) *Right,* Retinal capillary hemangiomas may be small and difficult to observe clinically.

exudates that seem to have a predilection for foveal involvement may appear. Exudative detachment often occurs in eyes with this tumor. Atypical variations include hemangiomas arising from the optic disc, where they may appear as encapsulated lesions or pseudopapilledema; or in the retinal periphery, where vitreous traction may elevate the tumor from the surface of the retina and make it appear to be floating free in the vitreous.

When a capillary hemangioma of the retina occurs as a solitary finding, the condition is generally known as *von Hippel disease.* This condition is familial in about 20% of cases and bilateral in about 50%. The lesions may be multiple in one or both eyes. If retinal capillary hemangiomatosis is associated with a cerebellar hemangioblastoma, the term *von Hippel–Lindau syndrome* is applied. The gene for von Hippel–Lindau syndrome has been isolated on chromosome 3. A number of other tumors and cysts may occur in patients with von Hippel–Lindau syndrome. The most important of these lesions are cerebellar hemangioblastomas, renal cell carcinomas, and pheochromocytomas. When this diagnosis is suspected, appropriate consultation and screening are critical for long-term follow-up of ocular manifestations and the associated systemic complications.

Fluorescein angiography of retinal capillary hemangiomas commonly demonstrates rapid filling of the feeder vessels to the tumor, rapid filling of the many fine blood vessels that make up the tumor itself, and massive leakage of dye into the tumor during the arteriovenous phase of the angiogram. Late staining of the entire tumor and leakage into the vitreous occurs as well as rapid arteriovenous transit by way of the blood vessels that constitute the hemangioma.

The treatment of retinal capillary hemangiomas includes photocoagulation for smaller lesions, cryotherapy for larger and more peripheral lesions, and scleral buckling with cryotherapy or penetrating diathermy for extremely large lesions with extensive retinal detachment. Eye-wall resection and charged-particle radiotherapy have also been employed. Visual prognosis is guarded for patients with large retinal lesions. Aggressive screening and early treatment may reduce the late complications of total exudative retinal detachment. Screening for systemic vascular anomalies (e.g., cerebellar hemangioblastomas) and malignancies (e.g., renal cell carcinoma) may reduce mortality.

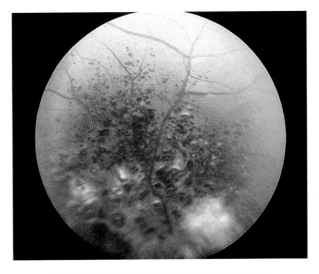

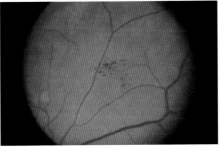

FIG XVIII-4—Retinal cavernous hemangioma. *Top,* Note multiple tiny vascular saccules and associated whitish fibroglial tissue. *Bottom,* When the lesions are small, the findings may be subtle.

Cavernous Hemangioma

Cavernous hemangioma of the retina is a rather uncommon retinal lesion that resembles a cluster of grapes in the retina (Fig XVIII-4). In contrast to Coats disease and retinal capillary hemangiomatosis, cavernous hemangiomas generally include no associated exudates. However, small hemorrhages and areas of gliosis and fibrosis may appear on the surface of the lesion. Within the vascular spaces of the hemangioma, a plasma–erythrocyte separation may appear that can be demonstrated best with fluorescein angiography. Cavernous hemangiomas occasionally occur on the optic disc, where their appearance resembles that in the extrapapillary retina. Cavernous hemangiomas of the retina are sometimes associated with similar skin and CNS lesions, and patients with intracranial lesions may have seizures.

Fluorescein angiography is virtually diagnostic in the case of cavernous hemangioma of the retina. In contrast to a retinal capillary hemangioma, a retinal cavernous hemangioma fills very slowly and the fluorescein often pools in the upper part of the vascular space, while the cellular elements (erythrocytes) pool in the lower part. The fluorescein remains in the vascular spaces for an extended period of time. Unlike Coats disease and retinal capillary hemangiomatosis, cavernous hemangiomas generally show no leakage of fluorescein into the overlying vitreous.

Histologically, cavernous retinal hemangioma consists of dilated, thin-walled vascular channels that are interconnected by small orifices. The dilated vessels may protrude upward beneath the internal limiting membrane, and associated gliosis and hemorrhage may occur. Treatment is rarely required.

Arteriovenous Malformation

Congenital retinal arteriovenous malformation (racemose hemangioma) is an anomalous artery-to-vein anastomosis ranging from a small, localized vascular communication near the disc or in the periphery to a prominent tangle of large, tortuous blood vessels throughout most of the fundus (Fig XVIII-5). If associated with an arteriovenous malformation of the midbrain region, this condition is generally referred to as *Wyburn-Mason syndrome*. Associated similar arteriovenous malformations may appear in the orbit and mandible.

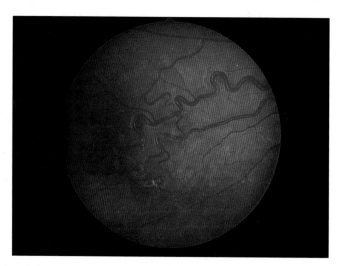

FIG XVIII-5—Retinal arteriovenous malformation, clinical appearance. Note the absence of capillary bed between the afferent and efferent arms of this retinal arteriovenous communication.

CHAPTER XIX

Retinoblastoma

The most common primary intraocular malignancy of childhood is retinoblastoma, second only to uveal malignant melanoma as the most common primary intraocular malignancy of all age groups. The frequency of retinoblastoma ranges from 1 in 14,000 to 1 in 20,000 live births, depending on the country. It is estimated that approximately 250–500 new cases occur in the United States each year. There is no sexual or racial predisposition, and the tumor occurs bilaterally in 30%–40% of cases. In the United States the mean age at diagnosis of retinoblastoma is

☐ Patients with unilateral disease: 24 months

☐ Patients with bilateral disease: 12 months

☐ Patients with a known family history of retinoblastoma: 4 months

About 90% of cases are diagnosed in patients under 3 years old.

Augsburger JJ, Oehlschlager U, Manzitti JE. Multinational clinical and pathologic registry of retinoblastoma. Retinoblastoma International Collaborative Study report 2. *Graefes Arch Clin Exp Ophthalmol.* 1995;233:469–475.

Rubenfeld M, Abramson DH, Ellsworth RM, et al. Unilateral vs. bilateral retinoblastoma: correlations between age at diagnosis and stage of ocular disease. *Ophthalmology.* 1986;93:1016–1019.

Sanders BM, Draper GJ, Kingston JE. Retinoblastoma in Great Britain 1969–1980: incidence, treatment, and survival. *Br J Ophthalmol.* 1988;72:576–583.

Genetic Counseling

Only 6% of retinoblastoma patients have a family history of retinoblastoma. In these cases the condition is inherited through an autosomal dominant gene with virtually complete penetrance. Sporadic cases constitute about 94% of all retinoblastomas. Approximately 15% of the sporadic unilateral patients are carriers of one so-called retinoblastoma gene (see p 146). Until recently, patients with a germinal mutation who would be likely to pass the tumor on to their offspring could not be distinguished clinically from patients with a somatic mutation who were not likely to perpetuate the tumor.

Although genetic counseling for retinoblastoma can be very complex, a few general principles apply (Fig XIX-1). Normal parents with one affected child with bilateral involvement run approximately a 5% risk of producing more affected children. If two or more siblings are affected, the chance that each additional child will be affected rises to 45%. The children of a retinoblastoma survivor who has the hereditary form of retinoblastoma have almost a 50% chance of being affected. If a

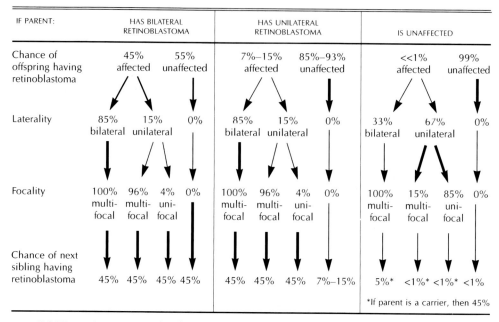

IF PARENT:	HAS BILATERAL RETINOBLASTOMA			HAS UNILATERAL RETINOBLASTOMA			IS UNAFFECTED		
Chance of offspring having retinoblastoma	45% affected	55% unaffected		7%–15% affected	85%–93% unaffected		<<1% affected	99% unaffected	
Laterality	85% bilateral	15% unilateral	0%	85% bilateral	15% unilateral	0%	33% bilateral	67% unilateral	0%
Focality	100% multi-focal	96% multi-focal	4% uni-focal	0%	100% multi-focal	96% multi-focal	4% uni-focal	0%	100% multi-focal	15% multi-focal	85% uni-focal	0%
Chance of next sibling having retinoblastoma	45%	45%	45% 45%	45%	45%	45% 7%–15%	5%*	<1%* <1%* <1%	

*If parent is a carrier, then 45%

FIG XIX-1—Genetic counseling for retinoblastoma. (Chart created by David H. Abramson, MD.)

patient has bilateral retinoblastoma, there is approximately a 98% chance that it represents a germinal mutation. See chapter XI, Retina, pp 145–151, for further discussion of the genetic origins of the retinoblastoma tumor as well as descriptions of histologic features. BCSC Section 6, *Pediatric Ophthalmology and Strabismus,* also discusses retinoblastoma in its chapter on ocular tumors in childhood.

Albert DM, Jakobiec FA, eds. *Principles and Practice of Ophthalmology.* 2nd ed. Philadelphia: Saunders; 1994;5:3328–3349.

Dryja TP. Assessment of risk in hereditary retinoblastoma. In: Albert and Jakobiec, pp 3220–3278.

Knudson AG Jr. Mutation and cancer: statistical study of retinoblastoma. *Proc Natl Acad Sci USA.* 1971;68:820–823.

Clinical Evaluation

The presenting signs and symptoms of retinoblastoma are determined by the extent and location of tumor at the time of diagnosis. The most common presenting signs of retinoblastoma in the United States are leukocoria (white pupillary reflex), strabismus, and ocular inflammation (Table XIX-1, Figs XIX-2, XIX-3). Other presenting features, such as heterochromia, spontaneous hyphema, and "cellulitis" are uncom-

TABLE XIX-1

PRESENTING SIGNS AND SYMPTOMS IN RETINOBLASTOMA

ABNORMAL FINDING	PERCENT
Leukocoria	50–62
Strabismus Esotropia (50%) Exotropia (50%)	20
Red, painful, glaucomatous eye	7
Poor vision, orbital cellulitis, unilateral fixed and dilated pupil, heterochromia, nystagmus, failure to thrive, extra digits, malformed ears, retardation	10
Well-baby examination	3

From Abramson DH. The diagnosis of retinoblastoma. *Bull NY Acad Med.* 1988;64:283–317.

mon. In rare instances a small lesion may be found on routine examination. Visual complaints are infrequent because most tumors present in pre–school-age children.

Balmer A, Chill DC. Retinoblastoma. In: Straub W, ed. *Turning Points in Cataract Formation, Syndromes, and Retinoblastoma.* New York: Karger; 1983:36–96.

Ellsworth RM. The practical management of retinoblastoma. *Trans Am Ophthalmol Soc.* 1969;67:462–534.

Shields JA, Augsburger JJ. Current approaches to the diagnosis and management of retinoblastoma. *Surv Ophthalmol.* 1981;25:347–372.

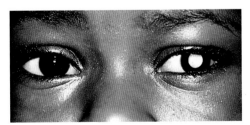

FIG XIX-2—Retinoblastoma, clinical appearance. Leukocoria associated with advanced introacular tumor. (Photograph courtesy of Paul Sternberg Jr, MD.)

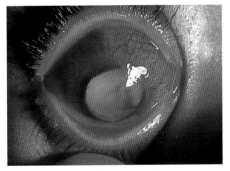

FIG XIX-3—Retinoblastoma, clinical appearance. Red eye with cloudy vitreous as a result of advanced endophytic tumor resembles endogenous endophthalmitis (masquerade syndrome).

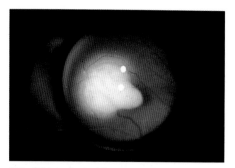

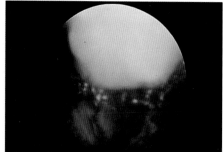

FIG XIX-4—Retinoblastoma, clinical appearance. Small, discrete white tumor supplied by dilated retinal blood vessels.

FIG XIX-5—Retinoblastoma, clinical appearance. Large white retinal tumor with associated tumor seeds into adjacent vitreous.

Small retinoblastoma lesions generally appear as translucent gray to white intraretinal tumors fed and drained by dilated, tortuous retinal vessels (Fig XIX-4). In more advanced cases extensive chalky white tumor may fill a large portion of the eye. A variant of retinoblastoma—*diffuse infiltrating retinoblastoma*—is often noted at a later age; is typically unilateral; and presents a greater diagnostic dilemma, occasionally being mistaken for atypical Coats disease.

As mentioned in chapter XI, retinoblastoma tumor cells may gain entrance into the vitreous where they appear as vitreous seeds (Fig XIX-5). When cells shed from retinoblastoma remain viable in the vitreous and subretinal space they may eventually give rise to viable tumor implants throughout the eye. Retinoblastoma cells may also enter the anterior chamber to produce a pseudohypopyon (Fig XIX-6). The anterior chamber cells may either aggregate on the iris to form nodules or settle inferiorly as a result of gravity to form a pseudohypopyon. Secondary glaucoma and rubeosis iridis occur in about 50% of such cases.

Tumor cells may invade the optic nerve and extend into the subarachnoid space, most commonly escaping from the eye by way of the optic nerve. Figure XI-36 illustrates bulbous enlargement of the optic nerve following invasion of retinoblastoma tumor; see p 150. Far-advanced retinoblastoma commonly extends outside the eye after invading the optic nerve and orbit. When the tumor erodes anteriorly through the sclera or exits the eye through the anterior chamber and trabecular meshwork and invades conjunctival lymphatics, the patient develops palpable preauricular and cervical nodes. Proptosis can occur in such situations (Fig XIX-7). In unusual cases, patients may present with systemic metastasis and intracranial extension at the time the ocular lesion is detected. The most frequently identified sites of metastatic involvement in children with retinoblastoma, as determined from autopsy series, include skull bones, distal bones, brain, spinal cord, lymph nodes, and abdominal viscera.

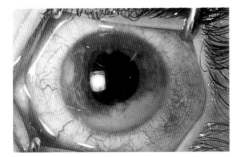 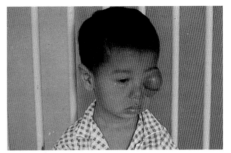

FIG XIX-6—Retinoblastoma, clinical appearance. Pseudohypopyon resulting from migration of tumor cells into the anterior chamber (masquerade syndrome).

FIG XIX-7—Retinoblastoma, clinical appearance. Proptosis caused by retinoblastoma with orbital invasion.

Clinical Examination

The diagnosis of retinoblastoma can generally be suspected on the basis of a complete ocular examination in the office. The initial examination should include an assessment of visual function, slit-lamp biomicroscopy of the vitreous and anterior segment if possible, and indirect ophthalmoscopy with scleral depression.

Children with retinoblastoma should have a complete general history and physical examination by a pediatrician or pediatric oncologist. Anesthesia is used with infants older than 2 months to permit complete assessment of the extent of ocular disease in all cases prior to treatment as well as in those cases when an awake examination is inadequate to confirm the diagnosis. Intraocular pressure and corneal diameters can also be evaluated during examination under anesthesia. Ultrasonography and CT scanning can be helpful in the diagnosis of retinoblastoma by demonstrating characteristic calcific densities within the tumor. Neuroimaging studies using MR or CT should evaluate both the orbital and CNS anatomy for extraocular disease. Recent studies have suggested that systemic metastatic evaluation, typically bone marrow and lumbar puncture, are not indicated in children without neurologic abnormalities or evidence of extraocular extension. Parents and siblings should be examined for any ophthalmoscopic evidence of untreated retinoblastoma or retinoma.

Differential Diagnosis

A number of lesions simulate retinoblastoma clinically. Lesions that resemble small to medium-sized retinoblastomas include retinal astrocytic hamartomas commonly seen in tuberous sclerosis; exudative deposits, such as those that occur with Coats disease and retinal capillary hemangiomatosis; and peripheral or posterior pole granulomas, such as those associated with nematode endophthalmitis. The differential diagnoses are different when the patient presents with leukocoria and a retinal detachment. The most common causes of leukocoria other than retinoblastoma include Coats disease, ocular toxocariasis, persistent hyperplastic primary vitreous

TABLE XIX-2

DIFFERENTIAL DIAGNOSIS OF RETINOBLASTOMA

CLINICAL DIAGNOSIS IN PSEUDORETINOBLASTOMA	265 CASES*	PERCENT	76 CASES**	PERCENT
Persistent hyperplastic primary vitreous	51	19.0	15	20.0
Retinopathy of prematurity	36	13.5	3	4.0
Posterior cataract	36	13.5	5	7.0
Coloboma of choroid or optic disc	30	11.5	7	9.0
Uveitis	27	10.0	2	3.0
Larval granulomatosis	18	6.5	20	26.0
Congenital retinal fold	13	5.0		
Coats disease	10	4.0	12	16.0
Organizing vitreous hemorrhage	9	3.5	3	4.0
Retinal dysplasia	7	2.5		
Assorted other disorders	28	10.5	9	12.0

*From Howard GM, Ellsworth RM. Differential diagnosis of retinoblastoma. *Am J Ophthalmol.* 1965; 60:610–618.
**From Shields JA, Stephens RT, Sarin LK. The differential diagnosis of retinoblastoma. In: Harley RD, ed. *Pediatric Ophthalmology.* 2nd ed. Philadelphia: Saunders; 1983:114.

(PHPV), and retinopathy of prematurity (Table XIX-2). Most of these conditions can be differentiated from retinoblastoma on the basis of a comprehensive clinical examination, history, and appropriate ancillary diagnostic testing.

Coats Disease

Coats disease is clinically evident within the first decade of life and is more common in boys. The lesion is typically characterized by unilateral retinal telangiectasia associated with progressive subretinal yellow exudation without a distinct mass (Fig XIX-8). Ultrasound evaluation documents the absence of a retinal tumor, and calcification is rare. Fluorescein angiography documents classic telangiectactic vascular alterations. Laser photocoagulation or cryoablation of the vascular anomalies eliminates the exudative component of the disease and may restore visual function. Diffuse retinoblastoma with its later presentation, absence of calcium, and diffuse retinal involvement may be missed and a mistaken diagnosis of Coats disease entertained. Serial evaluation and follow-up is critical for these patients.

Persistent Hyperplastic Primary Vitreous

Also known as *persistent fetal vasculature*, PHPV is typically recognized within days of birth. The condition is unilateral in two thirds of cases and is associated with a retrolenticular fibrovascular mass, cataract, indwelling of the ciliary processes, and microphthalmos. Indirect ophthalmoscopic examination often documents the vascular stalk arising from the optic nerve head. Ultrasound testing is often confirma-

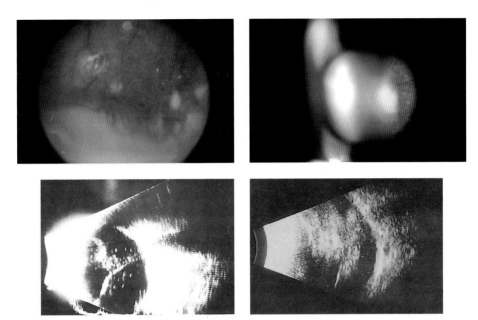

FIG XIX-8—Coats disease. *Upper left,* Clinical appearance of characteristic lightbulb aneurysms seen in a patient with Coats disease. There is an inferior exudative retinal detachment. *Upper right,* In advanced cases there can be a complete exudative retinal detachment. In this case the retina is visible behind the lens. *Lower left,* Patient with Coats disease shows an exudative retinal detachment on ultrasound. *Lower right,* In contrast, this ultrasound scan of a patient with retinoblastoma shows a total retinal detachment, but in this case a large tumor mass is also present.

tory of the diagnosis with evidence of persistent hyaloid remnants, shortened axial length, and absence of a retinal tumor and calcification. PHPV may be managed with combined lensectomy and vitrectomy approaches in selected cases. See BCSC Section 6, *Pediatric Ophthalmology and Strabismus.*

Ocular Toxocariasis

Ocular toxocariasis typically occurs in older children with a history of soil ingestion or exposure to puppies. It presents with organizing vitreoretinal tractional detachment associated with intraocular inflammation. Cataractous alterations may be noted. Ultrasound documents the involvement of the vitreous and absence of calcium. See BCSC Section 9, *Intraocular Inflammation and Uveitis.*

Astrocytoma

Retinal astrocytoma, or astrocytic hamartoma, generally appears as a small, smooth, white, glistening tumor located in the nerve fiber layer of the retina (Fig XIX-9). It may be single or multiple, unilateral or bilateral. In some cases it may become larger and calcified, resulting in a mulberry appearance. Astrocytomas occasionally arise from the optic disc; such tumors are often referred to as *giant drusen.* Astrocytomas

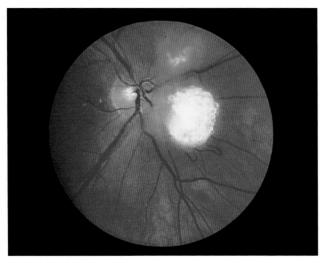

FIG XIX-9—Retinal astrocytic hamartomas, clinical appearance. Note the more subtle opalescent lesion superonasal from the optic disc and the larger mulberry lesion inferonasal from the disc.

of the retina commonly occur in patients with tuberous sclerosis, but most of these lesions are unassociated with any systemic syndrome.

Shields JA, Parsons HM, Shields CL, et al. Lesions simulating retinoblastoma. *J Pediatr Ophthalmol Strabismus.* 1991;28:338–340.

Shields JA, Shields CL. *Intraocular Tumors: A Text and Atlas.* Philadelphia: Saunders; 1992:341–362.

Retinoblastoma Classification

The Reese-Ellsworth clinical classification is the most commonly used grouping for intraocular retinoblastoma (Table XIX-3). It does not classify extraocular retinoblastoma. This classification takes into account the number, size, and location of tumors and the presence or absence of vitreous seeds. According to this classification, eye tumors are grouped from very favorable (group I) to very unfavorable (group V) by probability of eye preservation when treated with external-beam radiation alone. The Reese-Ellsworth classification does not provide prognostic information about patient survival or vision. Another clinical classification of retinoblastoma is the Essen classification (Table XIX-4).

Reese AB. *Tumors of the Eye.* 3rd ed. Hagerstown, MD: Harper & Row; 1976:90–132.

TABLE XIX-3

REESE-ELLSWORTH CLASSIFICATION OF RETINOBLASTOMA

GROUP	A	B
Group I (very favorable)	Solitary tumor 4 disc diameters (DD) at/behind equator	Multiple tumors 4 DD at/behind equator
Group II (favorable)	Solitary tumor 4–10 DD at or behind equator	Multiple tumors 4–10 DD at or behind equator
Group III (doubtful)	Any lesion anterior to equator	Solitary tumor 10 DD posterior to equator
Group IV (unfavorable)	Multiple tumors, some larger than 10 DD	Any lesion anterior to ora serrata
Group V (very unfavorable)	Massive tumor occupying half or more of retina	Vitreous seeding

TABLE XIX-4

ESSEN CLASSIFICATION

Group I	*Very favorable*
	Tumor(s) up to 4 disc diameters and 4 diopters elevation, except tumors near the macula or adjacent to the optic nerve head
Group II	*Favorable*
	Moderate-sized tumors of 8–10 DD, if not belonging in groups III or IV for other reasons
	Tumors near the macula, even if small
Group III	*Doubtful*
	Tumors with associated retinal detachment
	Tumors adjacent to the optic nerve head even if small
	Moderate-sized tumors with limited vitreous seeding over the surface
	Small highly elevated tumor, and therefore not separate from the ora serrata
	Tumors in this group only if not belonging in groups IV or V
Group IV	*Unfavorable*
	Extensive tumor with or without vitreous seeding or retinal detachment
	Large tumors adjacent to or overlapping the optic nerve head
	Large tumors not separable from the ora serrata by ophthalmoscopy
Group V	*Very unfavorable*
	Massive tumors involving half the retina, with or without vitreous seeding
	Totally detached retina

Modified from Hopping W. The new Essen prognosis classification for conservative sight saving treatment of retinoblastoma. In: Lammatzsch PK, Blodi FC, eds. *Intraocular Tumor.* Berlin: Akademie-Verlag; 1983: 497–508.

Treatment of Retinoblastoma

Enucleation

Management options currently used in children with retinoblastoma include enucleation, radiation therapy, photocoagulation, cryotherapy, and chemotherapy. Even though globe-conserving therapies are increasingly employed in the treatment of retinoblastoma, enucleation remains the treatment of choice in many children because the eye cannot be salvaged with any of these treatment modalities. Typically, enucleation is considered an appropriate intervention when:

☐ Tumor involves greater than 50% of the globe

☐ Orbital or optic nerve involvement is suspected

☐ Anterior segment involvement, with or without neovascular glaucoma, is noted

Enucleation techniques are aimed at minimizing the potential for inadvertent globe penetration while obtaining the largest length of resected optic nerve that is feasible, typically greater than 10 mm. Porous implants, such as hydroxyapatite or Medpor, are currently used by most surgeons.

Photocoagulative Ablation and Hyperthermia

Photocoagulation can be used for many retinoblastomas smaller than 3 mm in apical height and with basal dimensions less than 10 mm. Current laser photoablation techniques use direct confluent treatment over the entire tumor. Encircling laser treatment may also be effective by destroying the retinal vascular component of the tumor. Laser hyperthermia techniques that increase intrinsic tumor temperature coupled with direct tumor ablation are also employed.

Cryotherapy

Also effective for tumors in the size range of less than 10 mm in basal dimension and 3 mm in apical thickness, cryotherapy is applied under direct visualization with a triple–freeze/thaw technique. Typically, laser photoablation is chosen for posteriorly located tumors and cryoablation for more anteriorly located tumors. Repetitive tumor treatments are often required for both techniques along with close follow-up for tumor growth or treatment complications.

Chemoreduction Therapy

A significant advance in the management of intraocular retinoblastoma has occurred within the last decade. Systemic administration of chemotherapy has been noted to reduce tumor volume, allowing for consolidative ablative therapy with laser, cryo-, or radiotherapy. Current regimens include carboplatin, vincristine, and etoposide with or without cyclosporine. Children receive intravenous drug administration every 3 weeks for nine cycles of chemotherapy associated with examination under anesthesia and laser/cryoablation. Transpupillary laser ablation and hyperthermia are mainstays in this treatment. The National Cancer Institute has funded an international, multicenter, randomized clinical trial to evaluate the efficacy of this treatment in severe intraocular retinoblastoma.

Chemotherapy is generally advised for children with metastatic disease. Management of children with retinoblastoma requires a team approach including expertise in ocular oncology/pediatric ophthalmology, pediatric oncology, radiation oncology, and pediatrics. Drug regimens, routes of administration, and dose schedules should be determined by pediatric oncologists experienced in the management of children with retinoblastoma.

External-Beam Radiation Therapy

Retinoblastoma tumors are radiation responsive. Current techniques use focused megavoltage radiation treatments, often employing lens-sparing techniques, to deliver 4000–4500 cGy over a 4–6 week treatment interval. Typically, children with bilateral disease not amenable to laser and/or cryotherapy are treated with this globe-conserving strategy. Globe salvage rates are excellent, with up to 85% of eyes being retained. Visual function is often excellent and limited only by tumor location or secondary complications.

Two major concerns have limited the application of external-beam radiotherapy using standard techniques:

☐ The association of germline alteration of the RB gene with a lifelong increase in the risk of second, independent primary malignancies (e.g., osteosarcoma) that is exacerbated by exposure to external-beam radiotherapy

☐ The potential for radiation-related sequelae that include midface hypoplasia, radiation-induced cataract, and radiation optic neuropathy and vasculopathy

Recent evidence suggests that combined modality therapy that uses lower dose external-beam radiotherapy coupled with chemotherapy may allow for increased globe conservation with decreased radiation morbidity.

Abramson DH, Frank CM. Second nonocular tumors in survivors of bilateral retinoblastoma: a possible age effect on radiation-related risk. *Ophthalmology.* 1998;105: 573–580.

Plaque Radiotherapy (Brachytherapy)

Radioactive plaque therapy can be employed as salvage therapy for some eyes if other globe-conserving therapies have failed to destroy all viable tumor and as a primary treatment for occasional children with relatively small to medium-sized eye tumors. This technique is generally applicable for tumors less than 16 mm in basal diameter and 8 mm in apical thickness. Intraoperative localization with ultrasound may enhance local tumor control for iodine 125 plaque radiotherapy. A greater likelihood of radiation optic neuropathy or vasculopathy may be associated with this radiotherapy modality. Potentially, limiting the radiation dose to periocular structures may lower the incidence of secondary radiation-induced malignancies.

Abramson DH, Ellsworth RM, Kitchin FD, et al. Second nonocular tumors in retinoblastoma survivors: are they radiation-induced? *Ophthalmology.* 1984;91:1351–1355.

Albert DM, Jakobiec FA, eds. *Principles and Practice of Ophthalmology.* 2nd ed. Philadelphia: Saunders; 1994:3279–3298.

Bornfeld N, Gragoudas ES, Hopping W, et al, eds. *Tumors of the Eye.* New York: Kugler; 1991:83–144.

Eng C, Li FP, Abramson DH, et al. Mortality from second tumors among long-term survivors of retinoblastoma. *J Natl Cancer Inst.* 1993;85:1102–1103.

Roarty JD, McLean IW, Zimmerman LE. Incidence of second neoplasms in patients with bilateral retinoblastoma. *Ophthalmology.* 1988;95:1583–1587.

Shields CL, Shields JA, Baez K, et al. Optic nerve invasion of retinoblastoma: metastatic potential and clinical risk factors. *Cancer.* 1994;73:692–698.

Shields CL, Shields JA, De Potter P, et al. Plaque radiotherapy in the management of retinoblastoma: use as a primary and secondary treatment. *Ophthalmology.* 1993; 100:216–224.

Tucker MA, D'Angio GJ, Boice JD Jr, et al. Bone sarcomas linked to radiotherapy and chemotherapy in children. *N Engl J Med.* 1987;317:588–593.

Spontaneous Regression of Retinoblastoma

Retinoblastoma is one of the more common malignant tumors to undergo complete and spontaneous necrosis. Spontaneous regression is recognized clinically after involutional changes such as phthisis have occurred. The incidence of spontaneous regression is unknown, as no child with active retinoblastoma is observed in the hopes of spontaneous involution. Although the mechanism by which spontaneous regression occurs is not understood, its histologic appearance is diagnostic. The vitreous cavities of these phthisical eyes are filled with islands of calcified cells embedded in a mass of fibroconnective tissue. Close inspection of the peripheral portion of these calcified islands reveals the ghosted contours of fossilized tumor cells. The process is often accompanied by exuberant proliferation of retinal pigment and ciliary epithelia.

Associated Conditions

Retinocytoma

Retinocytoma is clinically indistinguishable from retinoblastoma. Chapter XI describes the histologic characteristics that distinguish retinocytoma from retinoblastoma; see Figure XI-38. The developmental biology of retinocytoma is subject to controversy. Some authorities consider retinocytoma to be retinoblastoma that has undergone differentiation, analogous to ganglioneuroma, the differentiated form of neuroblastoma. Many other authorities contend that retinocytoma is a benign counterpart of retinoblastoma.

Although histologically benign, retinocytoma carries the same genetic implications as retinoblastoma. A child harboring a retinoblastoma in one eye and a retinocytoma in the other should be considered capable of transmitting a faulty suppressor gene to offspring.

Trilateral Retinoblastoma

The term *trilateral retinoblastoma* is reserved for cases of bilateral retinoblastoma associated with ectopic intracranial retinoblastoma. The ectopic focus is usually located in the pineal gland or parasellar region and historically has been termed a *pineoblastoma*. This tumor affects 2%–5% of children with germline RB gene mutations. Reportedly, a child may present with ectopic intracranial retinoblastoma prior to ocular involvement. More commonly, this independent malignancy presents months to years after treatment of the intraocular retinoblastoma.

Several different observations support the concept of primary intracranial retinoblastoma. CT has helped to establish that intracranial tumors in some patients dying from retinoblastoma are anatomically separate from the primary tumors in the orbit. These intracranial tumors are not associated with metastatic disease elsewhere in the body, and, unlike metastatic retinoblastoma, they often demonstrate features of differentiation such as Flexner-Wintersteiner rosettes (see Figure XI-35). Embryologic, immunologic, and phylogenic evidence of photoreceptor differentiation in the pineal gland offers further support for the concept of trilateral retinoblastoma.

All patients with retinoblastoma should undergo baseline neuroimaging studies to rule out intracranial involvement. Patients with germline RB gene mutations (i.e., bilateral retinoblastoma; unilateral multifocal retinoblastoma; or unilateral retinoblastoma with a positive family history) should undergo serial imaging of the CNS. Recent studies suggest that MR serial imaging with and without contrast is most sensitive for CNS involvement and does not require even low-dose radiation exposure. Median survival of patients with retinoblastoma with CNS involvement is approximately 8 months.

> Holladay DA, Holladay A, Montebello JF, et al. Clinical presentation, treatment, and outcome of trilateral retinoblastoma. *Cancer.* 1991;67:710–715.

Prognosis

Children with retinoblastoma who have access to modern medical care have a very good prognosis for survival, with overall survival rates of over 95% for children in developed countries presenting with localized intraocular disease. The most important risk factor associated with death is extraocular extension of tumor, either directly through the sclera or more commonly by invasion of the optic nerve, especially to the surgically resected margin (see Figure XI-37). The importance of choroidal invasion is unclear. Multivariate analysis in a large series of cases has shown that choroidal invasion is not predictive of a fatal outcome. Some evidence suggests, however, that bilateral tumors may increase the risk of death because of their association with primary intracranial tumors (see discussion of trilateral retinoblastoma above).

> Kopelman JE, McLean IW, Rosenberg SH. Multivariate analysis of risk factors for metastasis in retinoblastoma treated by enucleation. *Ophthalmology.* 1987;94:371–377.

Children with bilateral disease who survive their retinoblastoma have an increased incidence of nonocular malignancies later in life. The mean latency for second tumor development is approximately 9 years from management of the primary retinoblastoma. The most common type of secondary cancer in these patients appears to be osteogenic sarcoma. Other relatively common secondary malignancies in these patients include pinealomas, brain tumors, cutaneous melanomas, soft tissue sarcomas, and primitive unclassifiable tumors (Table XIX-5). The RB gene mutation is associated with a 26.5% incidence of second tumor development within 50 years in patients treated without exposure to radiation therapy. External-beam radiation therapy to the eye appears to decrease the latency period, increase the proportion of tumors in the head, and increase the incidence of second tumors in the first 30 years of life. Estimates suggest that as many as 10%–20% of patients who have bilateral retinoblastoma will develop an apparently unrelated neoplasm within

TABLE XIX-5

NONRETINOBLASTOMA MALIGNANCIES IN RETINOBLASTOMA SURVIVORS

TUMORS ARISING IN THE FIELD OF RADIATION OF THE EYE		
PATHOLOGIC TYPE	NO. CASES	PERCENT
Osteosarcoma	25	40.3
Fibrosarcoma	6	9.7
Soft tissue sarcoma	5	8.1
Anaplastic and unclassifiable	5	8.1
Squamous cell carcinoma	3	4.8
Rhabdomyosarcoma	3	4.8
Assorted other	15	24.2
Total	62	

TUMORS ARISING OUTSIDE THE FIELD OF RADIATION		
PATHOLOGIC TYPE	NO. CASES	PERCENT
Osteosarcoma	12	36.4
Malignant melanoma	4	12.1
Pinealoma	3	9.1
Ewing sarcoma	2	6.1
Papillary thyroid carcinoma	2	6.1
Assorted other	10	30.3
Total	33	

From Abramson DH, Ellsworth RM, Kitchin FD, et al. Second nonocular tumors in retinoblastoma survivors. Are they radiation-induced? *Ophthalmology.* 1984;91:1351–1355.

20 years and that 20%–40% of such patients will develop an independent primary malignancy within 30 years. By 50 years the second tumor incidence is reported as high as 58.3%. The prognosis for survival in retinoblastoma patients who develop secondary sarcomas is less than 50%.

Albert DM, Jakobiec FA, eds. *Principles and Practice of Ophthalmology.* 2nd ed. Philadelphia: Saunders; 1994:2261–2266.

McLean IW, Burnier MN, Zimmerman LE, et al. *Tumors of the Eye and Ocular Adnexa.* Washington: Armed Forces Institute of Pathology; 1994:101–126.

Shields JA, Shields CL. Tumors of the retina and optic disc. In: Regillo CD, Brown GC, Flynn HW Jr, eds. *Vitreoretinal Disease: The Essentials.* New York: Thieme; 1999: 439–453.

Spencer WH, ed. *Ophthalmic Pathology: An Atlas and Textbook.* 4th ed. Philadelphia: Saunders; 1996:1332–1376.

CHAPTER XX

Secondary Tumors of the Eye

Metastatic Carcinoma

Since the first description in 1872 of a metastatic tumor in the eye of a patient with carcinoma, a large body of literature has indicated that metastatic tumor is the most common intraocular/orbital tumor in adults. Several comprehensive studies of tumor metastatic to the eye have been written. Some have reported the incidence of tumor metastases in a consecutive series in autopsies, some have dealt with tumor incidence in patients with generalized malignancy, and others have discussed a clinicopathologic approach.

> Albert DM, Jakobiec FA, eds. *Principles and Practice of Ophthalmology.* 2nd ed. Philadelphia: Saunders; 1994;5:3260–3270.

> Garner A, Klintworth GK, eds. *Pathobiology of Ocular Disease: A Dynamic Approach.* 2nd ed. New York: Marcel Dekker; 1994:1455–1459.

In a clinical survey Albert and coworkers found an incidence of ocular involvement in 10 of 213 patients with known metastatic disease. Bloch and Gartner, in a retrospective study of 737 consecutive autopsies, found 40 cases with metastasis to the eye or orbit, an incidence of 5.5%. They also reported that in a group of 230 consecutive patients who had died of metastatic carcinoma, 23 (10%) had metastatic foci in the eye. Projecting these findings to the estimated number of annual deaths in the United States from carcinomas (approximately 300,000), the incidence rate of intraocular metastases could be as high as 30,000 patients per year. This rate is in contrast to the estimated 1800 new cases of primary cancers of the eye per year.

Ferry and Font studied 227 cases of patients with ocular and orbital metastases. Of the 217 patients who could be followed, 192 died, with a median survival time of 7.4 months. The median age at onset of ocular symptoms was 33 years, and the average age was 52.5 years. The principal site of involvement was the eye in 196 cases, the orbit in 28 cases, and the optic nerve in 3 cases. No right or left eye preponderance was noted, and males and females were almost equally affected. However, the origin of the primary tumor was gender-dependent. The sites of overall primary involvement were

☐ Breast 40%

☐ Lung 29%

☐ Kidney 4%

☐ Testicle 3%

☐ Prostate 1%

☐ Pancreas, stomach, colon, and ileum less than 1%

TABLE XX-1

PRIMARY SITES OF CHOROIDAL METASTASIS

MALES (N = 137)	FEMALES (N = 287)
Lung (40%)	Breast (68%)
Unknown (29%)	Lung (12%)
Gastrointestinal (9%)	Unknown (12%)
Kidney (6%)	Others (4%)
Prostate (6%)	Gastrointestinal (2%)
Skin (4%)	Skin (1%)
Others (4%)	Kidney (<1%)
Breast (1%)	

Modified from Shields JA, Gross NE, Schwartz GP, et al. Survey of 520 eyes with uveal metastases. *Ophthalmology.* 1997;104:1265–1276.

From most to least frequent, the sites of primary tumors in males are lung, unknown primary, skin melanoma, and kidney; in females they are breast, lung, unknown primary, and gastrointestinal system. In Ferry and Font's report the breast was the site of the primary carcinoma in 77% of women, while the lung was the primary site in 49% of men and 11% of women. In 41 cases (18%) a primary site was not determined. Table XX-1 shows more up-to-date figures for choroidal metastasis from Shields et al.

Metastases to the eye are being diagnosed with increasing frequency for various reasons:

□ Increasing incidence of certain tumor types that metastasize to the eye (e.g., lung and breast)

□ Prolonged survival of patients with certain cancer types (e.g., breast cancer)

□ Increasing awareness among medical oncologists and ophthalmologists of the pattern of metastatic disease

□ Use of the indirect ophthalmoscope, facilitating easier and earlier detection

Mechanisms of Metastasis to the Eye

The mechanism of intraocular metastases depends on hematogenous dissemination of tumor cells. The anatomy of the arterial supply to the eye dictates the predilection of tumor cell deposits within the eye. Tumor cells enter the internal carotid artery directly from the aorta on the left side and indirectly from the innominate artery on the right. As larger cells tend to maintain a position in the slower part of the bloodstream (i.e., along the vessel wall), branches of the vascular tree provide a natural egress out of the major channels for these cells.

Tumor cells within the internal carotid artery enter the ophthalmic artery, which, in turn, gives off 10–20 short posterior ciliary arteries supplying the posterior uvea, two long ciliary arteries supplying the anterior uvea, and one central retinal artery supplying the retina. Accordingly, the posterior choroid, with its rich vascular supply, is the most favored site of intraocular metastases, and it is affected 10–20 times more frequently than is the iris or ciliary body. The retina and optic disc, supplied by the single central retinal artery, are rarely the sole site of involvement.

Bilateral ocular involvement has been reported in 20%–25% of cases, and multifocal deposits are frequently seen within the involved eye. It is also possible that some metastases enter the eye through tumor spread from the subarachnoid space, across the lamina cribrosa, and into the choroid. Most patients with ocular metastases also have concurrent CNS metastases.

Bloch RS, Gartner S. The incidence of ocular metastatic carcinoma. *Arch Ophthalmol.* 1971;85:673–675.

Ferry AP, Font RL. Carcinoma metastatic to the eye and orbit. I. A clinicopathologic study of 227 cases. *Arch Ophthalmol.* 1974;92:276–286.

Clinical Features

The clinical features of intraocular metastases depend on the site of involvement. Metastases to the iris and ciliary body usually appear as white or gray-white gelatinous nodules (Figs XX-1 through XX-3). The clinical features of anterior uveal metastases may include

☐ Iridocyclitis

☐ Secondary glaucoma

☐ Rubeosis iridis

☐ Hyphema

☐ Irregular pupil

Anterior segment tumors are best evaluated with slit-lamp biomicroscopy coupled with gonioscopy. High-resolution ultrasound imaging may quantitate tumor size and anatomic relationships.

Patients with tumor in the posterior pole commonly complain of loss of vision. Pain and photopsia may be concurrent symptoms. Indirect binocular ophthalmoscopy may reveal a nonrhegmatogenous retinal detachment associated with a placoid amelanotic tumor mass (Figs XX-4 through XX-6, pp 271–273). Multiple or bilateral lesions may be present in approximately 25% of cases, highlighting the importance of close evaluation of the fellow eye. The lesions are usually relatively flat and ill defined, often gray-yellow or yellow-white, with secondary alterations at the level of the RPE presenting as clumps of brown pigment.

The mushroom configuration frequently seen in primary choroidal melanoma from breakthrough of Bruch's membrane is rarely seen in uveal metastases. The retina overlying the metastasis may appear opaque and become detached. Rapid tumor growth with necrosis and uveitis are occasionally seen. Dilated epibulbar vessels may be seen in the quadrant overlying the metastasis.

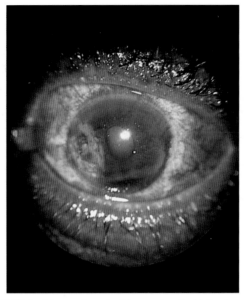

FIG XX-1—Metastasis to the iris associated with hyphema.

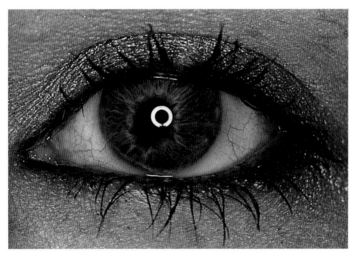

FIG XX-2—Metastasis from breast carcinoma to the iris. Note subtle mass at angle inferonasally associated with pupil irregularity.

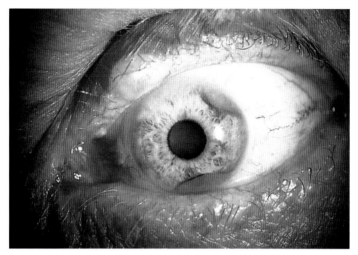

FIG XX-3—Metastatic cutaneous melanoma to the iris. Note both lesions at periphery.

Ancillary Tests

Fluorescein angiography may be helpful in defining the margins of a metastatic tumor, but it typically is less useful in differentiating this lesion from a primary intraocular neoplasm. The double circulation pattern and prominent early choroidal filling that are often seen in choroidal melanomas are rarely found in metastatic tumors.

Ultrasonography is diagnostically valuable in patients with metastatic tumor. B-scan shows an echogenic choroidal mass with an ill-defined, and sometimes lobu-

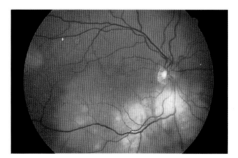

FIG XX-4—Multiple metastatic lesions to the choroid. Note the pale yellow color and relative flatness.

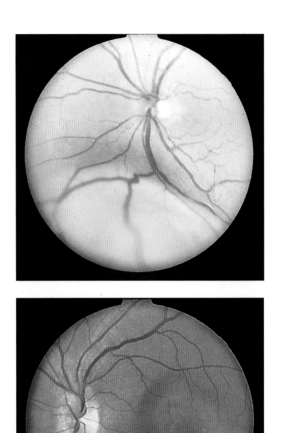

FIG XX-5—*Top,* Metastatic lesion to the choroid inferiorly, associated with bullous retinal detachment. *Bottom,* Subtle metastatic lesion to the choroid, near the fovea, associated with serous effusion.

lated, outline. Overlying secondary retinal detachment is commonly detected in these cases. A-scan demonstrates moderate to high internal reflectivity.

Fine-needle aspiration biopsy may be helpful in rare cases when the diagnosis cannot be established by noninvasive procedures. Although metastatic tumors may recapitulate the histology of the primary tumor, often they are less differentiated. Special histochemical and immunohistochemical stains can be helpful in the diag-

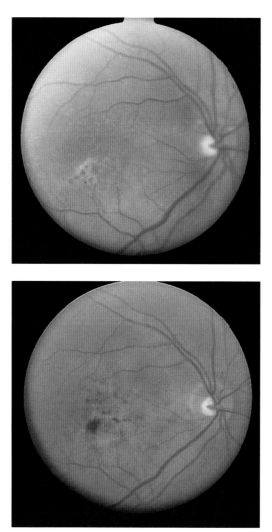

FIG XX-6—*Top,* Metastatic carcinoma to the choroid. Vision was reduced to finger counting because of macular involvement. Note irregular pigmentation on surface. *Bottom,* Same eye, 1 month after radiation therapy. Visual acuity has improved to 20/20. Note increased pigmentation, characteristic of irradiation effects.

nosis of metastatic tumors, but they are usually not helpful in determining the precise origin.

Metastases to the optic nerve may produce disc edema, decreased visual acuity, and visual field defects. Because the metastases may involve the parenchyma or the sheaths of the optic nerve, CT scan as well as ultrasonography may be valuable in detecting the presence and location of the lesion(s).

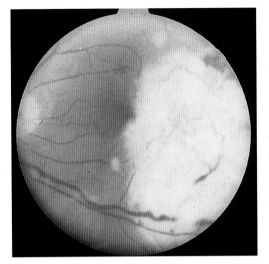 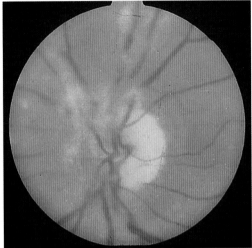

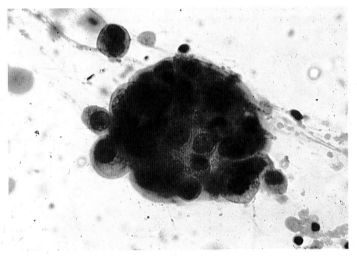

FIG XX-7—*Top left,* Metastatic lung carcinoma to the retina, involving the macula. Vision was reduced to finger counting. *Top right,* Same eye, showing characteristic perivascular distribution of metastases. *Bottom,* Vitreous aspirate from same eye, showing a morula of cells, characteristic of adenocarcinoma of the lung.

Metastases to the retina, which are very rare, appear as white, incohesive lesions, and they are often distributed in a perivascular location suggestive of cotton-wool spots (Fig XX-7). Because of secondary vitreous seeding of tumor cells, these metastases sometimes resemble retinitis more than they do a true tumor. Vitreous aspirates for cytologic studies may confirm the diagnosis.

Other Diagnostic Factors

One of the most important diagnostic factors in the evaluation of suspected metastatic tumors is a history of systemic malignancy. More than 90% of patients with uveal metastasis from carcinoma of the breast have a history of treatment prior to the development of ocular involvement. In the remaining 10% of patients the primary tumor can usually be diagnosed by breast examination at the time that the suspicious ocular lesion is detected.

Tumors metastatic to the uvea from other primary sites may represent the initial manifestation of cancer. About 70% of patients with ocular metastasis from the lung have no history of a pulmonary lesion. Patients with tumors that metastasize from gastrointestinal and genitourinary sites also may present initially with ocular manifestations.

Any patient with an amelanotic fundus mass suspected of being a metastatic focus should have a thorough systemic evaluation. The examination is conducted to locate the possible primary site in the breast, lung, bowel, or genitourinary tract as well as to determine any other organ sites of metastatic involvement.

Treatment

Indications for treatment include decreased vision, pain, diplopia, and severe proptosis. The patient's age, health status, and condition of the fellow eye are also critical in the decision-making process. Chemotherapy or hormonal therapy of sensitive tumors (e.g., breast cancer) may induce a prompt response to treatment. Typically, radiotherapy (either external beam or plaque) will be required for local tumor control; 3500–5000 cGy are given over 3–5 weeks in daily fractions. Radiation therapy frequently affects a patient's symptoms. Resolution of a serous detachment with improved vision may be observed soon after treatment. Occasionally, enucleation is performed because of severe, unrelenting pain.

Prognosis

The diagnosis of tumor metastatic to the uvea implies a poor prognosis, because dissemination of the primary tumor is usually widespread. In one report the survival time following diagnosis of metastases to the uvea varied from 1 to 67 months, depending on the primary cancer type. Metastatic carcinoid is associated with long survival times, and patients with metastatic breast carcinoma may survive for prolonged periods. Shorter survival time is typically seen in patients with lung carcinoma and carcinomas arising from the gastrointestinal or genitourinary tracts in which metastases herald the presence of the primary tumor. Although patients with breast carcinoma metastatic to the uvea survive an average of 9–13 months after the metastasis is recognized, cases with long-term survival have now been reported.

The goal in ophthalmic management of metastases to the eye is preservation or restoration of vision and palliation of pain. Radical surgical procedures and treatments with risks greater than the desired benefits should be avoided.

CHAPTER XXI

Lymphomatous Tumors

Malignant Lymphoma

Non-Hodgkin lymphomas occasionally infiltrate the intraocular tissues and become apparent clinically with protean manifestations. Immunocompromised individuals, particularly those with underlying systemic viral illness, show an increased incidence of intraocular lymphoma.

Of the different varieties of non-Hodgkin lymphomas, large cell lymphoma, historically referred to as *histiocytic lymphoma* or *reticulum cell sarcoma,* is the most significant in terms of ocular involvement. This type of lymphoma, which generally affects older adults, can infiltrate the uveal tract, subretinal space, sub-RPE space, retina, and vitreous. Diagnostic vitreous or subretinal biopsy may provide the only pathologic confirmation of the clinical findings. Most large cell lymphomas that involve the eye are believed to be B-cell malignancies.

Clinical Presentation

Ocular signs and symptoms may occur before systemic or CNS findings. In such cases the disease may simulate nonspecific uveitis, or masquerade syndrome (Fig XXI-1). The onset of bilateral posterior uveitis in patients over the age of 50 years should be considered suggestive of large cell lymphoma, as should "chronic" uveitis in patients within their fifth to seventh decades. Although 30% of patients present with unilateral involvement, delayed involvement of the second eye occurs in approximately 85% of patients.

FIG XXI-1—Large cell lymphoma, clinical appearance. Infiltration of vitreous simulates intraocular inflammation (masquerade syndrome).

Typically, diffuse fine vitreous cells are associated with deep subretinal yellow-white infiltrates. Often fine details of the retina are obscured by the density of the vitritis ("headlamp in the fog"). Retinal vasculitis, vascular occlusion, and exudative retinal detachment may be noted. The RPE may reveal characteristic clumping overlying the subretinal infiltrates. Anterior chamber reaction may be minimal.

Photographic and fluorescein angiographic studies document baseline clinical findings but are rarely helpful in defining a differential diagnosis. Ultrasound testing reveals discrete nodular or placoid infiltration of the subretinal space, associated retinal detachment, and vitreous syneresis with increased reflectivity. Clinical history and neurologic evaluation may reveal neurologic deficits in up to 10% of patients, and 60% of patients show concomitant CNS involvement at the time of presentation. If the diagnosis is suspected, neurologic consultation coupled with CT or MRI studies and lumbar puncture should be coordinated with diagnostic vitrectomy.

Diagnostic Evaluation

Diagnostic confirmation of ocular involvement requires sampling of the vitreous and, when appropriate, the subretinal space. Coordinated planning with the surgical pathologist prior to surgery regarding sample handling is critical. The surgical pathologist should be skilled in the handling of small-volume intraocular specimens and experienced in the evaluation of vitreous samples.

The best approach to pathologic evaluation of the specimen remains controversial. Complete diagnostic/therapeutic three-port pars plana vitrectomy is indicated to obtain an undiluted vitreous specimen. If a subretinal nodule is accessible in a region of the retina unlikely to compromise visual function, subretinal aspiration of the lesion can be performed. A single-vitrectomy biopsy may not be diagnostic, and repeat biopsy may be required. Evaluation of the vitreous/subretinal specimen may be performed using cytopathology, flow cytometry, and PCR analysis for gene rearrangements (see chapters III and IV).

The pathologic interpretation should be directed toward those techniques most familiar to the surgical pathologist, and it is recommended that a pathologist familiar with the diagnosis of intraocular large cell lymphoma evaluate the care. If adequate specimen is obtained, multiple pathologic approaches may be employed. Cytologic evaluation is essential in establishing the diagnosis, with flow cytometry and PCR serving as ancillary studies. Diagnostic specimens reveal malignant lymphocytic cells, thereby establishing the diagnosis (Fig XXI-2). Evaluation of cell surface markers may allow for subclassification of the tumor.

Management Strategies

Historically, treatment of localized intraocular disease has employed fractionated external-beam radiation therapy. Localized radiotherapy does not appear to improve mortality in patients with large cell lymphoma. Recent trends have advocated systemic chemotherapy, with or without combined radiotherapy, although combined CNS radiotherapy and chemotherapy appears to be associated with significant morbidity in elderly patients. A potential approach using staged chemotherapy with high-dose methotrexate followed by radiotherapy appears to prolong survival and may minimize the need for primary radiotherapy.

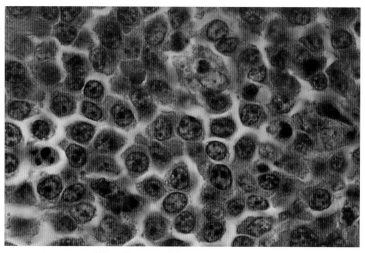

FIG XXI-2—Large cell lymphoma, cytology. Note unusual nuclei and prominent nucleoli of these neoplastic lymphoid cells obtained by fine-needle aspiration biopsy.

Prognosis

The prognosis for patients with large cell lymphoma is grim. Advances with early diagnosis and the staged approach mentioned above have produced a cohort of long-term survivors, however. Serial follow-up with consultative management by an experienced medical oncologist is critical to adequate treatment of this disease.

Uveal Lymphoid Infiltration (Reactive Lymphoid Hyperplasia)

Uveal lymphoid infiltration, or reactive lymphoid hyperplasia (RLH), typically presents in patients in the sixth decade. See also chapter XII. Involvement may be noted in the orbit, conjunctiva, or any uveal site. Patients typically notice painless, progressive visual loss. Ophthalmoscopically, a diffuse or, rarely, nodular amelanotic thickening of the choroid is noted. Exudative retinal detachment and secondary glaucoma may be present in up to 85% of eyes. Frequently, delay between the onset of symptoms and diagnostic intervention is significant.

This rare disorder is characterized pathologically by localized or diffuse infiltration of the uveal tract by lymphoid cells. The etiology is unknown. Clinically, this condition can simulate posterior uveal melanoma, metastatic carcinoma to the uvea, sympathetic ophthalmia, Vogt-Koyanagi-Harada syndrome, and posterior scleritis. Proptosis of the affected eye occurs in approximately 10%–15% of patients who develop simultaneous orbital infiltration with benign lymphoid cells. Ultrasound testing reveals a diffuse, homogeneous choroidal infiltrate with associated secondary retinal detachment. Extraocular extension or orbital involvement may be best demonstrated with echography.

Biopsy confirmation should be targeted to the most accessible tissue. If extra-ocular involvement is present, then biopsy of the involved conjunctiva or orbit may be considered. FNAB or pars plana vitrectomy with biopsy may be indicated for isolated uveal involvement. Coordination with the surgical pathologist is again paramount to obtain the greatest likelihood of appropriate confirmation and cell marker studies.

Historically, eyes with this type of lymphoid infiltration have generally been managed by enucleation because of presumed malignancy. Current management emphasizes globe-conservation therapy aimed at visual preservation. High-dose oral steroids may induce tumor regression and decreased exudative retinal detachment. Early intervention with low-dose ocular and orbital fractionated external-beam radiotherapy may definitively manage the disease.

The prognosis for life is excellent for patients with uveal lymphoid infiltration with the rare exception of those patients with systemic lymphoma. Preservation of visual function appears related to primary tumor location and secondary sequelae, including exudative retinal detachment or glaucoma. Early intervention appears to enhance the likelihood for visual preservation.

Bornfield N, Gragoudas ES, Hopping W, et al, eds. *Tumors of the Eye.* New York: Kugler; 1991.

Garner A, Klintworth GK, eds. *Pathobiology of Ocular Disease: A Dynamic Approach.* 2nd ed. New York: Marcel Dekker; 1994.

McLean IW, Burnier MN, Zimmerman LE, et al. *Tumors of the Eye and Ocular Adnexa.* Washington: Armed Forces Institute of Pathology; 1994.

Schachat AP, ed. Tumors. In: Ryan SJ, ed. *Retina.* 2nd ed. St Louis: Mosby; 1994.

Shields JA, Shields CL. *Intraocular Tumors: A Text and Atlas.* Philadelphia: Saunders; 1992.

Specht CS. Benign and malignant lymphoid tumors, leukemia, and histiocytic lesions. In: Albert DM, Jakobiec FA, eds. *Principles and Practice of Ophthalmology.* 2nd ed. Philadelphia: Saunders; 1994:3328-3350.

Spencer WH, ed. *Ophthalmic Pathology: An Atlas and Textbook.* 4th ed. Philadelphia: Saunders; 1996.

CHAPTER XXII

Leukemia

Ocular involvement with leukemia is common, occurring in as many as 80% of the eyes of leukemic patients examined at autopsy. Although the retina appears clinically to be the most frequently involved site, histologic studies show that the choroid is more often affected. Leukemic cells most commonly invade the uveal tract, but they are also found in the retina, optic disc, and vitreous (Fig XXII-1). Retinal hemorrhage and pseudo–Roth spots are common. Leukemic infiltration of the eye that is not apparent clinically may be recognized with ultrasonography.

Leukemic involvement of the iris is often manifested by a diffuse white thickening of the iris, in many cases with small nodules at the margin of the pupil (see Figure XVII-4e). Tumor cells can collect in the anterior chamber (a "sanctuary site") to form a pseudohypopyon, and infiltration at the angle can give rise to secondary glaucoma.

Retinal findings such as hard exudates, cotton-wool spots, and white-centered retinal hemorrhages (pseudo–Roth spots) are usually the result of associated anemia or thrombocytopenia. However, leukemic infiltrates can be seen as yellow deposits in the retina, the subretinal space, and the choroid. Gray-white nodules of various

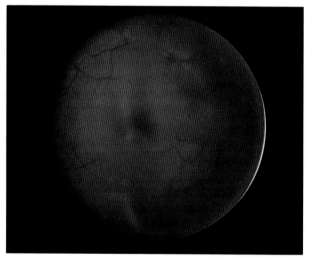

FIG XXII-1—Leukemic infiltration of the vitreous, clinical appearance. Note hazy fundus view resulting from dispersed tumor cells in the vitreous.

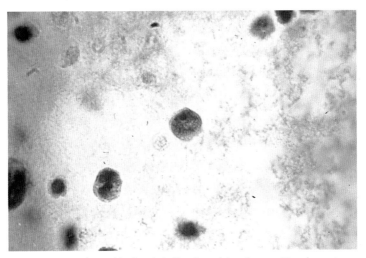

FIG XXII-2—Cytology of leukemic infiltration of the vitreous. Note large, irregular nuclei, prominent nucleoli, and scant cytoplasm of tumor cells obtained by diagnostic vitrectomy.

sizes have been seen in a case of chronic myelogenous leukemia. Occasionally, perivascular leukemic infiltrates can produce gray-white streaks along the blood vessels of the retina.

Leukemic deposits in the choroid may mimic lymphomatous infiltrates. Serous retinal detachments overlying these infiltrates are commonly seen and have been reported in various types of leukemia. Vitreous opacities are rare. Cytologic evaluation of vitreous deposits obtained by diagnostic vitrectomy establishes the diagnosis but is rarely needed (Fig XXII-2).

Patients with leukemia and allied disorders may be immunocompromised and thus susceptible to opportunistic infections. Endogenous infections must be considered in the differential diagnosis of leukemic infiltration.

Treatment of leukemic involvement of the eye generally consists of low-dose radiation therapy to the eye and systemic chemotherapy. The prognosis for vision depends on the type of leukemia and the extent of ocular involvement. Early irradiation can maintain good vision, and intrathecal chemotherapy can be given for optic nerve metastases.

CHAPTER XXIII

Rare Tumors

Medulloepithelioma

Medulloepithelioma, or diktyoma, is a tumor of the nonpigmented ciliary epithelium that occurs in both benign and malignant forms (see Figure XI-39). Medulloepitheliomas are congenital neuroepithelial tumors arising from primitive medullary epithelium. This type of tumor typically becomes evident clinically in children 4–12 years old, but it may also occur in adults. It usually appears as a lightly pigmented mass in the ciliary body but has also been documented in the retina and optic nerve. The tumor may erode into the anterior chamber and become visible at the iris root. Frequently, large cysts are evident on the surface of the mass. Chapter XI discusses the histologic features of medulloepithelioma.

Management usually consists of enucleation or observation. Surgical resection is specifically avoided for the majority of these tumors as a result of late complications and documented metastases associated with this treatment. Fortunately, metastasis is rare with appropriate management, even if the tumor appears frankly malignant on histologic examination.

Garner A, Klintworth GK, eds. *Pathobiology of Ocular Disease: A Dynamic Approach.* 2nd ed. New York: Marcel Dekker; 1994:1405–1413.

Leiomyomas, Neurilemomas, and Neurofibromas

Leiomyomas, neurilemomas, and neurofibromas of the uveal tract are extremely rare tumors that are usually misdiagnosed clinically as amelanotic primary uveal melanomas. The role of ancillary diagnostic tests for such lesions is uncertain.

Direct Intraocular Extension

Direct extension of extraocular tumors into the eye is rare. Intraocular extension most commonly occurs secondary to conjunctival carcinoma, but it also occurs with conjunctival melanoma and basal cell carcinoma of the eyelid. The sclera is usually an effective barrier preventing intraocular invasion. Only a small minority of carcinomas of the conjunctiva ever successfully penetrate the globe, but those that do are often variants of squamous cell carcinoma: mucoepidermoid carcinoma and spindle cell variant. These more aggressive neoplasms usually recur several times after local excision before they invade the eye.

BASIC TEXTS

Ophthalmic Pathology and Intraocular Tumors

Albert DM, Jakobiec FA, eds. *Principles and Practice of Ophthalmology.* 2nd ed. Philadelphia: Saunders; 1994.

Albert DM, Jakobiec FA, eds. *Atlas of Clinical Ophthalmology.* Philadelphia: Saunders; 1996.

Apple DJ, Rabb MF. *Ocular Pathology: Clinical Applications and Self-Assessment.* 5th ed. St Louis: Mosby; 1998.

Bornfeld N, Gragoudas ES, Hopping W, et al, eds. *Tumors of the Eye.* New York: Kugler; 1991.

Char DH. *Clinical Ocular Oncology.* 2nd ed. Philadelphia: Lippincott; 1997.

Cohen IK, Diegelmann RF, Lindblad WJ, eds. *Wound Healing: Biochemical and Clinical Aspects.* Philadelphia: Saunders; 1992.

Dutton JJ. *Atlas of Clinical and Surgical Orbital Anatomy.* Philadelphia: Saunders; 1994.

Garner A, Klintworth GK, eds. *Pathobiology of Ocular Disease: A Dynamic Approach.* 2nd ed. New York: Marcel Dekker; 1994.

Isenberg SJ, ed. *The Eye in Infancy.* 2nd ed. St Louis: Mosby; 1994.

Margo CE, Grossniklaus HE. *Ocular Histopathology. A Guide to Differential Diagnosis.* Philadelphia: Saunders; 1991.

McLean IW, Burnier MN, Zimmerman LE, et al. *Tumors of the Eye and Ocular Adnexa.* Washington: Armed Forces Institute of Pathology; 1994.

Nauman GOH, Apple DJ. *Pathology of the Eye.* New York: Springer-Verlag; 1986.

Rootman J, Stewart B, Goldberg, RA. *Orbital Surgery. A Conceptual Approach.* Philadelphia: Lippincott; 1995.

Sanborn GE, Gonder JR, Shields JA. *Atlas of Intraocular Tumors.* Philadelphia: Saunders; 1994.

Sassani JW, ed. *Ophthalmic Pathology with Clinical Correlations.* Philadelphia: Lippincott; 1997.

Shields JA, Shields CL. *Intraocular Tumors: A Text and Atlas.* Philadelphia: Saunders; 1992.

Spencer WH, ed. *Ophthalmic Pathology: An Atlas and Textbook.* 4th ed. Philadelphia: Saunders; 1996.

Yanoff M, Fine BS. *Ocular Pathology.* 4th ed. St Louis: Mosby; 1996.

Yanoff M, Fine BS. *Ocular Pathology: A Color Atlas.* 2nd ed. New York: Gower; 1992.

RELATED ACADEMY MATERIALS

Focal Points: Clinical Modules for Ophthalmologists

Helm CJ. Melanoma and other pigmented lesions of the ocular surface (Module 11, 1996).

Lane Stevens JC. Retinoblastoma (Module 1, 1990).

Margo CE. Nonpigmented lesions of the ocular surface (Module 9, 1996).

Stefanyszyn MA. Orbital tumors in children (Module 9, 1990).

Publications

Berkow JW, Flower RW, Orth DH, et al. *Fluorescein and Indocyanine Green Angiography: Technique and Interpretation* (Ophthalmology Monograph 5, 2nd ed, 1997).

Kline LB, ed. *Optic Nerve Disorders* (Ophthalmology Monograph 10, 1996).

Stewart WB, ed. *Surgery of the Eyelid, Orbit, and Lacrimal System* (Ophthalmology Monograph 8, 3 vols, 1993, 1994, 1995).

Wilson FM II, ed. *Practical Ophthalmology: A Manual for Beginning Residents* (1996).

Wirtschafter JD, Berman EL, McDonald CS. *Magnetic Resonance Imaging and Computed Tomography: Clinical Neuro-Orbital Anatomy* (Ophthalmology Monograph 6, 1992).

LEO Clinical Topic Updates

O'Brien JM, Gordon KB, Murray TG. *Ocular Oncology* (1996).

To order any of these materials, please call the Academy's Customer Service number at (415) 561-8540.

CREDIT REPORTING FORM

BASIC AND CLINICAL SCIENCE COURSE
Section 4

1999–2000

CME Accreditation

The American Academy of Ophthalmology is accredited by the Accreditation Council for Continuing Medical Education to sponsor continuing medical education for physicians.

The American Academy of Ophthalmology designates this educational activity for a maximum of 30 hours in category 1 credit toward the AMA Physician's Recognition Award. Each physician should claim only those hours of credit that he/she has actually spent in the educational activity.

If you wish to claim continuing medical education credit for your study of this section, you must complete and return the study question answer sheet on the back of this page, along with the following signed statement, to the Academy office. This form must be received within 3 years of the date of purchase.

I hereby certify that I have spent _____ (up to 30) hours of study on the curriculum of this section, and that I have completed the study questions. (The Academy, *upon request,* will send you a transcript of the credits listed on this form.)

☐ *Please send credit verification now.*

Signature _____
Date

Name: _____

Address: _____

City and State: _____ Zip: _____

Telephone: (_____) _____ *Academy Member ID# _____
area code

* Your ID number is located following your name on any Academy mailing label and on your Monthly Statement of Account.

Section Evaluation

Please indicate your response to the statements listed below by placing the appropriate number to the left of each statement.

1 = agree strongly	_____ This section covers topics in enough depth and detail.
2 = agree	_____ This section's illustrations are of sufficient number and quality.
3 = no opinion	_____ The references included in the text provide an appropriate
4 = disagree	amount of additional reading.
5 = disagree	_____ The study questions at the end of the book are useful.
strongly	

In addition, please attach a separate sheet of paper to this form if you wish to elaborate on any of the statements above or to comment on other aspects of this book.

Please return completed form to: **American Academy of Ophthalmology**
P.O. Box 7424
San Francisco, CA 94120-7424
ATTN: Clinical Education Division

Question	Answer	Question	Answer
1	a b c d	26	a b c d
2	a b c d	27	a b c d
3	a b c d	28	a b c d
4	a b c d	29	a b c d
5	a b c d	30	a b c d
6	a b c d	31	a b c d
7	a b c d	32	a b c d e
8	a b c d	33	a b c d e
9	a b c d	34	a b c d e
10	a b c d	35	a b c d e
11	a b c d	36	a b c d e
12	a b c d	37	a b c d e
13	a b c d	38	a b c d e
14	a b c d	39	a b c d e
15	a b c d e	40	a b c d e
16	a b c d e	41	a b c d
17	a b c d e	42	a b c d
18	a b c d e	43	a b c d
19	a b c d e	44	a b c d e
20	a b c d e	45	a b c d e
21	a b c d e	46	a b c d
22	a b c d e	47	a b c d
23	a b c d	48	a b c d
24	a b c d	49	a b c d
25	a b c d		

STUDY QUESTIONS

The following multiple-choice questions are designed to be used after your course of study with this book. Record your responses on the answer sheet (the back side of the Credit Reporting Form) by circling the appropriate letter. For the most effective use of this exercise, *complete the entire test* before consulting the answers.

Although a concerted effort has been made to avoid ambiguity and redundancy in these questions, the authors recognize that differences of opinion may occur regarding the best answer. The discussions are provided to demonstrate the rationale used to derive the answer. They may also be helpful in confirming that your approach to the problem was correct or, if necessary, in fixing the principle in your memory.

1. The most common primary malignancy of the eyelid is

   a. Basal cell carcinoma
   b. Squamous cell carcinoma
   c. Sebaceous carcinoma
   d. Melanoma

2. Sebaceous carcinoma

   a. Is more common in the lower than upper eyelid
   b. May arise from meibomian glands
   c. Is usually pigmented
   d. Is usually bilateral

3. Graves ophthalmopathy

   a. Usually involves extraocular muscle tendons
   b. Most commonly involves the inferior and medial rectus muscles
   c. Is manifested by granulomatous inflammation
   d. Is rarely bilateral

4. Orbital rhabdomyosarcoma

   a. Is the most common primary orbital tumor in adults
   b. Originates from extraocular muscles
   c. Does not require treatment
   d. May be embryonal, alveolar, or pleomorphic

5. Which of the following is correct? If a parent has bilateral retinoblastoma, each child

   a. Has an 85% chance of developing retinoblastoma
   b. Who develops retinoblastoma will have bilateral disease
   c. Will only be affected if male
   d. Has a 45% chance of developing retinoblastoma

6. The most common malignancy to involve the eye in adults is

    a.   Choroidal melanoma
    b.   Metastatic tumor
    c.   Melanocytomas
    d.   Hyperplasia of the retinal pigment epithelium

7. The preferred treatment for orbital rhabdomyosarcoma is

    a.   Enucleation
    b.   Exenteration
    c.   Chemotherapy alone
    d.   Combined radiation and chemotherapy

8. Which of the following statements about retinoblastoma is *false?*

    a.   Bilateral patients present at a younger age than unilateral patients.
    b.   Long-term survival of the unilateral patient is better than the bilateral
         patient.
    c.   Second nonocular tumors occur only in radiated patients.
    d.   Unilateral retinoblastoma is more common than bilateral.

9. Which of the following statements about uveal melanoma is true?

    a.   Uveal melanomas rarely metastasize.
    b.   Melanomas of the ciliary body have the best prognosis.
    c.   Metastases always occur within 2½ years of treatment.
    d.   Survival is directly related to tumor volume.

10. Blood vessels

    a.   Are continuously re-formed during life
    b.   Respond early in the healing of a clear corneal wound
    c.   Are made of stable cells
    d.   Grow into a healing wound as canalized tubes

11. In the final scar of the average wound

    a.   Myofibroblasts and fibroblasts contract
    b.   Most of the vessels persist
    c.   The recently laid collagen parallels the uninjured surrounding collagen
    d.   Macrophages remain, producing enzymes

12. When enucleated, most blind, painful eyes have either

    a.   Absolute glaucoma or expulsive hemorrhage
    b.   Phthisis bulbi or absolute glaucoma
    c.   Fibrous ingrowth or phthisis bulbi
    d.   Epithelial downgrowth or absolute glaucoma

13. Which answer accurately completes the following statement? Metallic intra-ocular foreign bodies made of

    a.   Less than 85% copper cause suppuration
    b.   Gold or silver are highly reactive
    c.   Aluminum are totally inert
    d.   Ferrous iron (Fe^{++}) damage the intraocular epithelia

14. Conjunctival and corneal epithelia

    a.   Never grow inside the eye
    b.   Can invade the eye by burrowing through intact cornea
    c.   Produce free-floating solid masses of cells in the eye
    d.   May grow down a tract or wound edge to the inside of the eye

15. All of the following conditions may be associated with congenital ectopia lentis *except:*

    a.   Marfan syndrome
    b.   Weill-Marchesani syndrome
    c.   Alport syndrome
    d.   Homocystinuria
    e.   Ehlers-Danlos syndrome

16. Which of the following statements about persistent hyperplastic primary vitreous (PHPV) is true?

    a.   Visual prognosis is excellent.
    b.   Early angle-closure glaucoma is common.
    c.   Retinal detachment is rare.
    d.   The eye is usually normal in size.
    e.   Cataract is uncommon.

17. Trisomy 21 (Down syndrome) commonly may include all of the following *except:*

    a.   Hyperopia
    b.   Keratoconus
    c.   Hypertelorism
    d.   Blepharitis
    e.   Esotropia

18. Diabetic oculopathy is characterized histologically by

    a.   Lacy vacuolization of the corneal endothelium
    b.   Relative loss of pericytes in the retinal capillaries
    c.   Microaneurysms in the retinal outer nuclear layer
    d.   Exudates in the retinal nerve fiber layer
    e.   Thinning of the ciliary epithelium basement membrane

19. Which of the following statements is true about peripheral retinal lesions?

    a. Typical peripheral cystoid degeneration is present in virtually 100% of adults.
    b. Paving-stone degeneration is caused by inner retinal ischemia.
    c. Lattice degeneration is seen only after posterior vitreous detachment (PVD).
    d. Typical peripheral cystoid degeneration may progress to typical degeneration retinoschisis, which may lead to retinal detachment.
    e. Atrophic retinal holes in lattice degeneration are frequently associated with retinal detachment.

20. Cotton-wool spots

    a. Are diagnostic of collagen vascular disease
    b. Contain swollen glial cells
    c. Never disappear once they are formed
    d. Are transudates from the superficial capillary plexus
    e. Represent coagulative necrosis of the nerve fiber layer

21. Prognosis for malignant melanomas of the uveal tract is related to all of the following *except:*

    a. Cytology of the tumor cells
    b. Breaks in Bruch's membrane
    c. Size of the tumor
    d. Location of the tumor
    e. Extraocular extension of the tumor

22. Medulloepitheliomas

    a. Are tumors arising from surface ectoderm–derived cells
    b. Are congenital lesions often containing cartilage
    c. Are usually malignant in nature
    d. Can be caused by trauma to the ciliary body
    e. Usually metastasize to the liver

23. A malignant tumor of epithelial origin is classified as a

    a. Carcinoma
    b. Sarcoma
    c. Leukemia
    d. Lymphoma

24. The most commonly used fixative in ophthalmic pathology is

    a. Glutaraldehyde
    b. Formalin
    c. B5
    d. RPMI

25. An appropriate use of surgical frozen sections is to

    a. Provide a rapid diagnosis for anxious family members
    b. Freeze all of the excised tissue
    c. Determine if representative tissue has been sampled
    d. Determine the margins of resection of PAM with atypia

26. A giant cell with an annulus of nuclei surrounded by a lipid-filled zone is classified as a

    a. Langhans giant cell
    b. Foreign body giant cell
    c. Tumor giant cell
    d. Touton giant cell

27. Which of the following tumors develops in the absence of a normal tumor-suppressor gene?

    a. Choroidal melanoma
    b. Melanocytoma
    c. Medulloepithelioma
    d. Retinoblastoma

28. Which of the following conditions is associated with basal laminar deposits?

    a. Choroidal neovascularization
    b. Retinal neovascularization
    c. Glomerulonephritis
    d. Pseudoexfoliation

29. Which of the following is *not* a feature of diabetic eye disease?

    a. Corneal epithelial basement membrane thickening
    b. Intraretinal microvascular abnormalities
    c. Peripheral corneal crystalline deposits
    d. Iris neovascularization

30. The average volume of the adult vitreous cavity is

    a. 3 cc
    b. 4 cc
    c. 5 cc
    d. 6 cc

31. Vitreous amyloidosis is associated with

    a. Peripheral neuropathy
    b. Cranial nerve paralysis
    c. Lattice dystrophy
    d. Peripheral vascular disease

32. All of the following statements regarding Descemet's membrane are true *except:*

    a. It is developmentally derived from the neural crest.
    b. It is elaborated by the corneal endothelial cells.
    c. It remains static throughout life.
    d. It is best demonstrated in histologic sections using the PAS stain.
    e. It is composed of type IV collagen.

33. Band keratopathy is characterized by

    a. Randomly distributed deposits in the cornea
    b. Calcium deposition within the deep corneal stroma
    c. Occurrence only in patients with hypercalcemia
    d. Involvement of the epithelial basement membrane and Bowman's layer
    e. Association with other congenital malformations

34. Which of the following statements regarding corneal dystrophies is true?

    a. They may occur unilaterally.
    b. They are inherited disorders.
    c. Their development often follows surgical or accidental trauma to the eye.
    d. They rarely cause visual symptoms or impairment.
    e. They are never associated with stromal thinning.

35. Marfan syndrome is characterized by all of the following *except:*

    a. Displacement of the lens (ectopia lentis)
    b. Diffuse thickening of the sclera
    c. Musculoskeletal and cardiovascular anomalies
    d. Mutations in the fibrillin gene on chromosome 15
    e. Axial myopia

36. Lens-related glaucoma may occur in all of the following *except:*

    a. Phacoantigenic endophthalmitis
    b. Pseudoexfoliation
    c. Ectopia lentis
    d. Mature cataract
    e. Phacolytic glaucoma

37. All of the following may be associated with congenital cataracts *except:*

    a. Anterior lenticonus
    b. Cerulean cataracts
    c. Aniridia
    d. Rubella
    e. Siderosis

38. All of the following statements regarding sympathetic ophthalmia are true *except:*

    a.   There is diffuse granulomatous inflammation of the uveal tract.
    b.   Dalen-Fuchs nodules are located under the retinal pigment epithelium.
    c.   Alopecia, poliosis, and vitiligo are typically observed.
    d.   Anterior chamber inflammation may be present.
    e.   The choriocapillaris is typically spared.

39. Rubeosis iridis may be associated with all of the following conditions *except:*

    a.   Diabetes mellitus
    b.   Posterior coloboma
    c.   Central retinal vein occlusion
    d.   Retinoblastoma
    e.   Coats disease

40. All of the following statements regarding melanoma of the uveal tract are true *except:*

    a.   Melanoma represents the most common intraocular malignancy in adults.
    b.   The prognosis is related to the cytologic cell type.
    c.   Melanosis oculi is a risk factor for developing melanoma.
    d.   Associated retinal detachments may be present.
    e.   Metastasis results from hematogenous spread of tumor to the liver.

41. Ocular adnexal lymphoid neoplasms involving which of the following sites have the highest association with systemic lymphoma:

    a.   Eyelid
    b.   Palpebral conjunctiva
    c.   Bulbar conjunctiva
    d.   Orbit

42. The conjunctival melanocytic proliferation most commonly associated with subsequent development of conjunctival malignant melanoma is

    a.   Ephelis
    b.   Nevus
    c.   Ocular melanocytosis
    d.   Primary acquired melanosis

43. Patients with rheumatoid arthritis are more likely to develop all of the following scleral inflammatory conditions *except:*

    a.   Anterior scleritis
    b.   Posterior scleritis
    c.   Simple episcleritis
    d.   Nodular episcleritis

44. Xanthelasma is associated with systemic hyperlipoproteinemia in approximately what percentage of patients?

    a. 0%–20%
    b. 21%–40%
    c. 41%–60%
    d. 61%–80%
    e. 81%–100%

45. The malignant eyelid neoplasm most commonly masquerading as a chronic conjunctivitis is

    a. Basal cell carcinoma
    b. Squamous cell carcinoma
    c. Sebaceous carcinoma
    d. Malignant melanoma
    e. Merkel cell carcinoma

46. The histologic classification of orbital rhabdomyosarcoma does *not* include

    a. Alveolar type
    b. Differentiated type
    c. Embryonal
    d. Pleomorphic

47. Pseudoexfoliation, or exfoliation syndrome, does *not* include

    a. A systemic deposition of fibrillin
    b. A history of infrared exposure
    c. Transillumination defects of the iris
    d. Deposition of flaky material on the lens zonule fibers

48. The best diagnosis for "a lymphoid infiltrate with a vaguely follicular pattern that includes the proliferation of monocytoid B lymphocytes and a heterogeneous mix of small lymphocytes and plasma cells" is which of the following?

    a. Reactive lymphoid hyperplasia
    b. Mucosa-associated lymphoid tissue (MALT)
    c. Small B-cell lymphoma
    d. Orbital inflammatory syndrome

49. Rosenthal fibers are a prominent feature in

    a. Some gliomas
    b. Some meningiomas
    c. Optic atrophy
    d. Duchenne muscular dystrophy

ANSWERS

1. Answer—a. Basal cell carcinoma is by far the most common primary malignancy of the eyelid. It is probably more common than squamous cell carcinoma, sebaceous carcinoma, and melanoma of the eyelid combined.

2. Answer—b. Sebaceous carcinoma may arise from meibomian glands or glands of Zeis. It is virtually always unilateral, is more common in the upper than lower eyelid, and may have a yellow appearance as a result of lipid.

3. Answer—b. Graves ophthalmopathy most commonly involves the inferior and medial rectus muscles, sparing the muscle tendons. The inflammation is non-granulomatous, and the disease is usually bilateral.

4. Answer—d. The histopathologic types of orbital rhabdomyosarcoma are embryonal, alveolar, and pleomorphic. The tumor most commonly occurs in children and rarely in adults. Orbital rhabdomyosarcoma arises from mesenchymal tissue, not extraocular muscle. Treatment includes chemotherapy and/or radiation therapy.

5. Answer—d. If a parent has bilateral disease, there is a 98% chance that he or she has a germinal mutation. If the parent had a germinal mutation, then the risk for each child is 45%. (See Figure XIX-1.)

6. Answer—b. While choroidal melanoma is the most common primary intraocular tumor, metastatic tumors are more frequent, with an estimated incidence in the United States of 30,000 a year. The incidence of new primary cancers of the eye is 1800 a year. Melanocytomas and hyperplasias of the RPE are benign lesions.

7. Answer—d. Neither enucleation nor exenteration provides a good long-term prognosis for patients with primary orbital rhabdomyosarcoma. The tumor is highly radiosensitive, and radiation combined with chemotherapy gives good results.

8. Answer—c. Second nonocular tumors occur in 10%–20% of patients with bilateral retinoblastoma within 20 years. As many as 70%–90% will develop a nonretinoblastoma tumor in 30 years. Radiation increases the risk, but many tumors occur outside the field of radiation or in nonirradiated patients.

9. Answer—d. Smaller uveal tumors have the best prognosis overall. Melanomas often metastasize, and 30%–40% of patients die within 5 years of metastatic disease. Ciliary body melanomas in a relatively hidden area often become large before symptoms develop and have a poorer prognosis. The mean duration from treatment to the onset of metastases of uveal melanoma is 7 years.

10. Answer—c. Blood vessels are made of stable cells that are not continuously mitotic during life. When stimulated at injury, the stable cells become mitotic and replace damaged or destroyed cells. Blood vessels do not participate in the healing of a clear corneal wound. Stable cells need factors in the milieu of cells and matrix to maintain viability. Blood vessels near a wound sprout solid buds that later form lumens.

11. Answer—a. The final scar shrinks because of the contraction of myofibroblasts and fibroblasts. The vessels decrease markedly as the scar matures, but a few remain, some as either arteries or veins. Part of the distortion of any scar occurs because the collagen laid down in the healing process is not in synchrony with that in the surrounding tissues. Macrophages, which produce many factors in the active healing stage, subside and are absent from the final scar.

12. Answer—b. Blind eyes may become painful after many years and are enucleated to relieve the pain. Most eyes develop either a high intraocular pressure and absolute glaucoma or cease to produce aqueous in adequate amounts to sustain the eye. In the latter case the eye shrinks and becomes phthisical. The other choices are serious conditions, and each may lead to either glaucoma or phthisis.

13. Answer—d. Intraocular iron produces siderosis bulbi in which the epithelia of iris, lens, ciliary body, and RPE absorb the iron, which damages intracellular micromolecular biochemical systems. Particles with greater than 85% copper content lead to suppuration. Gold, silver, and platinum are relatively inert and produce little reaction within the globe. Aluminum has an intermediate and variable reaction.

14. Answer—d. The epithelia gain access to the globe by migrating along a preexisting tract or wound edge; they are unable to invade normal tissues. Once in the globe, the epithelium usually grows as a sheet over available surfaces as posterior cornea or iris and may form cystic globules. Free-floating masses of solid epithelium do not form.

15. Answer—c. Alport syndrome consists of anterior lenticonus with hereditary nephritis and deafness.

16. Answer—b. PHPV commonly occurs in microphthalmic eyes and is associated with cataract and retinal detachment. Visual prognosis is poor.

17. Answer—a. Patients with trisomy 21 are usually myopic.

18. Answer—b. Diabetic oculopathy may show lacy vacuolization of the iris pigment epithelium. Microaneurysms occur in the deep capillary plexus at the junction between the inner nuclear and outer plexiform layers. Exudates are in the outer plexiform layer. Basement membranes throughout the body (including the ciliary epithelium) are thickened, not thinned.

19. Answer—a. Paving-stone degeneration is caused by outer retinal ischemia. Lattice degeneration is independent of PVD. Typical degenerative retinoschisis and lattice atrophic holes are benign and are not associated with detachment.

20. Answer—e. Cotton-wool spots are characteristic of, but not diagnostic of, collagen vascular disease; they occur in a variety of ischemic retinopathies. They contain swollen nerve fibers, not glial cells. They usually disappear with time. They are infarcts, not transudates.

21. Answer—b. The breaking of Bruch's membrane is not a prognostic sign in melanomas.

22. Answer—b. Medulloepitheliomas are derived from neuroectoderm. They are usually benign choristomas and, even if they are malignant, follow a benign course if the eye is removed with tumor confined to it. They are developmental lesions—so-called adult medulloepitheliomas are actually reactive hyperplasias of the ciliary epithelium and are usually related to ocular trauma.

23. Answer—a. Carcinoma is of epithelial origin. An example of an ocular carcinoma is squamous cell carcinoma of the conjunctival epithelium. Sarcoma is of soft tissue, or "mesenchymal" origin. Leukemia and lymphoma are of hematopoietic tissue origin.

24. Answer—b. Formalin is the most commonly used tissue fixative. Glutaraldehyde is used for fixing tissue for electron microscopic examination. B5 is a mercury-based fixative used for preservation of cytologic detail and is primarily used to fix lymphoid tissue. RPMI may be used for flow cytometry specimens.

25. Answer—c. Frozen sections are not used to satisfy the curiosity of the surgeon or relieve anxiety of the patient's family members. One should never freeze all of the excised tissue, since adequate fixation and avoidance of freezing artifact are needed to properly evaluate surgical specimens for diagnostic purposes. One should not try to evaluate margins of melanocytic proliferations, including melanoma, with frozen sections. Adequate specimen preservation and processing are needed for such evaluation. An appropriate use of frozen sections is to determine if representative tissue is being sampled; if so, more tissue should be submitted in a fixative for processing.

26. Answer—d. A Langhans-type giant cell has a horseshoe-shaped ring of nuclei around the periphery of the cytoplasm. Langhans giant cells may be encountered in tuberculosis and sarcoidosis among other diseases. Foreign body giant cells have haphazardly arranged nuclei. Some malignant neoplasms, including melanoma, may contain multinucleated tumor giant cells. Touton giant cells have central nuclei and a peripheral lipid-filled area. Touton giant cells may be seen in associated with chalazion, juvenile xanthogranuloma, xanthalesma, and xanthogranuloma among other diseases. Langhans, foreign body, and Touton giant cells are not diagnostic for any single disease process.

27. Answer—d. Choroidal melanoma, melanocytoma, and medulloepithelioma are not associated with a tumor-suppressor gene.

28. Answer—a. Basal laminar deposit and choroidal neovascularization may be present in age-related macular degeneration.

29. Answer—c. Peripheral corneal crystalline deposits are not a feature of diabetes.

30. Answer—b. The adult vitreous occupies four fifths of the eye, measures 4 cc, and weights 4 g.

31. Answer—a. Vitreous amyloidosis and peripheral neuropathy are associated with a transthyretin abnormality.

32. Answer—c. The production of Descemet's membrane by the endothelial cells begins during fetal development and continues throughout adulthood. Therefore, the thickness of Descemet's membrane slowly increases with age.

33. Answer—d. Band keratopathy involves the interpalpebral region of the cornea and consists of calcium deposition in the epithelial basement membrane and Bowman's layer. While band keratopathy may occur in patients with hypercalcemia, it also occurs in chronically inflamed eyes of patients with normal serum calcium levels. Band keratopathy is an acquired lesion and is, therefore, not associated with other congenital malformations.

34. Answer—b. The corneal dystrophies are primary, inherited, bilateral disorders. Patients may have symptoms of recurrent erosion or loss of visual acuity. Some of the dystrophies, such as macular dystrophy, may be associated with stromal thinning.

35. Answer—b. Axial myopia is commonly present in Marfan syndrome, and the sclera is often thinned.

36. Answer—b. Pseudoexfoliation, or exfoliation syndrome, results from deposition of a fibrillary proteinlike material on the anterior lens capsule and other intraocular structures; it is not an abnormality of the lens capsule per se.

37. Answer—e. Siderosis is caused by retention of iron-containing metallic foreign bodies in the lens, resulting in lens epithelial degeneration and necrosis. As such, it is an acquired condition rather than a congenital one.

38. Answer—c. Alopecia, poliosis, and vitiligo are all manifestations of Vogt-Koyanagi-Harada syndrome and not associated with sympathetic ophthalmia.

39. Answer—b. A coloboma occurs when there is an absence of tissue (such as iris or choroid), usually along the fetal fissure, and it is thus a congenital lesion. All of the other conditions listed may be associated with rubeosis iridis.

40. Answer—a. Metastatic tumors (usually from lung or breast carcinoma) represent the most common intraocular tumors in adults. Melanoma represents the most common primary intraocular malignancy.

41. Answer—a. Eyelid. Lymphomas manifesting in the eyelid are associated with systemic lymphoma in approximately 80% of cases; conjunctival and orbital lymphomas are more often localized than disseminated.

42. Answer—d. Primary acquired melanosis. PAM with atypia is associated with approximately two thirds of cases of conjunctival melanoma; preexisting nevi are seen in fewer than one fourth. Ocular melanocytosis is associated with an increased risk of uveal melanoma. Ephelis, or freckle, is not associated with melanoma.

43. Answer—c. Simple episcleritis, which has no association with systemic diseases.

44. Answer—b. Approximately one third of patients with xanthelasma will have an associated hyperlipoproteinemia, particularly types II and III.

45. Answer—c. Sebaceous carcinomas may mimic a chronic conjunctivitis and cause delays in diagnosis and appropriate treatment, with potentially serious adverse outcomes.

46. Answer—d. The histologic classification of orbital rhabdomyosarcoma does not include pleomorphic.

47. Answer—b. Pseudoexfoliation, or exfoliation syndrome, is not associated with a history of infrared exposure.

48. Answer—b. Mucosa-associated lymphoid tissue, or MALT, is the best diagnosis in this example.

49. Answer—a. Rosenthal fibers are a prominent feature in some gliomas.

INDEX

A-scan ultrasonography
  in choroidal hemangioma, 247*i*, 249
  in choroidal/ciliary body melanoma,
    232, 232*i*
  in metastatic eye disease, 272
Abrasions, corneal, 23
Acanthamoeba keratitis, 67–68, 68*i*
Accessory lacrimal glands
  of Krause, 172, 172*t*
  of Wolfring, 172, 172*t*
Acquired immunodeficiency syndrome
    (AIDS). *See* HIV infection/AIDS
Acral-lentiginous melanoma, 190
Actin, in immunohistochemistry, 40
Actinic (Labrador) keratopathy (spheroidal
    degeneration), 69, 69*i*
Actinic (solar) keratosis, 181–182, 182*i*
Acute retinal necrosis, 126–127, 126*i*
Adenocarcinoma, of retinal pigment
    epithelium, 245
Adenoid cystic carcinoma, of lacrimal
    glands, 197, 198*i*
Adenoma
  of ciliary epithelium, 245
  Fuchs (pseudoadenomatous
      hyperplasia), 152, 245
  pleomorphic (benign mixed tumor), of
      lacrimal gland, 196–197, 197*i*
  of retinal pigment epithelium, 245
Adipose tumors, of orbit, 207
Age-related macular degeneration,
    141–144
  drusen in, 141–142, 142*i*, 143*i*
  dry (nonexudative), 143, 143*i*
  melanoma differentiated from, 235
  wet (exudative), 143–144, 144*i*
Aging, syneresis and, 112, 112*i*
AIDS. *See* HIV infection/AIDS
Albinism, 122
Albinoidism, 122
Alcian blue stain, 38, 39*t*
Alizarin red stain, 39*t*
Alveolar rhabdomyosarcoma, 203
AMD. *See* Age-related macular
    degeneration

Amyloidosis/amyloid deposits, 177
  conjunctival, 53, 53*i*
  corneal
    in Avellino dystrophy, 75
    in lattice dystrophy, 74, 75*i*
  in eyelid, 177 178, 177*t*, 178*i*
  orbital, 195–196, 196*i*
  vitreous involvement in, 114–115, 114*i*,
    115*i*
Aneurysms, Leber miliary, 124–125
Angiography, fluorescein
  in choroidal hemangioma, 249
  in choroidal/ciliary body melanoma,
    230–232, 231*i*
  in metastatic eye disease, 271
  in retinal capillary hemangioma, 250
  in retinal cavernous hemangioma, 252
Angiomas (angiomatosis)
  encephalofacial (Sturge-Weber
      syndrome), 15*t*
    choroidal hemangioma in, 168, 247
  racemose (Wyburn-Mason syndrome),
      16*t*, 252, 252*i*
  retinal (angiomatosis retinae), 15*t*,
      249–250, 250*i*
Angiomatous tumors, 247–252. *See also*
    Angiomas (angiomatosis);
    Hemangiomas; Vascular tumors
Angle recession, traumatic, 28–29, 29*i*, 85,
    85*i*
  glaucoma and, 85, 86*i*
Aniridia, 14*t*, 156
  ectopia lentis in, 99*t*
Anomalies, congenital. *See* Congenital
    anomalies
Anterior basement membrane dystrophy
    (epithelial dystrophy), 72–73, 72*i*
Anterior chamber
  congenital anomalies of, 80–81
  degenerations of, 81–87
  depth of, 79
  disorders of, 79–88. *See also specific*
      type
  neoplastic, 88
  topography of, 79–80, 79*i*, 80*i*

Branch retinal artery occlusion, 137
Branch retinal vein occlusion, 137–138,
  139*i*
  neovascularization in, 136
BRAO. *See* Branch retinal artery occlusion
Brawny scleritis, 92, 92*i*
Brown and Brenn (B&B) stain, 39*t*, 67
Brown and Hopps (B&H) stain, 39*t*, 67
Bruch's membrane
  and choroidal neovascularization in age-
    related macular degeneration, 144,
    144*i*
  rupture of, 30
    by choroidal melanoma, 165, 166*i*
Brucke's muscle, 154
Brushfield spots, 224*t*, 225*i*
BRVO. *See* Branch retinal vein occlusion
Bullous keratopathy, 70, 71*i*
Buphthalmos (megaloglobus), 14*t*
  ectopia lentis and, 99*t*
Burkitt lymphoma, of orbit, 200
Busacca nodules
  in iridocyclitis, 224*t*
  in sarcoidosis, 159

Calcific drusen, 142
Calcific plaques, senile, 93, 94*i*
Callender classification, of uveal
  melanomas, 164
Cancer
  classification of, 20, 20*t*, 21*i*
  eyelid manifestations of, 180*t*
Candle wax drippings, in sarcoidosis, 159
Capillary hemangiomas
  of eyelid, 184–185
  orbital, 201, 202*i*
  retinal (angiomatosis retinae), 249–250,
    250*i*
Capsular glaucoma, 82
Carcinoma, 20*t*, 21*i*
  adenoid cystic, of lacrimal glands, 197,
    198*i*
  basal cell of eyelid, 183, 184*i*
    intraocular extension of, 282
  conjunctival, intraocular extension of,
    282
  of eyelid, 182–183, 183*i*, 184*i*
  of iris, 225*t*

metastatic, 267–265
  ancillary tests in evaluation of,
    271–274, 274*i*
  clinical features of, 269, 270*i*, 271*i*,
    272*i*, 273*i*
  diagnostic factors in, 275
  mechanisms of spread and, 268–269
  primary sites and, 267–268, 268*t*
  prognosis for, 275
  treatment of, 275
sebaceous, 185–186, 185*i*, 186*i*
squamous cell
  conjunctival, 55, 56*i*
  of eyelid, 182, 183*i*
  retinoblastoma associated with, 266*t*
thyroid, retinoblastoma associated with,
  266*t*
Carcinoma in situ, of cornea, 78
Carney complex, eyelid manifestations of,
  177*t*
Caruncle, 45
Caseating granulomas, 17, 18*i*
Cataract, 101–106
  anterior subcapsular, 102, 102*i*
  congenital and infantile, 14*t*, 98
  coronary (cerulean), 101
  disorders associated with premature
    formation of, 107
  exogenous agents causing formation of,
    107
  hypermature, lens protein leakage from,
    phacolytic glaucoma caused by,
    82–83, 84*i*, 99
  nuclear, 106
  in persistent hyperplasia of primary
    vitreous, 110
  posterior subcapsular, 103, 103*i*
  rubella, 98
  traumatic, 30
Cavernous hemangioma, 13
  of orbit, 201, 202*i*
  of retina, 251–252, 251*i*
Cavernous optic atrophy of Schnabel, 211,
  212*i*
Cellular atypia, in primary acquired
  melanosis, 60, 60*i*
  conjunctival melanoma and, 60, 61, 61*i*
Cellulitis, preseptal, 174, 174*i*

CLL lymphoma. *See* Chronic lymphocytic leukemia (CLL) type lymphoma
Clump cells, in iris, 153
  Koganei-type, 153
CME. *See* Cystoid macular edema
Coats disease, 125, 125*i*
  retinoblastoma differentiated from, 258, 258*t*, 259*i*
Cobblestone (paving-stone) degeneration, 130, 132*i*
Cogan microcystic dystrophy (epithelial dystrophy), 72–73, 72*i*
Cogan-Reese (iris nevus) syndrome, 81, 224*t*. *See also* Iris nevus
Collaborative Ocular Melanoma Study (COMS), 219, 239
Colloidal iron stain, 38, 39*t*
Colobomas
  optic nerve, 210
  uveal, 156
Colon cancer, in Gardner syndrome, fundus findings and, 236–237
Combined hamartoma, of retina and retinal pigment epithelium, 152, 246, 246*i*
Commotio retinae (Berlin disease), 30–31
Communication, between clinician and pathologist, 33
Complex choristomas, 46
Compound nevi
  conjunctival, 58, 59*i*
  of eyelid, 188, 189*i*
Computed tomography (CT scan)
  in choroidal/ciliary body melanoma, 233, 233*i*
  in retinoblastoma, 257
COMS. *See* Collaborative Ocular Melanoma Study
Congenital anomalies, 12–13, 12*i*, 14–16*t*. *See also specific type*
  of anterior chamber and trabecular meshwork, 80–81
  conjunctival, 45–47
  corneal, 63–66
  of lens, 97–98
  retinal, 122–125, 126*i*
  scleral, 90–91
  of uveal tract, 155–156
  of vitreous, 110–111, 110*i*

Congenital hereditary endothelial dystrophy, 63–64, 64*i*
Congenital hypertrophy of retinal pigment epithelium, 12, 12*i*, 125, 126*i*
  melanoma differentiated from, 235–237, 236*i*, 237*i*
Congenital/infantile cataract, 14*t*, 98
Congo red stain, 38, 39*t*
Conjunctiva
  amyloid deposits in, 53, 53*i*
  carcinoma of, intraocular extension of, 282
  congenital anomalies of, 45–47
  cysts of, 47, 48*i*
    nevi and, 59, 59*i*
  degenerations of, 51–53, 52*i*
  disorders of. *See also specific type*
    neoplastic, 53–61
  dysplasia of, 54, 54*i*
  epibulbar, 45
  epithelium of
    cysts of, 47, 48*i*
      nevi and, 59, 59*i*
    lesions of, 53–55, 56*i*
  forniceal, 45
  goblet cells in, 172, 172*t*
  infection/inflammation of, 47–51. *See also* Conjunctivitis
  intraepithelial neoplasia of, 54–55, 55*i*
  melanocytic lesions of, 58–61, 58*t*
  melanoma of, 61, 61*i*
    intraocular extension of, 282
    primary acquired melanosis and, 60, 61, 61*i*
  nevus of, 58–59, 58*t*
  palpebral, 45, 172
  topography of, 45, 46*i*
  tumors of, 53–61
    epithelial, 53–55, 56*i*
    subepithelial, 55–57, 56*i*, 57*i*, 58*i*
Conjunctival inclusion cysts, 47, 48*i*
  nevi and, 59, 59*i*
Conjunctival intraepithelial neoplasia (CIN), 54–55, 54*i*
Conjunctivitis, 47
  acute, 47
  bacterial, 49, 50*i*
  chronic, 47
  follicular, 48, 49*i*

Herpes simplex virus
    acute retinal necrosis caused by, 126,
        126*i*
    keratitis caused by, 67, 67*i*
Herpes zoster, acute retinal necrosis
        caused by, 126, 126*i*
High myopia, ectopia lentis and, 99*t*
Histiocytes, 17
Histiocytic lymphoma (reticulum cell
        sarcoma), 276
    of vitreous, 119
Histiocytoma, fibrous (fibroxanthoma)
    orbital, 204–205, 204*i*
    scleral, 94
HIV infection/AIDS, CMV retinitis and, 127
HLA antigens. *See* Human leukocyte (HLA)
        antigens
HMB 45, in immunohistochemistry, 40
Hodgkin disease, in orbit, 198
Homer Wright rosettes, in retinoblastoma,
        148, 149*i*
Homocystinuria, ectopia lentis in, 97, 99*t*
Hordeolum, external (stye), 173
Hormonal therapy, for metastatic eye
        disease, 275
Horner-Trantas dots, 48
HPV. *See* Human papillomaviruses
Hudson-Stähli line, 77
Human immunodeficiency virus infection.
        See HIV infection/AIDS
Human leukocyte (HLA) antigens, in Vogt-
        Koyanagi-Harada syndrome, 158
Human papillomaviruses, 54
    eyelid infections caused by, 174
Hyaline deposits, corneal, in Avellino
        dystrophy, 75
Hyaline (hard) drusen, 142, 142*i*
Hyalocytes, 110
Hyaloid artery, persistence of
        (Bergmeister's papilla), 111
Hyaloid face, of vitreous, 109
Hyaloideocapsular ligament, 109
Hyalosis, asteroid, 113–114, 114*i*
Hydrops, in keratoconus, 71
Hyperlipoproteinemia, xanthelasma
        associated with, 176, 177*t*
Hyperlysinemia, ectopia lentis in, 99*t*
Hypermature cataract, lens protein leakage
        from, phacolytic glaucoma caused by,
        82–83, 84*i*, 99

Hyperplasia
    lymphoid. *See* Lymphoid hyperplasia
    pseudoadenomatous (Fuchs adenoma),
        152, 245
Hyperthermia, diode laser
    for melanoma, 241
    for retinoblastoma, 262
Hyphema, glaucoma associated with, 84*i*,
        85

ICE. *See* Iridocorneal endothelial syndrome
Idiopathic orbital inflammation (orbital
        inflammatory syndrome/sclerosing
        orbitis/orbital pseudotumor), 194,
        195*i*
    orbital lymphoma differentiated from,
        200–201
Immunocompromised host, CMV retinitis
        and, 127, 127*i*
Immunohistochemistry, 40, 40*i*
Immunotherapy, for melanoma, 241
Implantation membrane, of iris, 224*t*
Inclusion cysts, epithelial, 47, 48*i*
    nevi and, 59, 59*i*
Index features, in diagnosis, 20
Indirect ophthalmoscopy, in
        choroidal/ciliary body melanoma, 229
    with transillumination, 229–230
Infection (ocular). *See also specific type or
        causative agent*
    conjunctival, 49, 50*i*. *See also*
        Conjunctivitis
    corneal, 66–68. *See also* Keratitis
    of eyelid, 173–174, 175*i*
    optic nerve, 210
    orbital, 192–193, 193*i*
    retinal, 126–128
    of uveal tract, 156–157
Inflammation (ocular), 13–19, 13*i*, 17*i*,
        18*i*, 19*i*
    acute, 23, 24*i*
    conjunctival, 47–51. *See also*
        Conjunctivitis
    corneal, 66–68. *See also* Keratitis
    of eyelid, 173–176
    granulomatous, 17, 18*i*
    lens-related, 98–100, 101*i*
    optic nerve, 210–211, 210*i*
    orbital, 192–194, 195*i*

retinoblastoma associated with, 266*t*
ring, 167, 167*i*, 227
superficial spreading, 190
tapioca, 225*t*
unsuspected, 234
Melanosis
benign acquired, 58*t*
primary acquired, 58*t*, 59*i*, 60, 60*i*
conjunctival melanoma and, 60, 61, 61*i*
Membranes, implantation, of iris, 224*t*
Meningioma, optic nerve, 214–216, 215*i*, 216*i*
Meningocele, 16*t*
Meningoencephalocele, 16*t*
Mesectodermal leiomyoma, of ciliary body, 169
Mesodermal dysgenesis. *See* Axenfeld-Rieger syndrome
Metastatic eye disease, 167, 168*i*, 267–275
carcinoma, 267–265
ancillary tests in evaluation of, 271–274, 274*i*
clinical features of, 269, 270*i*, 271*i*, 272*i*, 273*i*
diagnostic factors in, 275
mechanisms of spread and, 268–269
primary sites and, 267–268, 268*t*
prognosis for, 275
treatment of, 275
of choroid, 167, 168*i*, 269, 271*i*, 272*i*, 273*i*
of iris, 225*t*, 269, 270*i*, 271*i*
of optic nerve, 271
of orbit, 207
of retina, 274, 274*i*
of uvea, 167, 168*i*, 269, 271*i*, 272*i*, 273*i*, 275
Methenamine silver stain, 38, 67, 67*i*
Microaneurysms, retinal, ischemia causing, 135–136, 135*i*
Microglial cells, 208
degeneration of in retinal ischemia, 132–133
Mittendorf's dot, 111
Mixed tumor, benign (pleomorphic adenoma), of lacrimal gland, 196–197, 197*i*

Mohs' micrographic surgery, for basal cell carcinoma of eyelid, 183
Molecular pathology techniques, 42, 43*i*
Moll, glands of, 172*t*
Molluscum contagiosum, of eyelid, 174, 175*i*
Monocytes, in inflammation, 17, 17*i*
Morgagnian cataract, 104, 106*i*
Morgagnian globules, 104, 105*i*, 106*i*
Mucoepidermoid carcinoma, conjunctival, 55
Mucormycosis (zygomycosis), orbital, 192–193
Mucosa-associated lymphoid tissue (MALT) lymphoma, 200
Muir-Torre syndrome, eyelid manifestations of, 180*t*
Müller's muscle, 154, 172
Multinucleated giant cells, 17, 18*i*
Multiple sclerosis, optic nerve in, 210, 210*i*
Mutton-fat keratic precipitates, in sympathetic ophthalmia, 158
Mycotic keratitis, 67, 67*i*
Myelinated (medullated) nerve fibers, 124, 124*i*
Myoglobin, in immunohistochemistry, 40
Myopia, high, ectopia lentis and, 99*t*
Myositis, orbital, 194, 195*i*

Nanophthalmos, 91
Neoplasia, 19–20, 21*i*. *See also specific type and* Intraocular tumors
classification of, 20*t*, 21*i*
definition of, 19
Neovascularization
choroidal, 161, 161*i*
in age-related macular degeneration, 143–144, 144*i*
of iris (rubeosis iridis), 159–160, 160*t*
retinal
in age-related macular degeneration, 144
in retinal ischemia, 136, 136*i*
Nerve fiber layer, of retina, 121
Nerve fibers, myelinated (medullated), 124, 124*i*
Nerve (neural) sheath tumors
of orbit, 205, 206*i*
of uveal tract, 169

Neurilemoma (schwannoma)
  of orbit, 205, 206*i*
  of uveal tract, 169, 282
Neurofibromas
  of orbit, 205, 206*i*
  plexiform, 205, 206*i*
  of uveal tract, 169, 282
Neurofibromatosis (von Recklinghausen
      disease), 15*t*
  iris affected in, 225*t*, 226*i*
  optic nerve gliomas associated with, 214
  orbit affected in, 205
Neurosensory retina, 121–122, 121*i*. *See
  also* Retina
Neutrophils, in inflammation, 13, 13*i*, 17
Nevus
  of anterior chamber/trabecular
      meshwork, 88, 88*i*
  choroidal, 163, 163*i*, 221–222, 221*i*
    melanoma differentiated from, 234
  of ciliary body, 163, 221–222, 221*i*
  compound
    conjunctival, 58, 59*i*
    of eyelid, 188, 189*i*
  congenital, 186–187, 187*i*
  conjunctival, 58–59, 58*t*
  dysplastic, 188
  of eyelid, 186–188, 187*i*, 189*i*
  intradermal, 188, 189*i*
  iris, 81, 161, 220, 220*i*, 224*t*
  junctional, 187–188
  "kissing," 187*i*
  macular, 187
  magnocellular. *See* Melanocytoma
  melanocytic, 187–188
    giant congenital, 186–187
  nevocellular, 186–187, 187*i*
  of Ota (oculodermal melanocytosis), 14*t*,
      58*t*
    of iris, 225*t*
  Spitz, 188
  stromal, 59
  subepithelial, 59
NFL. *See* Nerve fiber layer
Nodular episcleritis, 91
Nodular fasciitis, episcleral tumor caused
    by, 94–95

Non-Hodgkin lymphomas, 276–278. *See
  also* Lymphomas
  orbital, 198–201, 199*i*, 200*i*
NPDR. *See* Diabetic retinopathy
Nuclear cataracts, 106
Nucleus, lens, 97
  degenerations of, 105–106, 106*i*

Ocular melanocytosis, 58*t*
  of iris, 225*t*
Ocular trauma, histologic sequelae of,
    28–31, 32*i*
Oculodermal melanocytosis (nevus of
    Ota), 14*t*, 58*t*
  of iris, 225*t*
Oil red O stain, 38
Oligodendrocytes, 208
Open-angle glaucoma
  pigment dispersion syndrome and, 87,
      87*i*
  trauma causing, 83–85, 84*i*, 86*i*
Ophthalmic artery, 209
Ophthalmic examination, in
    retinoblastoma, 257
Ophthalmic pathology, 9–216. *See also
    specific disorder or structure affected*
  of anterior chamber and trabecular
      meshwork, 79–88
  communication by health care team
      members and, 33
  congenital anomalies and, 12–13, 12*i*,
      14–16*t*
  of conjunctiva, 45–61
  of cornea, 62–78
  degeneration and dystrophy and, 19
  diagnostic electron microscopy in, 42
  of eyelids, 171–190
  fine-needle aspiration biopsy for, 42–44,
      219
  flow cytometry in, 41, 41*i*
  frozen section for, 44
  immunohistochemistry in, 40, 40*i*
  inflammation and, 13–19, 13*i*, 17*i*, 18*i*,
      19*i*
  of lens, 96–108
  molecular pathologic techniques in, 42,
      43*i*
  neoplasia and, 19–20, 20*t*, 21*i*
  of optic nerve, 208–216

Outer ischemic retinal atrophy, 132, 133*i*
Oxycephaly, ectopia lentis in, 99*t*

Pagetoid spread
  in primary acquired melanosis, 60
  of sebaceous carcinoma, 185*i*, 186*i*
Palpebral conjunctiva, 45, 172
PAM. *See* Primary acquired melanosis
Pannus, 70, 70*i*
  subepithelial fibrovascular, 70
Panuveitis, sympathetic ophthalmia and,
  157–158
Papillae
  Bergmeister's, 111
  limbal, 47–48, 49*i*
Papillary conjunctivitis, 47–48, 48*i*
  giant, 47
Papillomas
  conjunctival, 53–54, 54*i*
    squamous, 53–54, 54*i*
  of eyelids, 174
Papillophlebitis, 137. *See also* Central
  retinal vein occlusion
Parafovea, 122
Parafoveal telangiectasia, 124
Parasites, orbital infections caused by, 193
Parinaud oculoglandular syndrome, 51
Pars plana, 154
Pars plana vitrectomy, for intraocular
  lymphoma diagnosis, 277
Pars plicata, 154
PAS. *See* Periodic acid–Schiff stain
Paving-stone (cobblestone) degeneration,
  130, 132*i*
PCR. *See* Polymerase chain reaction
PDR. *See* Diabetic retinopathy,
  proliferative
Pearl cyst, of iris, 224*t*
Perifovea, 122
Perimetry, in choroidal/ciliary body
  melanoma, 233
Periodic acid–Schiff stain, 38, 39*t*
Peripheral cystoid degeneration, 129, 129*i*
Periphlebitis, in sarcoidosis, 159
Perls' Prussian blue stain, 39*t*
Persistent hyperplasia of primary vitreous
  (persistent fetal vasculature), 14*t*, 110,
  110*i*

retinoblastoma differentiated from,
  258–259
Peters anomaly, ectopia lentis and, 99*t*
Phacoantigenic (phacoanaphylactic/
  lens-induced granulomatous)
  endophthalmitis, 98–99, 100*i*
Phacolytic glaucoma, 82–83, 84*i*, 99, 104
Phakomatoses, 15–16*t*
Phakomatous choristoma (Zimmerman
  tumor), 173
Photoablation
  for melanoma, 241
  for retinoblastoma, 262
Photocoagulation
  for choroidal hemangioma, 249
  for diabetic retinopathy, 140, 140*i*
  for melanoma, 241
  for retinal capillary hemangioma, 250
  for retinoblastoma, 262
Photoreceptors, atrophy of, in macular
  degeneration, 143, 143*i*
PHPV. *See* Persistent hyperplasia of
  primary vitreous
Phthisis bulbi, 31, 32*i*
Pia mater, optic nerve, 208, 209*i*
Pigment dispersion syndrome. *See also*
  Pigmentations
  anterior chamber and trabecular
    meshwork affected in, 87, 87*i*
  cornea affected in, 76, 76*i*
  glaucoma and, 87, 87*i*
Pigment epithelium
  ciliary body, acquired hyperplasia of,
    245
  iris, 153, 154*i*
    cysts of, 224*t*, 226*i*
  retinal. *See* Retinal pigment epithelium
Pigmentations. *See also* Pigment dispersion
  syndrome
  corneal, 76–77
  trabecular meshwork, 86–87, 86*i*, 87*i*
Pilocytic astrocytoma, juvenile, of optic
  nerve, 214, 215*i*
Pinealoma, retinoblastoma associated
  with, 266*t*
Pineoblastoma, 264
Pinguecula, 51, 52*i*
Pits, optic, 15*t*, 209

317

Plaque radiotherapy (brachytherapy)
for choroidal hemangioma, 249
for melanoma, 240
for retinoblastoma, 263–264
Plasma cells, 18–19, 19*i*
Pleomorphic adenoma (benign mixed
tumor), of lacrimal gland, 196–197,
197*i*
Plexiform neurofibroma, of orbit, 205, 206*i*
Plica semilunaris, 45
PMN. *See* Polymorphonuclear leukocytes
PO (pupil–optic nerve) section, 35, 36, 37*i*
Polyarteritis nodosa, eyelid manifestations
of, 177*t*
Polychondritis, relapsing, eyelid
manifestations of, 177*t*
Polymerase chain reaction (PCR), 42, 43*i*
Polymorphonuclear leukocytes
(neutrophils), in inflammation, 13,
13*i*, 17
Polyneuropathy, familial amyloid, vitreous
involvement in, 115, 115*i*
Posterior embryotoxon, 80, 80*i*
Posterior keratoconus, 65, 65*i*
Posterior lenticonus, 101, 102*i*
Posterior uveal melanoma, 163–167, 165*i*,
166*i*, 167*i*, 227–245. *See also*
Choroidal/ciliary body melanoma
Posterior vascular capsule, remnant of
(Mittendorf's dot), 111
Posterior vitreous detachment, 115, 116*i*
in diabetic retinopathy, 140
Prealbumin. *See* Transthyretin
Prematurity, retinopathy of, 141
Preseptal cellulitis, 174, 174*i*
Primary acquired melanosis, 58*t*, 59*i*, 60,
60*i*
conjunctival melanoma and, 60, 61, 61*i*
Primary vitreous, 110
persistent hyperplasia of (persistent fetal
vasculature), 14*t*, 110, 110*i*
retinoblastoma differentiated from,
258–259
Proliferative vitreoretinopathy, 117, 118*i*
Propionibacterium acnes endophthalmitis,
100, 101*i*
Proptosis, 191
in retinoblastoma, 256, 257*i*
in thyroid orbitopathy, 193

Prussian blue stain, Perls,' 39*t*
Pseudoadenomatous hyperplasia (Fuchs
adenoma), 152, 245
Pseudoexfoliation (exfoliation syndrome),
82, 83*i*, 101, 102*i*
Pseudoglands of Henle, 47
Pseudogliomas, 145
Pseudohypopyon, retinoblastoma causing,
256, 257*i*
Pseudomelanomas, 234
Pseudomembrane, 47
Pseudotumor, orbital (idiopathic orbital
inflammation), 194, 195*i*
orbital lymphoma differentiated from,
200–201
Pterygium, 51, 52*i*
PVD. *See* Posterior vitreous detachment

Racemose angioma (Wyburn-Mason
syndrome), 16*t*, 252, 252*i*
Radial perivascular lattice degeneration,
130
Radiation therapy
for choroidal hemangioma, 249
for lymphoma, 277
for melanoma, 240–241
for metastatic eye disease, 275
for retinal capillary hemangioma, 250
for retinoblastoma, 263–264
Radioactive plaque therapy
(brachytherapy)
for choroidal hemangioma, 249
for melanoma, 240
for retinoblastoma, 263–264
Reactive lymphoid hyperplasia
of conjunctiva, 56*i*, 57, 57*i*
of orbit, 198, 199*i*
of uveal tract, 169, 278–279
REAL (Revised European-American)
classification, for lymphomas,
199–200
Red eye. *See also* Inflammation
in retinoblastoma, 255*i*, 255*t*
Reese-Ellsworth classification of
retinoblastoma, 260, 261*t*
Regeneration, 23. *See also* Wound repair
Relapsing polychondritis, eyelid
manifestations of, 177*t*
Reticular degenerative retinoschisis, 130

Uveitis
    anterior, granulomatous, iris nodules in, 224*t*
    sympathetic ophthalmia and, 157–158

Vascular system, of retina, 121
    anomalies of, 124–125, 125*i*
Vascular tumors, 247–252. *See also*
    Angiomas (angiomatosis);
    Hemangiomas
    of orbit, 201–202, 201*i*, 202*i*, 203*i*
Verhoeff von Gieson stain, 39*t*
Viruses
    conjunctivitis caused by, 49, 50*i*
    eyelid infections caused by, 174, 175*i*
    retinal infections caused by, 126–127, 126*i*
Vitrectomy, for intraocular lymphoma diagnosis, 277
Vitreoretinopathy, proliferative, 117, 118*i*
Vitreous
    amyloidosis involving, 114–115, 114*i*, 115*i*
    congenital anomalies of, 110–111, 110*i*
    cortex of, 109
    degenerations of, 112–118
    disorders of, 109–119. *See also specific type*
    neoplastic, 118–119
    inflammatory processes affecting, 111–112, 111*i*
    in leukemia, 280, 280*i*, 281, 281*i*
    primary, 110
        persistent hyperplasia of, 14*t*, 110, 110*i*
            retinoblastoma differentiated from, 258–259
    secondary, 110
    tertiary, 110
    topography of, 109–110
    wound healing in, 28
Vitreous detachment, posterior, 115, 116*i*
    in diabetic retinopathy, 140
Vitreous hemorrhage, 112–113, 113*i*
Vitreous seeds, in retinoblastoma, 147–148, 256, 256*i*
VKH syndrome. *See* Vogt-Koyanagi-Harada syndrome

Vogt-Koyanagi-Harada syndrome, 158
von Hippel, internal ulcer of (posterior keratoconus), 65, 65*i*
von Hippel disease, 250. *See also* Retinal capillary hemangioma
von Hippel–Lindau disease, 15*t*, 250. *See also* Retinal capillary hemangioma
von Kossa stain, 39*t*
von Recklinghausen disease (neurofibromatosis), 15*t*
    iris affected in, 225*t*, 226*i*
    optic nerve gliomas associated with, 214
    orbit involved in, 205
Vossius' ring, 30

Wedl (bladder) cells, 103, 103*i*
Wegener granulomatosis, eyelid manifestations of, 177*t*
Weill-Marchesani syndrome, ectopia lentis in, 99*t*
Wilms tumor, aniridia and, 156
Wolfring, glands of, 172, 172*t*
Wound contraction, 23, 24*i*
Wound repair, 23–31, 32*i*
    definition of, 23
    general aspects of, 12, 24*i*
    histologic sequelae of trauma and, 28–31, 32*i*
Wyburn-Mason syndrome (racemose angioma), 16*t*, 252, 252*i*

Xanthelasma, of eyelid, 176, 176*i*
Xanthogranuloma, juvenile, of iris, 224*t*
Xanthophyll, in macula, 122
Xeroderma pigmentosa, 16*t*

Zeis, glands of, 172*t*
Zimmerman tumor (phakomatous choristoma), 173
Zonular fibers
    ciliary muscle, 154
    lens, 97, 97*i*
Zoster (shingles), acute retinal necrosis caused by, 126, 126*i*
Zygomycosis (mucormycosis), orbital, 192–193

ILLUSTRATIONS

The authors submitted the following figures for this revision. (Illustrations that were reproduced from other sources or submitted by contributors not on the committee are credited in the captions.)

Harry W. Brown, MD: Figs V-2, V-4, V-5, V-7A, V-8, VIII-1 through VIII-7

Ben J. Glasgow, MD: Figs XIV-1, XIV-2, XIV-12, XIV-15

Hans E. Grossniklaus, MD: Figs I-1 through I-9, I-13, II-4 through II-9, III-1 through III-5, III-10, IV-1, IV-2, VII-2, VII-3, VII-7, VII-15, XI-30, XIV-6, XIV-7, XV-1, XV-2, XV-5, XV-7

Debra J. Shetlar, MD: Figs VI-2B, VI-3, VI-4, VI-8, VI-9, VI-12B, VI-13A, VI-14A, VI-15A, VI-16, VI-17, IX-1, IX-3, IX-8, IX-10, IX-11A, IX-12, IX-14A, IX-15A, IX-16 through IX-17, XII-1 through XII-6, XII-7B, XII-9, XII-19, XII-20

David J. Wilson, MD: Figs X-1 through X-4, X-6, X-7A, X-8 through X-11, X-13 through X-15, XI-1, XI-3 through XI-9, XI-15 through XI-18, XI-20, XI-24 through XI-26